No one has contributed more than Willis Harman to our ability to understand the world from an entirely new perspective, one that is more embracing of our humanity and our great human consciousness, business, science, and the planet. In a masterful weaving, he spins out a new worldview that can truly bring about the global mind change we all long for.

—Margaret J. Wheatley, co-author of
A Simpler Way and *Leadership and the New Science*

Willis Harman's work stands as a superb testament to the human spirit in the modern and postmodern world. *Global Mind Change* is one of his finest and most provocative statements, highlighting the utterly fundamental role of consciousness in the evolution of humanity—thus reflecting, as well as helping to bring about, the very changes it courageously announces.

—Ken Wilber, author of *Sex, Ecology, Spirituality*
and *The Marriage of Sense and Soul*

Willis Harman's key work foretold of today's hopeful forces underlying globalization. Before the velvet revolutions and the fall of the Berlin Wall, Harman predicted the worldwide spread of democracies and civic societies, citizens' movements of conscience networking for human rights, opportunities and responsibilities for self-reliant, moral development in harmony with nature.

—Hazel Henderson, economist, author
of *Building a Win-Win World*

Willis Harman's clarity of thinking about the most pressing issues of our time is extraordinary. His pioneering work in the study of consciousness has made this book a unique and invaluable contribution to creating a sustainable society. *Global Mind Change* is essential reading for everyone concerned with the fate of the Earth.

—Frances Vaughan, psychologist,
author of *Shadows of the Sacred*

When I was a young PhD, doing a postdoctoral fellowship at Stanford University, my mentor, concerned that I had interests that were too progressive, warned me to avoid a certain Professor Harman whose ideas might tempt me. Naturally, I sought Willis Harman out right away! He has always been an example to me of a unique combination of vision that was thoroughly grounded in reality. *Global Mind Change* is one of the best examples of the practical hope and vision he offers us.

—Charles T. Tart, professor emeritus,
University of California,
and author of *Living the Mindful Life*

The influence of Willis Harman's social thought has grown for several decades now, and will continue to grow for many years to come. *Global Mind Change* is perhaps his most important book. It challenges many current assumptions about human nature and the world in general, and it opens up new perspectives on science, business, ecology, and religion.

—Michael Murphy, author of *The Kingdom of Shivas Irons*
and co-founder of Esalen Institute

Willis Harman was a thinker of remarkable originality and this book sparkles with a host of provocative ideas for working with the far-reaching changes that we, our culture, and our planet now face.

—Roger Walsh, professor, University of California,
co-editor of *Paths Beyond Ego: The Transpersonal Vision*

GLOBALmindchange

GLOBAL mind change

The Promise Of The 21st Century

Willis Harman
Second Edition

INSTITUTE OF NOETIC SCIENCES

Berrett-Koehler Publishers, Inc.
San Francisco

Cover design by May Liang. Back cover photo by Victoria Rouse.

Berrett-Koehler Publishers, Inc.
450 Sansome Street, Suite 1200
San Francisco CA 94111-3320
Tel: 415-288-0260   Fax: 415-362-2512
www.bkpub.com

Institute of Noetic Sciences
475 Gate Five Road, Suite 300
Sausalito CA 94965
Tel: 415-331-5650   Fax: 415-331-5673
www.noetic.org

Ordering Information

Individual sales. Berrett-Koehler publications are available through most bookstores. They can also be ordered direct from Berrett-Koehler at the address above.

Quantity sales. Special discounts are available on quantity purchases by corporations, associations, and others. For details, contact the "Special Sales Department" at the Berrett-Koehler address above.

Orders for college textbook/course adoption use. Please contact Berrett-Koehler Publishers at the address above.

Orders by US trade bookstores and wholesalers. Please contact Publishers Group West, 1700 Fourth Street, Berkeley CA 94710. Phone 510-528-1444; fax 510-528-3444

Printed in the United States of America

 Printed on acid-free and recycled paper that is composed of 85% recovered fiber, including 15% post consumer waste.

Library of Congress Cataloging-in-Publication Data

Harman, Willis W.
     Global mind change: the promise of the twenty-first century /
  Willis W. Harman. -- 2nd ed., rev. and expanded
          p.   cm.
     Includes bibliographical references and index.
     ISBN 1-57675-029-9
     1. Social change.   2. Attitude change.   I. Title.
HM101.H28   1998
303.4--dc21
                                                   98-21139
                                                      CIP

Second Edition
03   02   01   00   99   98   10 9 8 7 6 5 4 3 2 1

DEDICATION

I wish to dedicate this book to four persons
who have profoundly affected the latter part
of my life: Alfred M. Hubbard and Judith
Skutch Whitson, who were my teachers in
the truest sense, and Paul Temple and Henry
Rolfs, whose generosity, through the Institute of Noetic Sciences, has given me the
freedom to serve in the best way I know.

CONTENTS

PREFACE XI

FOREWORD BY HAZEL HENDERSON XV

CHAPTER ONE 1
The Scientific Heresy: Transformation Of A Society

The Copernican Revolution 2
Intimations Of Paradigm Change 8
Unconscious Belief 12
The Lesson Of Hypnosis 15

CHAPTER TWO 19
Consciousness As Causal Reality

The Shaping Of The Scientific Worldview 20
Unspoken Assumptions Of Conventional Science 24
Choose Your Metaphysic 28
Three Metaphysical Perspectives 30
The Plausibility Of M-3 Dominance 32

CHAPTER THREE 37
Challenges To Positivism And Reductionism

The Mind In Health, Illness, And Healing 38
Attention And Volition 43
Mind, Instinct, And Evolution 45
Exceptional Capabilities 49

CHAPTER FOUR 55
The New Paradigm In Science

The Difficult Task Of Being Open-Minded 56
Scientific Objectivity And Reliability 61
Multiple Persons In A Single Body 63
Affirmation And Inner Imagery 69
The Limits Of Creativity 70
The 'Perennial Wisdom' In Religion 73
Science And The 'Perennial Wisdom' 76

CHAPTER FIVE 83
Legitimising The Transpersonal

The Issue Of Unembodied Existence 85
Toward A More Comprehensive Science 88
Scientific Causality: A Philosophical Comment 101
Toward A More Adequate Epistemology 112
Considering The Possibility Of
Different Ontological Assumptions 115
A Concluding Comment 116

CHAPTER SIX 119
Transforming The World Macroproblem

A Different Perspective 122
Origins Of The World Macroproblem 126
Clues From Social Movements 130
Value Emphases Of The Trans-Modern World 137
Symbol Of A New Relationship With The Earth 140
The Greeks Had A Word For It 143
The New Business Of Business 144

CHAPTER SEVEN 149
Aspects Of The World System Change

Four Challenges To The Present Order 150
The 'Central Myth' Of Modern Society 160
The Necessity For Redefining Work 161
Money, Banking, And Debt 171
Redefining Global Development 174
Finding Global Security 178
Politics And Values 185
Leading Edge Change: An Example 189
Concluding Thoughts 194

References And Further Reading 195
Index 197
About The Author 205
About The Institute Of Noetic Sciences 206
About Berrett-Koehler Publishing 209

PREFACE

If the world that science tells us about is reality,
how does it happen that we don't feel more at home in it?

The factors and forces to bring about a global mind change are already in motion.

Throughout history, the really fundamental changes in societies have come about not from dictates of governments and the results of battles but through vast numbers of people changing their minds—sometimes only a little bit.

Some of these changes have amounted to profound transformations—for instance the transition from the Roman Empire to Medieval Europe, or from the Middle Ages to modern times. Others have been more specific, such as the constitution of democratic governments in England and America, or the termination of slavery as an accepted institution. In the latter cases, it is largely a matter of people recalling that no matter how powerful the economic or political or even military institution it persists because it has legitimacy, and that legitimacy comes from the perceptions of people. People give legitimacy and they can take it away. A challenge to legitimacy is probably the most powerful force for change to be found in history.

To the empowering principle that the people can withhold legitimacy, and thus change the world, we now add another: By deliberately changing the internal image of reality, people can change the world. Perhaps the only limits to the human mind are those we believe in.

The first twenty years of my professional life were spent teaching electrical engineering and systems analysis at a major university. The next twenty were as a social scientist and futurist in a contract research organization, helping clients in government and business do strategic planning over a very wide range of practical policy issues. My particular task was to help them think about the issues in the context of the future environment in which the consequences of their decisions would manifest. To deal with these puzzles full time, day after day, was an unusual privilege, and I learned much. As the years went on, I found that a picture was forming in my mind of the meaning of our times and of many plausible alternative futures. The picture got clearer, and by the time I retired from that career and moved on to a third (the present one), I had little remaining doubt about the fundamental nature of the transformation we are living through. Although I was aware that some aspects seemed preposterous to most, I was convinced (and my conviction continues to strengthen) that the real action today is changing *fundamental assumptions*.

In 1977 I accepted the invitation of Edgar Mitchell and the board of the Institute of Noetic Sciences to join them in "expanding knowledge of the nature and potentials of the mind, and applying that knowledge to the advancement of health and well-being for humankind and the planet." (The word "noetic," from the Greek word "nous" meaning mind, intelligence, understanding, implies the three ways in which we gain knowledge: the reasoning processes of the intellect, the perception of our experiences through the senses, and the intuitive, spiritual or inner ways of knowing. Noetic Sciences is the systematic study of these all-inclusive ways of knowing, which form the basis for how we see ourselves, each other, and the world.)

Since the work of the Institute is at the heart of the contemporary "paradigm change"—it is precisely in this area that the basic assumptions underlying modern Western society are most called into question—I knew I had found an ideal place to be.

But the task is not easy. People are threatened by the awareness (conscious or unconscious) of impending change in their lives. The prospect that "truths" they have known all their lives might be superseded by some other beliefs can be especially threatening. Thus there is a tendency to "fight back"—to actively oppose the change. Note the fundamentalist reaction in all parts of the globe to modern society's embodiment of change as a way of life—technological change, increasing power of institutions, weakening of older value commitments.

You can imagine that critical examination of the basic assumptions undergirding modern society itself will be all the more threatening. Sociological and historical researches show that during similar revolutionary changes there are, typically, increases in frequency of mental illness, social disruption and use of police to quell the disruption, violent crime, terrorism, religious cultism, and acceptance of sexual hedonism. These signs are, of course, visible today, and they may well intensify before they return to more normal levels. They are all basically responses to the underlying anxiety and uncertainty to the unconscious threat of change.

Understanding the necessity of change probably reduces the threat as one sees that world society can not continue much longer on its current, increasingly nonviable tract. But societal change implies individual change, and it is that which brings on the sharpest anxiety.

The next decade or two are particularly critical. I believe the key challenge is not to try to resist a change that may well be inevitable, nor is it to be zealous in fomenting a change prematurely. It is, rather, trying to help our society understand the nature and necessity of the forces of historical change we are experiencing, to go through the change with mutual cooperation and caring, with as little misery as possible.

Through truth-telling and dialogue and sincere attempts to see the world through the other person's eyes, together we can come to an understanding of what it is that needs doing, and to a joint commitment that it gets done. All my life I have heard the admonition "Don't just talk; get out there and do something!" The problem is that in times like these we are all too likely to do what turns out to be the wrong thing. If it is to represent the best advice for such uncertain times, the maxim should probably be turned around: *Don't just do something; get out there and talk.*

In this third career what I feel most keenly to be my own mission is to promote that dialogue and contribute to that understanding. This book is a step in that direction; I hope it is a helpful one.

Willis W. Harman
Sausalito, California
September 1987

ADDENDUM FOR THE SECOND EDITION:

In a way I am surprised how much of the previous text of this book stands up a decade after it was written. The changes made, while significant, are chiefly extensions resulting from my increased understanding. These are mainly in two areas.

First, the ongoing work of the Institute of Noetic Sciences has resulted in a much more satisfactory understanding of what must be done in science. This has resulted in the addition of a completely new Chapter 5.

Second, a sharpening of the issue of the unsustainability of the modern way of life has increased the clarity with which some of the issues in Chapters 6 and 7 are discussed, particularly as regards the crucial role of business in this transitional period.

Willis W. Harman
Sausalito, California
October 1995

ACKNOWLEDGMENTS

I would like to acknowledge with gratitude the insights that have come to me from many people, particularly Brendan O'Regan, Tom Hurley and Barbara McNeill, staff members at the Institute of Noetic Sciences. Thanks also to Institute staff members Christian de Quincey, Carol Guion and David Johnson for their invaluable aid in producing the book, and to May Liang for the cover design.

Foreword

Hazel Henderson

I AM DEEPLY HONORED to help refocus attention on Willis Harman's crucial work. Willis considered *Global Mind Change* his most succinct "signature" book, and made this revised edition his last task in life. During his final few weeks, Willis and I communicated briefly. He was ready for his next journey, and I promised to stay committed to the spirit of his work—opening minds to the dazzling array of possibilities that await humans and their societies as we shed our self-imposed historical, cultural, and conceptual blinders.

Willis and I shared—along with many others now swelling into millions—this passion for the possible. I first discovered it in myself as a child—it was embodied in the pristine, magical world of nature, in the misty depths of the English countryside, the chattering robins in the hedgerows, the carpets of bluebells in the woods, the delicious fruits and vegetables my mother grew in our garden, and the intrepid seagulls heading out into the adventurous Atlantic ocean. I, too, headed westward to the United States of America, a beacon of possibilities to generations of Europeans who related deeply to its Constitution, Bill of Rights, and the daring dream of pursuing life, liberty, and happiness.

I first met Willis Harman in 1972 in Washington, DC, at a confusing multi-dimensional event, the White House Conference on the Industrial World Ahead. I was invited as a "dissident" from the general celebratory monoculture of progress: overwhelmingly white, middle-aged male corporate executives and financiers. As a European and a cultural "outsider," I spoke freely of the new global agenda of human responsibilities—from cleaning up our environmental life-support system to harnessing capitalism and materialism to social justice, higher ethical behavior, and global standards. I encountered Willis Harman standing in a corridor. We caught each other's eye, and I blurted out, "I feel like a Martian here!" Willis grinned and nodded. He had articulated views similar to mine from his perspective as a futurist at the Stanford Research Institute. Willis shared concerns with me about bringing broader, longer-range perspectives into Congress, the White House, and Washington policy circles.

Willis and I worked together launching the Congressional Institute for the Future, on whose original board we served—together with Elise Boulding (now Professor Emerita, Dartmouth College), whose *Building a Global Civic Culture* helped a generation to envision today's uprising of millions of empowered citizens. Elise Boulding showed us the outline of a third sector beyond business and government: those "grassroots globalists" the late Jonas Salk called "cultural mutants who have the audacity to take responsibility for the whole human species."

When *Global Mind Change* was published in 1987, I savored every word, and I still do. Even though our paths rarely crossed, Willis and I were and are metaphysically and soulfully connected. *Global Mind Change* helped to restore my faith after my second book, *The Politics of the Solar Age*, published in 1981, was banished from Washington policy debates as Ronald Reagan ascended the presidency. Futurists like me, predicting the end of the fossil-fueled Industrial Age and the dawning of the Solar Age, were deemed doomsayers, Luddites, or subversives. Yet the steady empowerment of millions with broader awareness, longer time frames, and higher consciousness could not be suppressed by the dominant culture's reductionist view of material progress via the global reach of positivist science and corporate industrialism.

Willis and I had shared our visions of more humane, equitable, and ecologically sustainable forms of development since our first meeting in 1972. Today, we can all see more clearly the outline of this vision emerging into our material reality. The United Nations Conference on Climate Change in Kyoto in 1997 saw the emergence of a scientific consensus on the need to phase out fossil fuels and move to solar-based technologies more in harmony with nature. Today, more US citizens visit alternative healthcare providers than doctors of the medical-industrial complex. Opinion surveys identify growing millions who are "downsizing" their material lives to better their overall quality of life and the rise of "cultural creatives" documented during the late 1990s. A new interpretation of human evolution is emerging from the dismal neoclassical economics of individual powerlessness to shape the blind forces of the market. From the statistical submergence in the Law of Large Numbers, the individual is emerging as a key actor in evolution of human societies, as David Loye shows in *The Evolutionary Outrider: The Impact of the Human Agent on Evolution* (1998) and *Darwin's Lost Theory* (1998).

Enormous dangers remain, dangers we humans have created—from still-stockpiled nuclear, chemical, and biological weapons to radioactive waste, toxic chemicals in our food, water, air, and soils. These are, as Willis says, *"symptoms"* of our state of mind, reflected as problems "out there." I called them "crises of perception"—and we see new symptoms in the expected computer crashes that will greet the year 2000. Already, billions of dollars have been spent to correct this seemingly minor programming error. This millennium "glitch" is now expected to cause a drop in productivity across the board in all industrial societies and will cost several hundred billions more before we are finished. Perhaps such systemic lessons, whether the Asian meltdown of 1997-98, stock market crashes, or a cascading shutdown of computerized services, are necessary to accelerate the shift to holistic, integrated, expanded planetary awareness.

Such learning experiences may help us see our current values and belief systems more clearly. The Greeks had a word for it—*hubris*: blind, overreaching pride in our own self-righteousness. One might add: short-termism, economism, and sheer states of denial. Let us hope that this new edition of *Global Mind Change* can help dispel this denial *of the rest of who we are*: evolving, creative beings with powerful minds, loving hearts, and the vision to see vast vistas of opportunities and possibilities that beckon us toward a future of our choosing.

—St Augustine, Florida
February 1998

INTRODUCTION

Imagine yourself a historian looking back from some time in the twenty-first century. What do you judge the most important thing that happened for the world in the twentieth century? Was it putting a man on the moon? Or creation of the United Nations? Or the development of nuclear weapons, or of computers and artificial intelligence?

My guess is that it will be something much less conspicuous to those of us who are living now, something whose significance will not be fully apparent for decades to come. It will be something as quiet as a change of mind, a change of mind that is bubbling up out of the unconscious depths, spreading around the world, changing everything.

It is much easier, of course, to answer that question about the seventeenth century. In retrospect, we can easily see that the most important development for the world was not the Thirty Years' War and the Peace of Westphalia, nor the ending of the Ming dynasty in China, nor even the establishment of colonies along the Atlantic seaboard of North America. Most people would probably agree, after some thought, that the winner is that total change of view which we call the scientific revolution. The scientific revolution started in Western Europe and ultimately affected the lives of people all over the Earth, in ways so fundamental it is hard to find a comparable transformation anywhere else in history.

It may seem an outrageous hypothesis that in the last third of the twentieth century we should be going through another such basic mind change, one at least as profound and far more rapid. Yet that is the thesis of this book.

We are already well into the mind change. It is altering the way we interpret science; it is drastically modifying our concepts of healthcare; it is revolutionizing our concepts of education; it is causing major changes in the world of business and finance; it is in the process of delegitimating war and causing a total rethinking of the means of achieving national and global security.

Yet its effects are relatively invisible. It does not show up clearly in survey research on values and lifestyles; its incursion into science thus far appears minor indeed; its examples in the corporate world are impressive, but represent a tiny fraction of the whole. The mind change is perhaps most visible in the reperceiving of healthcare and total fitness, yet even there its broader implications are not widely and openly discussed.

Few today doubt that the world is going through some sort of structural transition. The evidence suggesting this is omnipresent. How major the structural change will be is more disputable. For some the pattern of a fundamental transformation fairly jumps out of the evidence; for others it is a much more problematic conclusion.

Most of us are hesitant to fancy that we might be living through one of the most fundamental shifts in the history of Western civilization. There is a certain reluctance to appear arrogant about our own times: Doesn't every generation think it is living in a unique historical period?

Yet the possibility must be taken seriously.

This small volume explores the hypothesis that a change is taking place at the most fundamental level of the belief structure of Western industrial society. The book is deliberately small, because its purpose is not to make a case with finality but to stimulate a critical dialogue—the few references cited are placed at the end of the book rather than placed throughout as footnotes. We may not be able to reach consensus on the correct interpretation of our times. But the stakes are high and the attempt is worth making.

However we view it, the present-day world situation is hazardous for civilization. The passengers on planet Earth have a rough passage ahead. Our ability to travel that passage together without a wreck depends on keeping levels of understanding high and anxiety low. Whatever conclusions one reaches participating in this dialogue will increase that needed understanding.

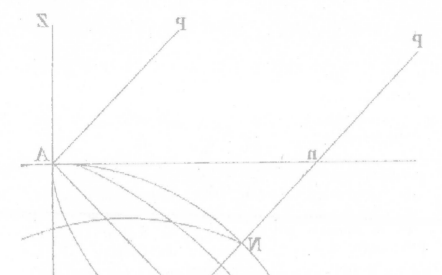

The Scientific Heresy: Transformation Of A Society

1

Every transformation . . . has rested

on a new metaphysical and

ideological base; or rather, upon

deeper stirrings and intuitions whose

rationalized expression takes the

form of a new picture of the cosmos

and the nature of man.

—Lewis Mumford

Once upon a time there was a merchant's son named Nicolaus Copernicus who lived in a small city in Poland. He was a student of law and medicine and mathematics. While still in his twenties he was internationally eminent as a lecturer in mathematics. Most of all, however, he was fascinated by the mathematical intricacies of astronomy . . .

The story is familiar to everyone. It is retold here because of its contemporary relevance. *Why did the Copernican ideas have such reverberations throughout all of Western Europe? How were such powerful transformational forces set in motion? Suppose a similar transformation were underway today—would we recognize the signs?*

THE COPERNICAN REVOLUTION

Copernicus did not intend a heresy, let alone a "revolution." He was a canon and lawyer at the Cathedral of Frauenberg, the northernmost Catholic diocese in Poland; however, he actually devoted much of his time to astronomical studies. As these studies progressed, he became increasingly dissatisfied with the prevailing theoretical system, that of the Alexandrian scholar Ptolemy. This interpretation of the heavens had become firmly entrenched in astronomical thought, virtually as an article of faith, having been used and taught for fourteen centuries. It was essentially geocentric, with the firmament a vast spherical crystalline shell revolving around the spherical Earth, and additional mechanisms supporting the sun, moon, and planets. The scheme involved an elaborate system of basic circular orbits with superimposed circular motions, called epicycles, added as necessary to account for observed irregularities in the motions of the planets. As observations had become progressively more accurate, more epicycles had to be added, and the whole system had become very unwieldy; it was increasingly difficult to use it for predicting future positions of the heavenly bodies.

Copernicus was a competent Greek scholar, and poring over ancient Greek writings he found that some of them had proposed a heliocentric model. In this view the apparent motions of the sun, moon, and planets were accounted for by imagining the Earth to rotate daily on its axis, and to revolve around the stationary sun once a year. At first blush this idea of the Earth moving around the sun seemed absurd,

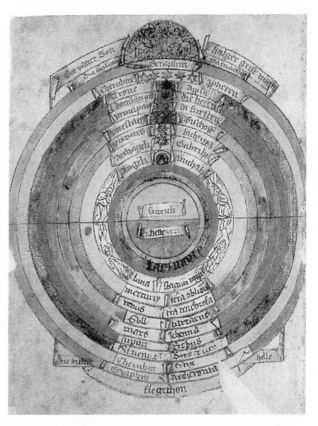

How Christian Europe saw the universe before Copernicus' time: with the Earth at its center. From a German manuscript, c. 1450.

but when Copernicus applied it to his data (retaining, however, the concept of uniform circular motions) he found the result was aesthetically superior and the model somewhat simpler, when compared with the Ptolemaic system.

At first he circulated the new ideas quietly only among his friends. Meanwhile, he developed his argument further with diagrams and mathematical computations. In order to have his model fit astronomical observations he found it necessary to add numerous complications. In the end, Copernicus' scheme was more elegant than Ptolemy's, but not particularly simpler. (It was Johannes Kepler, a contemporary of Galileo, who later added the notion of elliptical

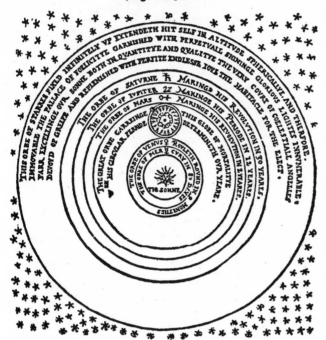

Nicolaus Copernicus established mathematically that the Earth moves around the sun in On the Revolution of the Celestial Spheres (1543).

orbits, and formulated the descriptive laws of planetary motion in a far simpler form.)

After three decades of gestation, Copernicus' book *On the Revolution of the Celestial Spheres* was finally published in the year of his death, 1543; a second edition was printed in 1566, and by the end of the century it was well distributed in both Protestant and Catholic countries of Western Europe. His work not only offered an alternative system to the Ptolemaic, on several points it was in direct conflict with the venerated ideas of Aristotle. For instance, Aristotle had argued for the fixity of the Earth, and had taught that bodies fall to the ground because that is their "natural place"—closer to the center of the universe. If Copernicus was right, a new explanation for the behavior of falling bodies was clearly needed, since the Earth no longer held a singular position. (The re-examination of this matter eventually led to Newton's concept of universal gravitation.)

Throughout Western Christendom Aristotle's doctrines had become elevated almost to the level of religious dogma. To some, the new ideas of Copernicus amounted to heresy. To others, however, who had found the Aristotelian dogma stifling of intellectual development, the break with traditional doctrines actually added to the attractiveness of the Copernican theory.(For example, in his *Dialogue on the Two Chief Systems of the World* [1632], Galileo argues pointedly, through discussion between fictional characters, that it is most reasonable that the Earth moves and is not the center of the universe, and hence Aristotle's whole cosmology is baseless. The feeble defense of Aristotle is left to true-believer Simplicius, whose loyalist arguments are mercilessly attacked.)

The implications of Copernicus' ideas went much further, however. The dethronement of the Earth from the center of the universe caused profound shock. No longer could the Earth be considered the epitome of creation, for it was only a planet like the other planets. No longer was the Earth the site of all change and decay with the changeless universe encompassing it. And the belief in a correspondence between man, the microcosm, as a mirror of the surrounding universe, the macrocosm, was no longer valid. Actually, the implication was that man might not have such a special place in creation after all. The Copernican ideas became one focus of tremendous controversies in religion, philosophy, and social theory, which set the tenor of the modern mind; they catalyzed a major transition in Western values. In truth, the Copernican revolution amounted to a successful challenge to the entire system of ancient authority, requiring a complete change in the philosophical conception of the universe. It was heresy on the grand scale. Ultimately the "scientific heresy" prevailed, and we now look back on it as an unqualifiedly positive evolutionary step.

Today we know that the transformation in thought that is symbolized by the Copernican episode reached far outside astronomical and philosophical debate; it was part of an even broader transformation, involving the whole way of looking at the world—the transformation that we now call "the scientific revolution." The revolutionaries saw themselves as attacking the traditional ways of thinking and educating. The heresy was directed at the authority system known as Scholasticism. Scholasticism assumed a living world created and guided by God for man's benefit. Its understandings were largely arrived at by citing authorities, either philosophical or scriptural. The primary function of this knowledge was to rationalize sense experience in harmony with revealed religion. In contrast, the new way was empirical: *What is true is what is found by scientific inquiry to be true. Ultimate authority resides in observation and experiment rather than tradition.*

Thus in 1600 an educated man (most educated persons were men) knew that the Earth was the center of the cosmos—the seat of change, decay, and Christian redemption—while above it circled the planets and stars, themselves pure and unchanging but moved by some sort of intelligent or divine spirits and also signaling and influencing human events by their locations and aspects. A hundred years later this man's equally Christian descendant, say his great-grandson, knew (unless he lived in a church-controlled Catholic country) that the Earth was but one of many planets orbiting around one of many stars, moving through and separated by unimaginable distances—all still under the overall guidance of God, but with an important difference. The outlook of the first individual was *teleological*: The universe is alive and imbued with purpose; all creatures are part of a Great Chain of Being, with man between the angels and the lower animals; events are explained by divine purpose or by their function in a meaningful world. To his great-grandson, by contrast, it is essentially a dead universe, constructed and set in motion by the Creator, with subsequent events accounted for by mechanical forces and lawful behaviors. The great-grandfather, as a reasonable man, would accept the overwhelming evidence for the working of enchantments, the occurrence of miracles, the existence of witches and other beings with supernatural powers; his descendant, with equal certainty, would dismiss all those stories as the results of charlatanry and delusion.

The scientific revolution amounted to a new way of seeking and validating knowledge. Knowledge was no longer to be regarded as the established property of a priesthood; it was to be sought in open inquiry, and validated in public by agreed-upon means. Authority was to be sought in experience, rather than orthodoxy. Gradually the role of Providence was transferred to the "natural laws" whereby God was thought to operate. Rather than resulting from the "grace" of Divine intervention, change was increasingly thought of as "evolution" and "stages of advancement" and "material progress." The development of the scientific method (effectively articulated by Francis Bacon) was to bring about creation of vast accumulations of knowledge, and the eventual application of that knowledge to manipulation of the physical environment—to the presumed betterment of man's condition on Earth. Progress in the arts and sciences became linked with material well-being and spiritual fulfillment—on Earth, rather than at some future time in Heaven.

Nor did the changes stop there. In retrospect, historians and social scientists can now see that the time of Copernicus marked a historic watershed. Before that were centuries of the period we call, broadly, the Middle Ages. After the Copernican impact the course was irrevocably set for what we now call modern times. To be sure, society was changing during the entire period of the Middle Ages, and the changes in one part of Europe were quite different from those in another. In addition, there were other critical developments taking place around the same time as the scientific revolution—the Protestant Reformation, for example, and the economic or capitalist revolution. Furthermore, modern times in the late twentieth century are not the same as modern times in the 1950s, or the 1920s. Thus to pick out a particular period as characterized by extraordinary change is somewhat of an artificiality. Still, there is something to that idea of a watershed. Modern times really *are* fundamentally different from the Middle Ages (as those in turn were different from the days of the Roman Empire). The most basic difference is in the underlying view of reality.

Lewis Mumford dealt with this matter of fundamental societal change in a little book published almost half a century ago called *The Transformations of Man* (1956). Some change is taking place all the time, of course, and yet there seem to be particular periods in history when society goes through a more fundamental kind of change, involving all its institutions and even more basic aspects of its culture. Mumford claimed that there have not been more than four or five such "transformations" in the entire history of Western civilization. The most recent one is that marking the end of the Middle Ages.

Mumford observes that "Every transformation of man . . . has rested on a new metaphysical and ideological base; or rather, upon deeper stirrings and intuitions whose rationalized expression takes the form of a new picture of the cosmos and the nature of man." Turning this statement around, the hallmark of transformation is a change at the deepest level of the social structure. Every society ever known rests on some set of largely tacit basic assumptions about *who we are, what kind of universe we are in, and what is ultimately important to us*. Some such set of assumptions can be found to underlie the institutions and mores, patterns of thought and systems of value, that characterize a society. They are typically not formulated or taught because they don't need to be—they are absorbed by each person born into the society as though by osmosis. They are accepted as given, as obviously true—and throughout most of history, by most people, never questioned.

A word made popular by Thomas Kuhn in his study of *The Structure of Scientific Revolutions* (1970) has often been used (sometimes quite loosely) to speak of societal transformation in terms of "paradigm change." When used this way, the dominant paradigm of a society refers to *the basic ways of perceiving, thinking, valuing, and doing, associated with a particular view of reality.* What was so earth-shaking about the Copernican revolution was that *the fundamental view of reality* was shifting; with that shift came major changes in "the basic ways of perceiving, thinking, valuing, and doing"—changes that heralded the modern era.

It would not have been possible for someone in the early part of the seventeenth century, say, to forecast what the consequences of the paradigm change would be—if, indeed, one were able to recognize that such a fundamental belief-system shift was taking place. The best one could have hoped to do would be to suggest some broad characteristics of the new society. Similarly, if such a transformation is taking place today, we can identify that fact and anticipate some characteristics of post-transformation, trans-modern society. But even that could be extremely useful and is what we will be attempting in this book.

INTIMATIONS OF PARADIGM CHANGE

What manner of evidence could justify such an extravagant comparison as implied by the phrase the *second* Copernican revolution, or might cause us to think of "a *new* heresy" that could change the world as much as the "scientific heresy" did? We shall give a preliminary answer here and then explore the subject in more detail in later chapters.

Roger Sperry of the California Institute of Technology shared the 1981 Nobel Prize in Physiology or Medicine for his work in human split-brain studies. Sperry's research, involving extensive observation of patients whose brains had actually been divided by severing the corpus callosum joining the two halves, showed that there are important differences in functioning between the left and right halves of the brain. (Not as much difference, perhaps, as one might be led to believe from the "left-brain, right-brain" myth of pop psychology, but nevertheless a significant difference.) As an accompaniment to this honor, he was invited to write the lead article for the 1981 *Annual Review of Neuroscience.*

Now the traditional summary article in an annual review is, as one would gather from the title, a review of the past year's accomplishments in the particular area, plus some strong intimations that much more could be done if there were only more funding. Sperry's paper, entitled "Changing Priorities," did not follow the traditional pattern. Instead, he wrote of the importance of the previously neglected area of subjective experience, and noted a profound development, which he describes as follows:

> Current concepts of the mind-brain relation involve a direct break with the long-established materialist and behaviorist doctrine that has dominated neuroscience for many decades. Instead of renouncing or ignoring consciousness, the new interpretation gives full recognition to the primacy of inner conscious awareness as a causal reality.

It is probably not true that Sperry's colleagues all agree with him, and it is certain that much of the scientific community does not. We shall have to see, later on, what kinds of evidence can be adduced to support this statement. But for the moment just assume it is true. Think of how revolutionary a thought this is, that science should now accommodate consciousness as a *causal reality.*

Throughout most of the history of most kinds of science, scientific research and theory have been based in an implicit metaphysic that is both *reductionistic* and *positivistic.* That is to say, scientists have sought to explain phenomena in terms of more elementary happenings (for example, color explained in terms of wavelength, gas pressure in terms of the motion of the gas molecules); and what is real (or at least discussible) is taken to be that which can be *measured*—that is, what is ultimately discernible to the physical senses, either directly or by the use of scientific instrumentation.

This bias was a most useful one for many purposes. It was especially so for distinguishing scientific explanations from such prescientific interpretations as the whims of the gods, or the intervention of divine grace, or such "natural tendencies" as bodies seeking to come to rest near the center of the universe and nature abhorring a vacuum.

It was the hallmark of the behavioral sciences emphasis of the 1950s that only behavior and forces (stimuli) that were ultimately measurable could be talked about scientifically; the realm of subjective experience could be dealt with only in terms of these externally observable phenomena. Thus the study of consciousness, in scientific terms, was reduced to examination of behavior (such as awareness, responsiveness) that could be observed from outside the organism. Early approaches to dealing with inner conscious awareness in its own terms (that is, introspectionism) had been discredited. Tough-minded behavioral scientists insisted that it would be impossible to build a reliable science based on self-reports of inner, subjective experience (as the phenomenologists and gestaltists had tried to do).

The behavioral predilection became quite strong by mid-century, particularly in the United States. Nevertheless, there remained the sneaking suspicion on the part of many, scientists as well as nonscientists, that something important was being left out. After all, the only experience of reality that we have *directly* is our own conscious awareness. There was something very unnatural about a science that seemed to deny consciousness as a causal reality when everyday experience seemed to confirm again and again that it is my *decision* to act that causes action.

There were other poses that one had to assume in order to be in accord with the sophisticated scientific view of the day, which felt equally artificial. One tried to accept that it is the brain that is real, and conscious awareness is an "epiphenomenon" (that is, something to be explained in terms of more fundamental matters). The question "Does mind exist?" seemed a serious one. The complex products of creative imagination were supposed to have come about through some sort of random cycling of a brain-computer, together with some kind of selection of "best fit." We were supposed to believe that the complex instinctual behaviors of animals and complex physiological systems such as the two eyes that give us binocular vision had developed through our evolutionary past exclusively as a result of random mutations plus natural selection.

Besides, there were the anomalies to remind us that all was not well with the orthodox scientific worldview. Down through the centuries a variety of anomalous phenomena, including clairvoyant remote viewing, telepathic communication, levitation and teleportation, "instantaneous" spiritual healing, and other "psychic" phenomena, had been reported. Various explanations had been offered as to why these reports were probably mistaken. Famous and competent scientists had arrayed themselves on both sides of the debate. A half-century ago it seemed fairly clear that in spite of the claims of a few people doing research in parapsychology, or "psychic research," the better educated and more sophisticated public felt confident that scientific advance was making the genuineness of the phenomena decreasingly plausible.

What was common to all of these anomalous psychic phenomena was that *mind* seemed to have some effects in the physical world—directly, as in the reported instances of dramatic healing, or indirectly, as in the presumed telepathic communication. But that was true in everyday and commonplace phenomena as well. I decide to raise my right arm, and behold!—it goes up. Attitudes toward one's work bring about tension and stress, and an ulcer results. Patients told that a plain sugar pill has curative powers experience remission of the symptoms of their illness (the placebo effect). In our everyday experience it would seem strained and artificial to deny that what goes on in our minds has effects on our actions. Yet *as scientists*, more than one generation of students were trained to engage in that denial.

It is in the light of these decades of *denial* of consciousness as causal reality that Roger Sperry's pronouncement comes with such impact. It is similar to the impact of Copernicus' theories after centuries of denying that the Earth, being the assumed center of the universe and special focus of Divine attention, could possibly move.

As "the Earth goes around the sun" became the somewhat inadequate summary of the Copernican revolution, so "consciousness as causal reality" is that of the "second Copernican revolution."

But as we recognize "inner conscious awareness as causal reality" we are immediately reminded of Sigmund Freud's insistence that unconscious processes are also causal with regard to our behavior. In assessing how and how much these new elements are going to change things, the most useful starting point for our purposes is the idea of *unconscious beliefs*.

UNCONSCIOUS BELIEF

This concept of unconscious beliefs and the extent to which they are capable of shaping and distorting our perceptions of everything around us—and within us—is so central to understanding the global mind change that we shall make a temporary digression to look into it more deeply.

Each of us holds some set of beliefs with which we conceptualize our experience—beliefs about history, beliefs about things, beliefs about the future, about what is to be valued, or about what one ought to do. What may be less obvious is that we have unconscious beliefs as well as conscious ones. (There are many ways in which people have attempted to talk about the processes and contents of the conscious and unconscious minds. In the following discussion we will use a way that is adequately powerful, yet as free as possible of psychological jargon. It employs the concept of the conscious and unconscious *belief system* as introduced by psychologist Milton Rokeach in *The Open and Closed Mind* [1960].)

People may not realize they have these unconscious beliefs, but the beliefs can be inferred from behavior—from slips of the tongue, compulsive acts, "body language," and so on. A familiar example from psychotherapy is an unconscious belief in one's inadequacy or inferiority. Individuals may consciously feel adequate and equal, at least most of the time, but under certain circumstances the behavior, body posture, and so on may betray that they unconsciously believe something else to be the case.

Thus we cannot take at face value what people say they believe. They may be deceiving us deliberately, or they may be rationalizing, not knowing what they deeply believe. We have to infer a person's unconscious beliefs from everything he or she says and does. That is as true of ourselves as it is of others. We do not know what we believe unconsciously, but it is almost certainly not what we consciously believe we believe.

The person's *total belief system* is an organization of beliefs and expectancies that the person accepts as true of the world he or she lives in—verbal and nonverbal, implicit and explicit, conscious and unconscious.

The belief system does not have to be logically consistent; indeed, it probably never is. It may be compartmentalized, containing logically contradictory beliefs that typically do not come into conscious awareness at the same times. The person unconsciously wards off evidence that might reveal such an inner contradiction. Notice that this decision to *not* become consciously aware of something is unconscious. We *choose* as well as believe unconsciously.

The belief system can be conceived of as comprising "concentric" regions or shells. The outermost region contains beliefs that are relatively accessible to conscious awareness and relatively easy to change (as by education). Somewhat more deeply embedded in the system are intermediate-level beliefs, less accessible and more resistant to change. Some of these intermediate-level unconscious beliefs are worked with in psychotherapy (such as the judgments of the "internalized parent"). This intermediate region contains beliefs about the nature of authority (for example, whether I trust my own experience or accept the interpretation of some external authority). In the innermost core of the belief system are basic unconscious assumptions about the nature of the self and its relationship to others, and about the nature of the universe. Typically a person may go through most of life with these core beliefs essentially unchanged. When they do change, the shift is likely to be accompanied by a rather stressful period in the person's life.

Belief systems serve two powerful and conflicting sets of motives at the same time. One is the need for a cognitive framework to interpret new experience—to perceive and understand and act responsively. The other is the need to ward off threatening aspects of reality. Our belief systems are our way of making sense out of raw experience. However, they may also distort if necessary to preserve the illusion of order—as, for instance, when we "forget" an incident that doesn't "fit in." (Repression of early childhood memories of traumatic experiences is a familiar example.)

A belief system may be defined as *open* to the extent that new data can enter and affect existing beliefs. A person will be open to information insofar as possible, but will unconsciously reject it, screen it out, or alter it insofar as is necessary to ward off threat and anxiety. The closed mind can distort the world and narrow it down to whatever extent is needed to serve these protective goals and still preserve the illusion of understanding it. The more closed the belief system, the more it can be understood as a tightly woven network of cognitive defenses against anxiety, designed to shield a vulnerable mind.

As was just suggested, we not only believe unconsciously, we also choose unconsciously. This shows up with particular clarity in the case of subliminal perception. In one form of this well-known phenomenon an image is flashed on a screen for a very brief interval—so brief that the person is not consciously aware of having seen anything. However, a physiological response (such as a change in the electrical conductivity of the skin indicating an emotional reaction, or an "event-related potential" in the brain indicating surprise) or a psychological response (for example, influenced free-association) may make it clear that at an unconscious level the person indeed did perceive the image, analyze its meaning, and "choose" an appropriate response.

We need not have gone to the laboratory for an example, of course. Unconscious choosing is evident in everyday life. For instance, I may consciously choose to carry out a certain action that contradicts an unconscious belief (possibly implanted very early in childhood) that the action is *bad*. As a result of an unconscious choice, then, a feeling is telegraphed to the conscious mind—a feeling we call *guilt*. From still another part of the mind, the deep intuition, may come another choice: to reconcile the conflict and get rid of the guilt feelings.

This is but one example of a more general observation, namely, that the typical individual is psychologically fragmented. While the conscious mind is making one set of choices, other fragments of the mind, outside of conscious awareness, are choosing other things. (A rather old-fashioned term describes the individual who had more or less integrated these various fragments into a whole, capable of conflict-free decision: a person of *integrity*.)

Few findings in the social sciences are as well established as the fact that the greater portion of our total mental activity goes on outside of conscious awareness: *We believe, value, choose, and know unconsciously as well as consciously.* Furthermore, our perceptions, values, attitudes, and behavior are influenced far more by what is going on in the unconscious mind than by what is easily accessible to the conscious mind. Although this fact is quite well publicized in our day, we typically live, think, and behave without taking seriously its many implications. (Think, for example, how differently education would be viewed if this fact were taken seriously.)

The way we perceive reality is strongly influenced by unconsciously held beliefs. The phenomena of denial and resistance in psychotherapy illustrate how thoroughly one tends not to see things threatening to deeply held images conflicting with deeply held beliefs. Research on hypnosis, self- and experimenter-expectations, authoritarianism and prejudice, subliminal perception, and selective attention has demonstrated over and over that our perceptions and "reality checks" are influenced, far more than is ordinarily assumed, by beliefs, attitudes, and other mental processes of which a large portion is unconscious. We perceive what we expect, what it has been suggested to us we should perceive, what we "need" to perceive—to an extent that we might be shocked by if we realized it consciously.

This influence of beliefs on perception is intensified when a large number of people believe the same thing. Cultural anthropologists have thoroughly documented how persons who grow up in different cultures perceive literally different realities. We can fool ourselves collectively as well as individually.

THE LESSON OF HYPNOSIS

The phenomena of hypnosis, in particular, emphasize dramatically how changes in unconscious beliefs, brought about in this case by suggestion, can alter perception and experience. The suggestion of the hypnotist, for example, can lead the subject to perceive an object or a person that, as far as any onlooker is concerned, really isn't there. Or the subject can be led to fail to perceive something that is there. The suggestion of a solid wall can become so real to the subject that his fist is bruised upon "striking" it. The suggestion that a pencil is a hot soldering iron causes it, when laid on the back of the hand, to raise the physical signs of a burn. Acceptance of the hypnotic suggestion that one cannot lift a light object produces a complete inability to do so. On the other hand, a more positive suggestion may lead to the body being able to perform feats it could not otherwise do—form a rigid bridge between two chairs, for example, or lift a heavy weight.

One of the most persuasive yet easily accessible experiences to emphasize this point is the firewalking seminar. Since these seminars were introduced into the United States and Europe in the early 1980s, many thousands of people have performed this feat, which defies all ordinary expectations about the effect of having flesh come in contact with fire. The essence of the experience is that a smooth bed of burning coals is prepared from a wood fire, and participants, having internalized the suggestion that no harm will ensue, walk barefoot over the coals. The seminars have been carried out with groups ranging in size from a few individuals to several hundred. It is not uncommon for nearly everyone to walk, and for nearly everyone to be unharmed. Yet the coals are hot (1200 to 1400 degrees Fahrenheit), hot enough to burn the soles of the feet badly in the absence of the protecting belief. Skeptics have claimed that there is a "physical" explanation such as low heat conductivity of charcoal, insulating layer of ash, "leidenfrost effect" of a thin layer of evaporated perspiration. But whatever the intermediating mechanism, the fact remains that when people change the unconscious belief that burning coals will barbecue the feet, they are insulated from harm; change the belief back again and severe third-degree burns can result. The experience is powerful because any doubter can experiment by changing the belief and suffering the painful result.

The conclusion we are aiming at does not depend upon any single bit of evidence, so there is no need to strain at explaining away the firewalking phenomenon. (Some skeptics have insisted that it is not necessary to believe that the fire will not harm; it is sufficient to believe strongly that it is not necessary to believe! The suggested "explanations" that appear regularly in the media and scientific literature are much like adding epicycles to the Ptolemaic model— they give comfort to the explainer but add little to our real understanding.) The fundamental fact, powerful and empowering in its implications, is that our experiencing of reality is strongly affected by our internalized beliefs. Our beliefs, in turn, are affected by our experiencing of what we perceive as reality—which most of the time reinforces the beliefs. When it doesn't, we generally feel very uncomfortable—and may be on the way to learning something valuable.

Now each of us, from infancy onward, is subjected to a complex set of suggestions from our social environment, which in effect teaches us how to perceive the world. We may from time to time, especially in early childhood, have experiences that do not conform to this cultural norm—but we eventually "correct" these perceptions and cease experiencing the anomalies, through the power of the socializing process. And so each of us is literally *hypnotized* from infancy to perceive the world the way people in our culture perceive it.

In the modern world this "cultural hypnosis" extends to experiencing a world in which "scientific laws" are always obeyed—whereas in other, more "primitive" cultures, "violations" of these laws may be relatively commonplace. For example, the phenomenon of changing inner beliefs to such an extent that one can with impunity walk barefoot over burning coals, just mentioned, is one which has for centuries been observable in a variety of pre-modern societies. In some cases persons would stand in the fire for half an hour or more, or ladle handfuls of burning coals over their heads in a fiery shower.

In some "primitive" societies, remote perception (of the whereabouts of cattle that may have strayed out of sight, or of the well-being of distant relatives, for example) is regularly employed. In modern society the phenomenon of "remote viewing" was generally assumed to be physically impossible. How could one possibly "see" what was happening at distances of, perhaps, hundreds or thousands of miles? Yet in recent years, as interest developed in the possible utility of this phenomenon for purposes of military intelligence, there has been research with positive results in both the United States and the Soviet Union.

Reports from the Indian subcontinent of extraordinary capabilities of yogis to mentally control bodily processes were treated with considerable skepticism until the advent of biofeedback training showed that we all have the potential ability, to a far greater extent than had earlier been recognized, to control brain waves, blood flow, heartbeat, and the like.

These several examples emphasize the difficulty of distinguishing the extent to which the "reality" we perceive is peculiar to our cultural hypnosis. We tend to find it curious that other "primitive" or "traditional" cultures should perceive reality in the way they do—so obviously discrepant with the modern scientific worldview. It is harder to entertain the thought that we in modern Western society might have our own cultural peculiarities in the way we perceive the world—that our reality might be as parochial in its way as that of the Middle Ages appears to us now. Since Western science is the "best" knowledge system yet devised, it seems reasonable to consider our values "normal," our predilections "natural," and our perceived and measured world "real."

We now begin to see that comparing our times with the Copernican revolution is not as far-fetched as it may have seemed at first. It was not a comfortable matter, in the early seventeenth century, for an individual to admit into his or her personal belief system data that challenged the traditional beliefs—even granting that those beliefs had a few difficulties that would have to be patched up. It was hard to "see" challenging information precisely because the old belief system provided a coherent picture of the world that *worked*. Likewise it is not comfortable for some of us, in the late twentieth century, to recognize the parochial nature of our prevailing belief system (even though it may seem to be based on the best science available). It is hard for us to "see" evidence that doesn't fit in, and that suggests that the conventional worldview may be in a state of fundamental change. Despite our discomfort, it is essential to consider that possibility.

Consciousness As Causal Reality

2

Recent developments in the mind-brain

sciences rejecting reductionism and

mechanistic determinism on the one side,

and dualisms on the other, clear the way

for a rational approach to the theory and

prescription of values and to a natural

fusion of science and religion.

—Roger Sperry

I T MAY SEEM STRANGE that the consideration of consciousness as a "causal reality" is such an innovation. Doesn't it happen all the time, one wonders, that my *inner decision* to act *causes* something to happen in the objective world? Of course consciousness is a causal reality, one thinks. How could we have ever thought otherwise?

THE SHAPING OF THE SCIENTIFIC WORLDVIEW

We need to recall how the science we know came into being. The modern worldview that began to take shape in the seventeenth century was the result of a revolt of what seemed to be common sense against a system of thought that had come to seem repugnant. It was a declaration of faith in the senses as opposed to the speculative mind, and in the visible world as opposed to the unseen. It emphasized the empirical (as a reaction against the authority of Scholasticism) and the reductionist (as a better explanation than the medieval "spiritual forces").

There were also ample grounds for separating the objective, which can be viewed by all, from the subjective, which is viewed in the privacy of one's own mind. There were good reasons to concentrate on the objective—one was simply that more rapid progress could be made, but an equally cogent one was avoiding a territorial clash with the institutions of religion. The early scientists could now explore anew such areas as astronomy, mechanics, and anatomy without confronting too directly the religious dogmas of the day, but to venture into the human mind—to deal with matters of personal human purpose, destiny, and will—was more hazardous.

Attempting to probe into the mind and spirit was also likely to feel inappropriate to the scientist himself. Many scientists (beginning with Descartes, a profoundly religious man) recognized the limited applicability of the new approach. They assumed a demarcation between those areas of human experience suitable for the scientific method because of their essentially impersonal and mechanical character and those not.

Thus the scientists felt free to devote themselves to their new exploration unencumbered by responsibility for the ultimates of existence, leaving that to theologians, philosophers, and poets. This division of realms gave the scientists a relatively free hand in physical discovery. It provided a respected barrier behind which they might conveniently pursue their research, untrammeled by the constraints of personal conscience and/or political and religious censorship.

Again we need to qualify the implication that the seventeenth century was a sharp watershed. History and social evolution do not come quite so neatly packaged nor proceed in such linear fashion. It appears that in the florescence of the Middle Ages, in the twelfth and thirteenth centuries, there was not only concentration on the spiritual and the hereafter, but also a keen interest in economic, political, and social matters that concern life on Earth. As early as the thirteenth century there was a blooming of invention in Western Europe, bringing forth such crucial developments as the iron axe and plow, the horse collar, horseshoe, and stirrup, the windmill and waterwheel, and numerous craft techniques. For some reason, this technological impetus declined in the fourteenth and fifteenth centuries, and flowered again in the seventeenth and eighteenth centuries—the period we now think of as the beginning of the industrial revolution and the modern work ethic. Thus although the timing and form of the scientific revolution were indeed shaped by the evolution of the encompassing, broader society, the interaction of the two was complex.

By the nineteenth century science had expanded its activities into new areas of investigation, at the same time making increasingly exclusive claims for the cognitive. The scientific became equated with the reliably measurable, excluding a vast realm of human concern now discounted as "subjective" or "metaphysical."

In this regard the history of science is somewhat like the well-known story of the inebriate who had lost his house key in the dark down the street and was searching for it under the corner streetlight because "the light is better here." For quite understandable reasons, in its early centuries the new search for truth called empirical science concentrated "where the light was better"—on exploration of the quantitatively measurable aspects of the physical environment, ignoring issues of the human mind and spirit central to the humanities and the religions. And because science was acquiring tremendous prestige, the implication grew that there *was* nothing more to say. (It is as though the above mentioned searcher eventually came to conclude that there really isn't any street other than that area illuminated by the street lamp.)

Every knowledge system is shaped by the characteristics of the society that produces it. We are accustomed to considering the flow in the opposite direction, seeing how scientific and technological advances have shaped modern society. But it is of critical importance to recognize both flows. We have the kind of society we have in part because of the fruits of science and technology. But the converse is also true: We have the kind of science we have in part because of the particular nature of the society in which it was developed.

Thus one way of viewing the scientific revolution is as a shift in the sort of knowledge that was valued by society. Medieval society was not strongly interested in technology. A new dynamism entered with the interrelated developments we call the Reformation, the rise of capitalism, and the scientific revolution. The underlying belief-system shift included increased emphasis on manipulation of the physical environment through technology. That in turn required a valuing of that knowledge which is useful for the development of technology—namely, knowledge that will enable prediction and control. Increasingly, through the first two-thirds of the twentieth century, scientific knowledge and the "scientific method" were identified with prediction-and-control knowledge. It went largely unnoticed that other societies (such as in ancient Greece, India, Europe in the Middle Ages) had valued other kinds of knowledge, useful for other purposes than the technological conquest of nature.

Another example of this shaping of science by society is seen in the current funding and support pattern. In the United States today, government funding of scientific research is, as a matter of policy, almost exclusively dedicated to pursuit of knowledge that will (a) aid the economy, (b) contribute to military technological capabilities, or

(c) enhance medical high-technology. Other funding sources such as foundations are also strongly inclined in these directions.

In general, any society finds certain questions to be of great interest to it (such as, What knowledge will add to technological capability?), and others very much less so (for example, What kinds of inner exploration lead to a sense of deep meaning and purpose in life?). Thus *every society's knowledge system is parochial*—even modern science.

Furthermore, every lasting knowledge system satisfies the tests that it is put to. That is, human experience tends to confirm it, or it would not retain the commanding position that it holds. Thus there are cultures in which all of nature is alive and in communication with human beings, and there are cultures in which the weather, harvests, and game are managed by assorted gods. Whatever the belief system of a particular culture, it *works*. It has been subjected to tests, and reality is perceived as conforming to the belief system.

Part of the problem with the modern scientific worldview is that it hasn't worked in a critical area of individual and social life—the area of choosing and implementing fundamental value commitments. As Roger Sperry pointed out in his landmark paper on "Changing Priorities":

> Beliefs concerning the ultimate purpose and meaning of life and the accompanying worldview perspectives that mold beliefs of right and wrong are critically dependent, directly or by implication, on concepts regarding the conscious self and the mind-brain relation and the kinds of life goals and cosmic views which these allow. Directly and indirectly social values depend . . . on whether consciousness is believed to be mortal, immortal, reincarnate, or cosmic . . . localized and brain-bound or essentially universal. . . . Recent conceptual developments in the mind-brain sciences rejecting reductionism and mechanistic determinism on the one side, and dualisms on the other, clear the way for a rational approach to the theory and prescription of values and to a natural fusion of science and religion.

Thus the Western neglect of the realm of subjective experience has had serious consequences in our confusion about values. For it is ultimately in this realm of the subjective, the transcendent, and the spiritual that all societies have found the basis for their deepest value commitments and sense of meaning.

UNSPOKEN ASSUMPTIONS OF CONVENTIONAL SCIENCE

It is humbling to the educated Westerner to realize that to an indeterminable extent science, like the traditional belief systems of "primitive" cultures, describes a world that is shaped by its built-in assumptions. To illustrate this, consider the following set of ten premises which, if encountered in a textbook a few decades ago, would hardly have aroused question:

A Rational Set Of Premises For A Scientific Age

1. The only conceivable ways in which we can acquire knowledge are through our physical senses, and perhaps by some sort of information transmission through the genes. The sole way in which we extend our understanding of the nature of the universe is through empirical science—that is, the exploration of the measurable world through instrumentation that augments our physical senses.

2. All qualitative properties (at least the ones we can talk about scientifically) are ultimately reducible to quantitative ones (for example, color is reduced to wavelength, thought to measurable brain waves, hate and love to the chemical composition of glandular secretions).

3. There is a clear demarcation between the objective world, which can be perceived by anyone, and subjective experience, which is perceived by the individual alone, in the privacy of his/her own mind. Scientific knowledge deals with the former; the latter may be important to the individual, but its exploration does not lead to the same kind of publicly verifiable knowledge.

4. The concept of free will is a prescientific attempt to explain behavior that scientific analysis reveals is due to a combination

of forces impinging on the individual from the outside, together with pressures and tensions internal to the organism.

5. What we know as consciousness or awareness of our thoughts and feelings is a secondary phenomenon arising from physical and biochemical processes in the brain.

6. What we know as memory is strictly a matter of stored data in the central nervous system, somewhat analogous to the storage of information in a digital computer.

7. The nature of time being what it is, there is obviously no way in which we can obtain knowledge of future events, other than by rational prediction from known causes and past regularities.

8. Since mental activity is simply a matter of dynamically varying states in the physical organism (primarily in the brain), it is completely impossible for this mental activity to exert any effect directly on the physical world outside the organism.

9. The evolution of the universe and of man has come about through physical causes (such as random mutation, natural selection), and there is no justification for any concept of universal purpose in this evolution, or in the development of consciousness, or in the strivings of the individual.

10. Individual consciousness does not survive the death of the organism; or if there is any meaningful sense in which the individual consciousness persists after the death of the physical body we can neither comprehend it in this life nor in any way obtain knowledge about it.

Scanning the scientific and philosophical literature of the earlier part of the century, one can find endless statements confirming that the above premises are not an exaggeration of the assumptions typically held. For instance:

Chemistry and physics account for so much of what the cell does, and for so much to which years ago physical science could at that time offer no clue, that it is justifiable to suppose that the still unexplained residue of the cell's behavior (and hence, man's behavior) will prove resolvable by chemistry and physics.

—Sir Charles S. Sherrington, physiologist

The Astonishing Hypothesis is that "You," your joys and your sorrows, your memories and your ambitions, your sense of personality and free will, are, in fact, no more than the behavior of a vast assembly of nerve cells and their associated molecules.

—Sir Francis Crick, Nobel laureate neurobiologist

The hypothesis that man is not free is essential to the application of scientific method to the study of human behavior. The free inner man who is held responsible for the behavior of the external biological organism is only a prescientific substitute for the kinds of causes which are discovered in the course of a scientific analysis.... Science insists that action is initiated by forces impinging upon the individual, and that [freedom] is only another name for the behavior for which we have not yet found a cause.

—B. F. Skinner, psychologist

That man is the product of causes which had no prevision of the end they were achieving; that his origin, his growth, his hopes and fears, his loves and beliefs, are but the outcome of accidental collocations of atoms; that no fire, no heroism, no intensity of thought and feeling, can preserve an individual life beyond the grave; that all the labours of the ages, all the devotion, all the inspiration, all the noonday brightness of human genius, are destined to extinction in the vast death of the solar system, and the whole temple of Man's achievement must inevitably be buried beneath the debris of a universe in ruins—all these things, if not quite beyond dispute, are yet so nearly certain, that no philosophy which rejects them can hope to stand.

—Bertrand Russell, philosopher

In science we have to act as if the mechanistic theory of life were true, but we are in no way committed to it as a metaphysically valid statement. . . . Scientific progress can be made only by those who experiment as if mechanism is true.

—Joseph Needham, biologist

The child derives his identity from a social environment. The social environment remains to his death the only source for validating that identity. . . . The remarkable convergence of twentieth-century thinkers . . . is the elaboration of the idea that human meaning is arbitrary. . . . The world of human aspiration is fundamentally fictitious. If we do not understand this, we understand nothing about man.

—Ernest Becker, philosopher

On the other hand, the ten assumptions just listed would seem totally alien to any other than modern Western culture. Furthermore there is, in anecdotal accounts and in the existing research on consciousness and exceptional capabilities, an impressive amount of evidence that seems to contradict each of the premises listed.

Yet it was essentially on the basis of such assumptions that the increasingly prestigious scientific worldview was able, in the past, to dismiss as of secondary consequence the spiritual, aesthetic, and intuitive experiences of humankind, and hence to discredit value systems based in those subjective experiences.

However, as we have seen, it is well established from research in hypnosis and other areas of experimental psychology that once a person has an internalized picture of reality, further experience tends to confirm that picture. Reality is experienced in accordance with the established picture, sometimes at the cost of gross perceptual distortion and elaborate rationalization to make it all hold together. For example, it has been demonstrated over and over that the hypnotized subject not only sees reality in accordance with the internalized suggestions, but has very logical-sounding explanations as to why reality "really" is that way. Research on authoritarianism and prejudice shows clearly that people of a certain ethnic origin tend to be seen as having characteristics expected of that ethnic group. The Polish anthropologist Bronislaw Malinowski observed that the Trobriand Islanders, who believed that all characteristics are inherited from the father, regularly failed to see the child's resemblance to members of the mother's family. Anecdotal accounts in psychotherapy give countless examples of patients' rationalizing their obsessive-compulsive behavior.

Thus, to summarize again, we see the very important dual relationship between the experienced world and the science that is developed. The scientific knowledge that has been gained influences the way we perceive the world. But the way the world is experienced in a particular culture influences what kind of science gets developed by that society.

CHOOSE YOUR METAPHYSIC

That a society's basic experiencing of reality shapes its science, as well as the reverse, may be a profoundly disturbing thought if one pursues its implications. We who have been educated in modern society naturally and confidently assume that our scientific view of reality is essentially correct and other "prescientific" or "primitive" views are wrong. But we have to consider the possibility that some of those other views are seeing reality through other cultural windows, and emphasize other aspects of the total human experience; they are not so much wrong as complementary. There is also the possibility that some sort of "trans-modern" view in the future may be quite different from our own—and at least equally correct.

Improbable as it may seem to many, we appear to be going through another such profound change comparable to that of the scientific revolution. Again at the heart of it is a challenge to the prevailing knowledge authority system. So far, the evidence for this sea change is scanty. We can invite the reader to observe the pattern; we cannot claim it is demonstrable.

Science And Metaphysics

In his *Introduction to Metaphysics* the eminent French philosopher Henri Bergson said of the "much-desired union of science and metaphysics" that it would "lead the positive sciences, properly so-called, to become conscious of their true scope, often far greater than they imagine." It may be that the time for realization of that dream has arrived.

As a matter of fact, it might be more accurate to speak instead of the *reunion* of science and metaphysics, for throughout the early history of science the two were strongly linked. The Royal Society, founded in 1660, greatly influenced the early development of science; during this early period science and metaphysics were so intertwined as to be two aspects of a single endeavor. For the first three decades of the Society's existence " . . . 'Rosicrucianism,' Freemasonry, and the Royal Society were not just to overlap, but virtually to be indistinguishable from one another." (Baigent and Leigh, 1989; p. 145) The founders of the Royal Society, including Robert Boyle and Christopher Wren, and the first president, Robert Moray, were steeped in the esoteric metaphysical traditions of Freemasonry, Rosicrucian, Neo-Platonic, and Hermetic thought. Isaac Newton, president of the Royal Society from 1703 to 1727, was strongly influenced by the Hermetic tradition throughout his life. When Benjamin Franklin was inducted into the Royal Society, in 1756, it was still strongly oriented toward the worldview of Freemasonry.

The word "metaphysics" has two quite different meanings in common usage, which fact can lead to some confusion. The first meaning is a branch of philosophy comprising *ontology*, dealing with the questions "What is reality?" and "How did it come to be?," and *epistemology*, concerned with the question "How do you know?" The second meaning is the study of the transcendent or supersensible, the contacting of the reality that lies "beyond the physical." It is the second sense to which Bergson was referring in his statement, and to which the early members of the Royal Society were aligned. But for the union to take place, it turns out to be necessary to re-examine the metaphysical (first sense) assumptions underlying modern science.

Three Metaphysics

Oversimplifying somewhat for clarity, let us think in terms of three basically different kinds of implicit metaphysic (first sense):

• M-1. In the first of these, the basic stuff of the universe is matter-energy. We learn about reality from studying the measurable world. (The positivist assumption is that that is the only way we can learn.) Whatever consciousness is, it emerges out of matter (that is, the brain) when the evolutionary process has progressed sufficiently far. Whatever we can learn about consciousness must ultimately be reconciled with the kind of knowledge we get from studying the physical brain, for consciousness apart from a living physical organism is not only unknown, it is inconceivable.

• M-2. An alternate metaphysic is dualistic. There are two fundamentally different kinds of basic stuff in the universe: matter-energy stuff and mind-spirit stuff. Matter-energy stuff is studied with the present tools of science; mind-spirit stuff must be explored in other ways more appropriate to it (such as inner, subjective exploration). Thus there develop, in essence, two complementary kinds of knowledge; presumably there are areas of overlap (such as the field of psychic phenomena).

• M-3. Yet a third metaphysic finds the ultimate stuff of the universe to be consciousness. Mind (or consciousness, or spirit) is primary, and matter-energy arises in some sense out of mind. The physical world is to the greater mind as a dream image is to the individual mind. Ultimately the reality behind the phenomenal world is contacted, not through the physical senses, but through the deep intuition. Consciousness is not the end-product of material evolution; rather, consciousness was here first!

These three basic metaphysical perspectives are summarized briefly in the following table:

THREE METAPHYSICAL PERSPECTIVES
• M-1 Materialistic Monism
(Matter giving rise to mind)

• M-2 Dualism
(Matter plus mind)

• M-3 Transcendental Monism
(Mind giving rise to matter)

The fundamental change that we are suggesting is happening in Western society can be put in terms of these metaphysics. Essentially, it is a shift of dominant metaphysic from M-1 to M-3. At first thought this may seem as outrageous a proposition as the heliocentric universe did to many in early seventeenth century Europe. M-3 seems quite foreign to the Western mind, or certainly would have a generation or two ago. (It is not nearly so alien as it was even a third of a century ago, if we may judge from increased overt interest in the Eastern philosophical religions; purchases of books based on some sort of transcendental theme; appearances of "metaphysical" and Eastern transcendental concepts, such as reincarnation, karma, life-changing near-death experiences, in motion picture themes and innuendoes; participation in meditative practices, workshops and seminars; widespread interest in the phenomenon of "channeling"; and other indicators.)

Although Descartes postulated a dualistic universe, by the twentieth century science was rather firmly committed to an M-1 metaphysic. Within the past decade or so some scientists, recognizing that the extreme positivist position simply doesn't square with human experience, have been writing and speaking about the need to re-base science on an M-2 metaphysic. (Nobel laureate Sir John Eccles is one example.) Quietly, a number of scientists find that when they take their total experience into account, the M-3 metaphysic fits best; besides, that seems to be implicit in the esoteric "perennial wisdom" of the world's spiritual traditions. For the present, that position seems a long way from the picture of the world that emerges out of our various sciences. (However, in the long run it may very well be where science ends up—but that is a point to be explored more fully in a later chapter.)

It is important to not misunderstand the M-3 position. It does not necessarily deny the "reality" of the material world. A dream is "real," for that matter; it's just that when you look at it from a different vantage point you see another reality behind the dream. So the world studied by physicists is real enough; nevertheless, from a different vantage point there appears to be *a reality behind the physical world that modern science, in its present form, is in no position either to affirm or deny.*

The above trichotomy, with its accompanying discussion, is deliberately somewhat oversimplified in the interest of clarity. A number of variants of these three metaphysical assumptions are preferred by one or another philosopher or scientist. For example, the late Roger Sperry espoused a position he called *mentalism*, which we might designate M-1a. The mentalist concept assumes mind (that is, mental phenomena) to be emergent in the material evolution of the brain, not in any sense prior to the development of very complex neural circuitry. Once it is present, however, it makes possible a kind of "downward causation" (subjective mental state affecting physiological phenomena, for example). This is to be contrasted with the "upward causation" assumed throughout most science (for example, chemical changes in the body causing a subjective state). Another position, which we might term M-1b, is called *panpsychism*, and is much discussed in some forms of "postmodern" thought. This is the assumption that besides the physically observable properties of matter there has always existed an "inside aspect" of matter which resembles mind.

We should recognize that although science in its present form essentially evolved within an M-1 worldview, it is perfectly compatible with either the M-2 or M-3 metaphysic. It is compatible, but in those views it is found to be inherently incomplete as a picture of the total universe.

It is furthermore critically important to recognize that one does not set out to *prove* the validity of a metaphysic. Reality is far too rich to be adequately captured in any conceptualization of it—any conceptualization whatever. We are potentially capable of understanding aspects of reality that can never be adequately expressed in exact verbal form. It is not an appropriate question, then, to ask: Which of these three metaphysics is *true*? It is appropriate to ask: Which one seems to make the best fit with the *totality* of human experience?

THE PLAUSIBILITY OF M-3 DOMINANCE

This is indeed a bold claim we are making, namely, that the M-1 dominance is declining, and the M-3 metaphysic is on its way to becoming the dominant metaphysic not only of this society, but of most of the world as well. The fact that no such fundamental change has occurred in Western society since the Copernican revolution, nearly four centuries ago, suggests the aptness of the phrase "the second Copernican revolution." Whereas the original Copernican revolution reordered our concepts of outer space, this one is concerned with our understanding of *inner* space.

First of all we should note that the M-3 orientation is by no means new in human history. As we shall show in more detail in Chapter 4, for thousands of years it has been part of the esoteric, inner-circle understanding, or *gnosis*, in most of the world's spiritual traditions. So also has been the concept of a cultural hypnosis (*maya*, in the Vedanta conception) that, although it differs in specific content from one culture to another, nevertheless tends to conceal an inner understanding that is akin to what we termed M-3. Throughout Western (and Eastern) cultural history there has been an esoteric tradition of the potentiality for the individual to become "dehypnotized" or "enlightened." A few quotations will serve as reminder of this fact:

> In the ordinary waking state . . . man does not see the real world. . . . He lives in hypnotic sleep. . . . "To awaken" for man means to be "dehypnotized."
> —P. D. Ouspensky, *In Search of the Miraculous*

> Humanity is asleep, concerned only with what is useless, living in a wrong world.
> —Sanai of Afghanistan, 1130 CE

> Our conscious thinking has all the characteristics of a dream. . . . The representation that it gives us of the world is illusory. . . . In [a higher awareness state] consciousness is awakened in a way which is no longer exclusive or attached . . . it is liberated from usual hypnosis.
> —Hubert Benoit, Zen scholar

> Everything you see is the result of your thoughts. There is no exception to this fact.
> —*A Course in Miracles*

> We do not want to attain truth. We do not want anyone to
> break our dream.
>
> —Swami Vivekananda

How are we to think of physical reality, then? The dream analogy, already mentioned briefly, is a good place to start. When we dream, there is typically a "story line"—events happen, and there seen to be some sorts of causal relations among them. While we are dreaming, everything in the dream seems real enough. When we awaken, we recognize that what felt so real was actually a dream. The law of causality is other than it seemed to be when we were asleep. In the dream it may have seemed that one event was the cause of something else, and so on. To the awakened self it is apparent that "I, the dreamer" am cause of the dream—events, interrelationships, and all.

Now try to imagine the analog. In our ordinary state the world seems real; various kinds of events take place, and there are apparent causal relationships among them. Some of these relationships are so dependable, in fact, that we discover "scientific laws" to describe them. (Only rarely does mind seem to intrude in the physical world in such a way that anomalous phenomena occur.) But suppose one "awakens" from the "dream" of the physical world. It then becomes apparent that the causality law is different from what we thought (and were taught): "I, the dreamer" (or "We, the collective dreamer") am the cause of the events and the relationships. The out-of-consciousness collective/universal mind is creator of the world that the conscious individual mind experiences.

This way of looking at reality must seem so strange to the Western educated mind that it is hard to take it seriously. In fact, although it may seem to be more characteristic of the Eastern philosophies, it is also present in the Western traditions and, as we have seen, it does not necessarily contradict the usual scientific view.

Remember, we are not arguing here that the M-3 metaphysic is *true*. We are merely trying to understand how it might be that some people—including some with rather sophisticated educational training—could have come to conclude that this way of seeing the world is more congenial to the totality of human experience than is the positivistic, reductionistic scientific worldview.

Most of the rest of this book will be directed toward examining some of the areas of human experience that seem to suggest the M-3 metaphysic, and exploring the implications for society if indeed it comes to predominate.

Challenges To Positivism And Relativism

3

Unless there is a giant conspiracy involving highly

respected scientists in various fields, many of them

originally hostile to the claims of the psychic

researchers, the only conclusion the unbiased observer

can come to must be that there are people who obtain

knowledge existing in other people's minds, or in the

outer world, by means yet unknown to science.

—H. J. Eysenck

THERE ARE SOME AREAS, such as the ones we will explore in this chapter, that cannot be studied properly in the context of a science based on an M-1 metaphysic (see page 29) because positivism and reductionism don't seem to fit them. It is by no means clear what some future science based on an M-3 metaphysic might be like, but surely such a science will handle these areas more adequately.

THE MIND IN HEALTH, ILLNESS, AND HEALING

Let us start with health, illness, and healing. One of the most marvelous characteristics of the human organism is its ability to protect and maintain its health. In general, when we fall ill it is because this capability has been interfered with—and the chief interfering agent is the state of mind.

Essentially, each of us relies on three complex and highly interconnected bodily systems to maintain our well-being—the nervous system, the stress response system, and the immune system. The nervous system consists of the brain, the spinal cord, and the nerve pathways that extend to all parts of the body. It is the communication and command network for both external and internal changes, and the regulator of external and internal responses.

The nervous system has as subsystems the voluntary nervous system and the autonomic nervous system. The latter has two basic operating modes called the sympathetic and parasympathetic responses. The parasympathetic response is a condition of rest, relaxation, healing, and physical repair and regeneration. Food is digested, muscles relax and replenish energy supplies, tissues regenerate, all without attention from the conscious mind. The sympathetic response, in contrast, is a pattern of general alarm, arousal, and readiness to operate physically against external threat or dangers to the body. The sympathetic response (also called the fight-flight reaction) is triggered instinctively (unconsciously), without conscious direction. It typically is accompanied by (or evoked by) emotions of rage or fear. Its actions on the body may include acceleration of the heart rate, increased force of contraction of the heart, increased blood pressure and respiratory rate, shunting of blood supply from the inner organs to the muscles, secretion of sweat, dilation of the pupils, and other preparations for the intense activity involved in offense, defense, or escape.

The response of the sympathetic nervous system is one of the triggers of the second self-protective system, the stress response. The "hardware" of the stress-response system consists of the hypothalamus, pituitary, adrenal, and other glands, about a dozen or so in all, which together make up the endocrine system. (Stress response is only one of the functions of the endocrine system, which also has a number of regulatory and integrative functions in the body.) The stress-response system responds to external or internal sources of stress with a wide range of protective, regenerative, self-protective reactions, all of which are regulated by free-circulating body chemicals called hormones. For example, strong emotion associated with perception of a life-threatening situation results in several glands of the endocrine system releasing specific hormones into the bloodstream. This in turn increases the rate and force of contraction of the heart and constricts the peripheral blood vessels, thus raising blood pressure and circulation; dilates the bronchioles, aiding respiration; dilates the eye pupils for better vision; and increases the blood clotting ability to handle a potential injury. These effects help prepare the organism for either fight or flight.

The third self-protective bodily network is the immune system. This system is quite decentralized, and involves the white blood cells (leukocytes), the circulatory system, the lymphatic system, and certain glands and specialized areas. The key actors in it are about a trillion (10^{12}) lymphocytes (a form of white blood cell) and about 100 million trillion (10^{20}) molecules called antibodies that are produced and secreted by the lymphocytes. These comprise a sort of internal army that searches out and destroys invaders and enemies that break through the skin or enter the body from the air or in food. (Were the immune system to suddenly cease functioning, the microbes in the body would cause it to putrefy as rapidly as it would when kept in a warm environment after death.)

When activated, the immune system sends various protective cells and substances through the bloodstream and via the internal conduits of the lymph system, rushing to the site of the danger—an infection, puncture, cancer cell, or foreign body, for example. Multiplying rates of the white blood cells go up to replace those that may be lost in battle. Certain white cells (B-lymphocytes) manufacture specific substances (antibodies) that can attack and destroy the particular invader. (Because there are millions of different types of possible invaders, and because the antibodies are so specific to the foreign entities, there must be millions of different types of antibodies—and the right ones must be produced to attack the specific invaders.) Other actors in the system repair the damage and scan for further injury.

It has recently been discovered that these three systems—the central nervous system, the hormonal system, and the immune system—communicate with one another through "molecular messengers" called neuropeptides. "Messages" can originate in any part of the body; it appears that emotions and mental activity are far less centralized in the brain than used to be thought.

Good health depends upon the coordinated, constant effort of all three of these systems. Each of them can function perfectly well without conscious effort on our part. When the systems malfunction, we become ill. The role of the mind in creating illness has been increasingly appreciated as psychosomatic disorders and stress have become better understood.

For example, stress is our psychophysical response to perceived external changes and difficulties. Excessive or misplaced reaction to these external stressors takes a severe physiological toll on the body over time, and in the presence of an existing weakness in part of the body can cause physical disease. It is now quite clear that attitudes leading to stress can be a causative factor in a wide variety of illnesses, including gastric and duodenal ulcers, cardiovascular disease, migraine and tension headaches, arthritis, and asthma. Certain personality types are found to be predisposed to these stress disorders—in particular, cardiovascular disease. Stress disorders have long since replaced infectious diseases as the major health afflictions of modern society.

Stress also can interfere with the functioning of the body's immune system. If the immune system is not functioning well, it can fail to intercept disease-causing viruses or bacteria, and illness may result. Or, it can fail to ferret out and destroy cancer cells when they occur, resulting in malignancy that gets completely out of control. Yet other diseases occur when the body's ability to produce antibodies is impaired. Still other ailments called autoimmune diseases (such as rheumatoid arthritis and multiple sclerosis) result when the immune system inappropriately attacks its own body's cells. Again, patterns of attitudes—personality types—are found to differ in their suscepti-bility to immune system disorder, and to the diseases that result.

Scientific descriptions of these protective systems elaborate on the mechanisms in far greater detail than we have here. The more one learns about the complexities of, for instance, the immune system the more miraculous the picture appears, and the less the purely mechanistic picture "feels right." Critical questions go largely unanswered—for instance: How do all the separate parts of the system communicate and function together to detect the specific invaders, to create just the right kinds of antibodies, to kill off or incapacitate the attacking bodies, and to clean up the mess after-wards? How do thoughts in the mind translate into interferences with immune system functioning?

If the role of the mind in creating illness is amazing, the role of the mind in healing is no less so. One specific form of this interaction is known as the "placebo effect." The basic phenomenon appears to be akin to hypnosis. If a patient accepts the suggestion that an inert substance (for example, a sugar pill) is in fact a powerful remedy, the result may be a healing—clearly brought about by the patient's mind since there is no medical consequence from the inert substance itself.

A now-famous case was described a number of years ago by Philip West, one of the pioneer researchers of psychological factors in illness. He was treating a man with severe cancer, who begged to be given the experimental drug Krebiozen. At that time Krebiozen was being touted by its proponents as a miracle cancer cure. After only one dose of the drug, the patient's tumor masses "melted like snowballs on a hot stove." Whereas he had once needed an oxygen mask to breathe, he soon became so active that he even began piloting his own plane. Shortly thereafter, however, he read about studies indicating that Krebiozen was ineffective. His cancer began to spread again, and he was hospitalized. His doctor, reacting to this dramatic turn of events, decided to lie to the patient, telling him not to believe the studies, and promised treatment with a new, more potent Krebiozen. In fact, the man was given only water, but nevertheless his condition improved significantly. His recuperation continued until one day he read in an article that the American Medical Association and the Food and Drug Administration had conclusively proved the worthlessness of Krebiozen. He immediately suffered a relapse, and died several days later.

Regeneration is a phenomenon closely related to healing. A portion of the body is destroyed—a small wound, let us say. At the same time the immune system is cleaning up the wound, the rest of the body goes ahead with restoring the missing tissue. The right kinds of cells multiply and fill in the empty space, stopping when the area is restored to its original shape. The accelerated growth of tissue does not go on and on, ending up with an unsightly bulge of scar tissue; it "knows when to stop." Regeneration in humans is not as spectacular as in some nonmammalian creatures. We do not grow back an amputated leg, for example, as a lobster will grow back an amputated claw. Nonetheless, the central feature remains the same. There appears to be a stored pattern that governs the regenerative process. If our science is based in the M-1 metaphysic, the pattern "must" be stored physically, perhaps in the cells or in the central nervous system—and we strain to believe that it is so. If the dominating metaphysic is, instead, M-2 or M-3, then the pattern can be a thought or an image, something like the image in the mind of a sculptor before she or he creates a masterpiece.

Let us again insert the reminder: We are not suggesting that the phenomena of healing—or any other phenomena—prove the incorrectness of the M-1 metaphysic. The positivistic, reductionistic scientific paradigm can be strained to fit almost anything, much as the Ptolemaic picture could be strained to fit increasingly accurate astronomical measurements. Perhaps it is essentially an aesthetic sense that in the end opts for the metaphysic or conceptual framework that can be adapted to experience with the least strain.

ATTENTION AND VOLITION

The most recently dominant metaphor in cognitive science is that of information processing. Let Morton Hunt, in his popular summary of the area, *The Universe Within*, describe how consciousness is dealt with here: "What has seemed to philosophers to be mind—a different sort of stuff from the brain—is not a separate stuff at all, but a series of processes of immense complexity, the integration of millions or billions of neural events. We call some of these macroevents 'ideas,' but they are actually sets of physical microevents—concatenations of impulses, coded and processed and stored in memory. . . . [The] mind is . . . the brain's total set of symbol manipulations. . . . Mind is to the brain as digestion is to the stomach: The brain is what *is*, the mind is what the brain *does*."

The contents of consciousness are "actually sets of physical microevents." One could hardly find a more concise statement of the positivistic and reductionistic assumptions. With our cultural conditioning it may sound like a perfectly reasonable thing to say—but it just doesn't feel like the whole story.

One of the most problematic aspects of human experience when viewed from the M-1 standpoint is *volition*. Nothing is more central to the sense of self than the experience of volition—of "I choose," "I decide." The apparent conflict between the sense of volition and the deterministic assumption of positivistic science is one of the oldest problems in psychology. "Does free will exist?" was a common formulation of the puzzle.

In the M-1 outlook free will does indeed seem to present a paradox. For if we assume the omnicompetence and determinism of science and the universality of physical laws, then free will would seem to be no more than the feeling associated with a determined action. That is to say, I act in a way determined by all the external and internal forces acting upon me, and feel that it is my choice to do so. If we thus take free will to be an illusion, then we would also have to abandon such concepts as liberty, moral action, rational behavior, and so on.

Now there is a meaningful sense in which the feeling of freely choosing can indeed be self-deception, and we need to distinguish that from the more fundamental puzzle. We have already noted that we seem to choose unconsciously as well as consciously. Thus when I rationally decide that it is a poor idea to leave uneaten food on my dinner plate, that may in fact turn out to be a consequence of my having internalized the parental insistence that leaving food on my plate is *bad*. But it is one thing to recognize unconscious along with conscious choice. It is quite another to insist that both are illusory, and there is no such thing as a choosing self.

One observation has long bothered those who may have felt that science must be deterministic—that however well one may defend this position rationally it is impossible to behave as though it were true. However logically sound the deterministic hypothesis may be, it never *feels* true to life.

Sir John Eccles, in his book (with Sir Karl Popper) *The Self and Its Brain* (1981), refers to the work of H. H. Kornhuber to bring out an interesting feature of volition. Kornhuber discovered the existence of electrical potentials generated in the cerebral cortex following the occurrence of will to action and prior to the actual performance of motor activity. He consistently observed an interval of a fraction of a second between the conscious act of will and the activity resulting from it. During this brief interval there is an observable flurry of electrical potentials that quickly focus on the appropriate cerebral area to bring about the action desired. But the delay between willing and willed activity is quite measurable. Eccles observes, "We can regard these experiments as providing a convincing demonstration that voluntary movements can be freely initiated independently of any determining influences that are entirely within the neuronal machinery of the brain."

On the other hand, there appears to be some work with evoked potentials that indicates the contrary—namely, electrical potentials in the nervous system that appear before the individual is consciously aware of having decided to act. Then there are those emergency situations in which one responds instantaneously with a corrective or preventive action, and only afterward is aware of having made the right action decision "instinctively." Whatever may turn out to be the best way to understand volition, fitting it into the M-1 metaphysic remains a strain.

Let us look at one rather well-known experiment by hypnosis researcher Ernest Hilgard (1977) that bears on the question Who is choosing? A subject was hypnotized and told that his left (non-writing) hand would feel no pain. He was then instructed to place that hand in a container of ice-cold water and ice cubes. Although this would normally be quite painful, the subject reported—as expected—that he felt quite comfortable. Meanwhile, the subject was asked to engage in "automatic writing" with his right hand—to simply let the hand write "anything it wanted to" without the subject's paying any particular attention to it. After several minutes, when asked how his immersed hand felt, the subject replied that it was fine. At the same time, however, his other hand was complaining bitterly by writing such things as "it hurts" and "ouch." Thus one part of the psyche (including the conscious, reporting mind) is unaware of the pain, while another part is experiencing it and giving expression to it. This "other part of the psyche" Hilgard terms the "hidden observer."

Volition is obviously not a simple matter. Closely related to this phenomenon is that of attention. Sitting in my study I can pay attention to what I am reading. Alternatively, my mind can wander to something that happened yesterday, or I can pay attention to whether my body is comfortable—free from itches, aches, and the like, or I may shift my attention to a noise that has been present, unobtrusively, while I was reading.

Attention is more important than it may first appear to be, for how I attend will affect what I perceive, and what I perceive will affect how I interpret my experience. If I listen to a person's words I may have a very different interpretation of a conversation than if I attend to the person's body language and observe the subtle messages that come to me from shifty eyes, posture, and gestures.

But with attention as with volition, we have an everyday phenomenon that fits only with great strain into an M-1 worldview. Who is the self that chooses? Who is the self that attends?

Mind, Instinct, And Evolution

The complex instinctual behaviors of animals is another area that raises similar questions. Myriad examples could be brought forth; let us take one cited by Rupert Sheldrake in his book *A New Science of Life* (1981).

The European cuckoo lays its eggs in the nests of birds of other species. The young, hatched and reared by these unwitting foster parents, never see their real parents. Toward the end of the summer, the adult cuckoos migrate to their winter habitat in southern Africa. About a month later, the young cuckoos congregate and then they also migrate to the same region of Africa, where they join their elders. They instinctively know that they should migrate and when to migrate; they instinctively recognize other young cuckoos and gather together; and they instinctively know in which direction they should fly and what their destination is.

Do the cuckoos have some elaborate computer-like program stored in their genes? The answer of M-1 science tends to be "It must be so." Or do the young cuckoos tune in to the Great Cuckoo Mind in the Sky and take their directions from there? It sounds absurd, yet something like that is what Sheldrake suggests with his concept of "formative causation."

According to this concept, systems are organized in the way they are now because similar systems were organized that way in the past. The characteristic behaviors of biological organisms are influenced by invisible organizing fields operating across space and time. These hypothesized *morphogenic fields* are a sort of cumulative record of past behaviors, weighted in favor of those behaviors that worked for the species—in somewhat the same sense as natural selection. Thus, for instance, the spider learns to spin and repair a web—not through imitating its parents, nor from some genetic programming, but from the nonmeasurable cumulative morphogenic field that contains the trial-and-error learning of all generations past.

One of the examples offered by Sheldrake involves a series of experiments carried out by Harvard psychologist William McDougall in the early 1920s, aimed at testing whether learned behavior patterns are inherited. McDougall placed rats in a specially constructed water tank from which they could escape by swimming to an unlighted gangway. If, instead, a rat swam to a brightly lighted gangway, it would receive an electric shock. The rats' rates of learning were measured by counting the number of errors they made before learning to swim straight to the unlighted gangway. Quite surprisingly, it turned out that later generations of rats learned more rapidly than the generations preceding them. The experiment was continued for 32 generations and took 15 years to complete. From first to last generations of rats there was over a tenfold increase in their rate of learning. Much more surprisingly, when separate studies in Scotland and Australia were designed to replicate McDougall's experiments, the first generation of rats learned almost as rapidly as McDougall's 32nd generation. A number of the rats even "learned" the task immediately, without making a single error.

These results are completely inexplicable in conventional terms. Not only is learned behavior not supposed to be inherited, there is no way of accounting for transmission of learning between completely isolated groups of rats. The Sheldrake concept of accounting for behavior patterns through a cumulative nonphysical morphogenic field, not spatially confined, fits the observed results easily. This idea may seem in an M-1 frame of mind to be an outrageously wild hypothesis. But the concept does not seem so strange viewed from the standpoint of an M-2 or M-3 metaphysic, in which consciousness is not constrained to fit our usual physicalistic expectations.

Most scientists would agree that instinctual behaviors, whatever their origins, are among the characteristics that arise through the process of evolution and are genetically transmitted to each succeeding generation of the species.

The origin of the diverse forms of life on the Earth, as generally understood, is familiar enough in outline. Some fifteen billion years ago the present universe began, with the "Big Bang." Around three billion years ago the first life appeared on the Earth, and two-tenths of a billion years ago, the first mammals. Although some aspects of the origin of life remain uncertain, scientists ordinarily assume it came about through some sort of chance combining of nucleic acids and proteins. Thereafter, more and more different forms of life appeared, essentially through the process of random mutation and natural selection. Along this evolutionary path there evolved the attribute of mind or consciousness. (Nonmaterial consciousness is assumed to appear out of a material world—a world of matter and energy. As we saw earlier, one attempt to deal with this paradox is to argue that the mind is simply process—it is "what the brain does.")

Darwin's theory of evolution is essentially based on a very few assumptions. One of the most central is that there is a continual struggle for survival, in which the great majority of contestants lose.

Another is that there is a natural range of variation in all species, both in trivial traits and in essential ones. In highly competitive organisms, some of these variations must confer an advantage or a disadvantage in the struggle for the means of survival. Thus there is a natural selection, whereby organisms that are less well fitted to their conditions of life tend to be eliminated, while those that are better fitted are more likely to survive and to leave progeny. The result is a gradual modification of species in the direction of greater adaptedness.

The main source of variation within organisms of the same species is now known to be mutations of the genetic material, the genes based on deoxyribonucleic acid (DNA). Mutations are small changes in the molecular structure of the DNA that arise as a consequence of some damaging chemical or radiation, and are essentially random.

A number of challenges have been put to the neo-Darwinist evolutionary hypothesis (that is, the Darwinist theory modified by what has since been learned about the genetic mechanisms of inheritance). One of these challenges is the Lamarckian concept of inheritance of acquired or learned characteristics. (This was the hypothesis McDougall was testing in the experiments just described.) In the sense of acquired characteristics being genetically transmitted to succeeding generations, this hypothesis is generally discarded. However, in the sense of the cumulative learning of the species being somehow preserved in the morphogenic field, as proposed by Sheldrake, the idea may be showing signs of revitalization.

Another challenge has been to the assumption that gradual transformation involving small changes each generation could account for the tremendous diversity of organisms existing on the Earth. Apart from anything else, the organisms differ in the number and structure of their chromosomes, so that some more abrupt and major changes must have occurred.

Most puzzling of all in the neo-Darwinist conceptualization of the evolutionary path is the appearance of complex structures and behaviors that seem to have survival value only in the final form, not in intermediate stages. An often-cited example is binocular vision. Binocular vision is found in mammals and many other creatures. The eye itself is an exquisitely designed instrument for visual perception;

the binocular feature using two eyes gives added depth perception. Once the two eyes are present it is easy enough to see their survival value. But how can we imagine a gradual evolution of binocular vision in tiny stages, each step a result of random mutation, and each step having sufficient survival value so that it is favored as the characteristics are passed on to successive generations? Or alternatively, can we imagine the accidental appearance of an organism that in one leap arrives at rudimentary binocular vision with sufficient survival value that through successive generations of natural selection it gets perfected to the present form? Although such kinds of explanation leave a tremendous lot to "accident," they are nonetheless the preferred form of explanation in a science committed to an M-1 metaphysic.

Consider another kind of explanation which speaks of some sort of teleological "pull" in the evolutionary process, of evolution toward increased awareness, complexity, freedom—in short, of evolution *going somewhere* (not in a predetermined sense, but in the sense of preferred direction). In that kind of evolutionary explanation the organism developed two eyes because at some deep level of inner understanding it wanted to see better! Perhaps a species on the long path of evolutionary development is not only pushed by random mutations and natural selection, but also directed by the kind of teleological force implied in Henri Bergson's *Creative Evolution* and much more forthrightly in Teilhard de Chardin's *The Phenomenon of Man*. In this kind of explanation *mind is prior to brain*, and evolution is characterized both by the organism's freedom to choose and by its inner sense of "right" direction. This has been a totally unacceptable form of explanation in modern scientific debate—yet it is much more congenial to the emerging view that consciousness has somehow to be factored into our total scientific picture of the universe.

Exceptional Capabilities

Throughout all the debates pertaining to the limitations of M-1 science there is one area that has generated the most heated controversy of all—the area of exceptional capabilities, particularly those that seem in some way to contradict the basic scientific picture of reality. In Chapter 2 we listed ten tacit assumptions of conventional science. We refer now to capabilities and phenomena that appear to challenge one or more of those assumptions.

In Chapter 1 we mentioned one such phenomenon that has recently become in vogue as a powerful demonstration of the power of suggestion—firewalking. There have been many valiant attempts to somehow accommodate this experience to the M-1 metaphysic— insulating ash, insulating layer of steam, and so forth. Whatever intermediating mechanism one assumes, the fact of the matter appears to be that if one holds one's consciousness or attention one way the bare feet will quickly receive third-degree burns from the burning coals and if one holds the mind a different way the feet stay free from harm.

In all traditional societies stories are told of men and women with seemingly miraculous powers, and such powers are recognized by all religions. In many parts of the world various paranormal abilities are said to be cultivated deliberately within esoteric systems such as shamanism, sorcery, tantric yoga, and spiritualism. And even in modern Western society there are persistent reports of apparently inexplicable phenomena, such as telepathy, clairvoyance, precognition, memories of past lives, hauntings, poltergeists, psychokinesis, and so on—supported by data from scientific research. Although there have been some cases of fraud and delusion, and some supposedly paranormal events that turned out to have reasonable normal causes, a residue remains of occurrences that appear to defy explanation in terms of any known physical principles. Moreover, numerous experiments designed to test for so-called extrasensory perception or for psychokinesis have yielded results with the odds against chance explanation being millions to one and higher.

Insofar as these phenomena cannot be explained in terms of the known laws of physics and chemistry, from the standpoint of the M-1 metaphysical assumptions they ought not to happen. If they appear to occur nevertheless, then they depend either on laws of physics as yet unknown, or on nonphysical causal factors or connecting principles.

One common classification of psychic phenomena is given below:

- EXTRASENSORY PERCEPTION (when information appears to be obtained under conditions that rule out the known sensory channels)

–Telepathy (in which this communication appears to be mind-to-mind)

–Clairvoyance (in which there appears to be direct apprehension of information that would not normally be assumed to be accessible—for example, the phenomenon of remote viewing)

–Precognition (in which one seems to have information regarding events that have not yet happened—sometimes occurring in the form of a "memory" of something happening some time hence)

–Retrocognition (in which there appears to be knowledge of, or "memory" of, events that happened in the past but which the person could not know about in ordinary ways)

- PSYCHOKINESIS (when the state of a person's mind appears to exert a direct effect on the physical environment)

  –Simple psychokinesis (in which the state of mind apparently results in something being moved or physically affected at a distance and without physical intervention of the ordinary sort, for example, the reported metal-bending demonstrations)

  –Levitation (of oneself)

  –Teleportation (apparent disappearance of an object from one location and reappearance at another)

  –Materialization and dematerialization (generation of material forms apparently out of nowhere; and the disappearance of material forms)

  –Thought photography (in which a held image or mental state apparently results in an image on photographic film)

  –Psychic healing and psychic surgery (healing of body organs through intention apparently without any intervention of physical instruments or energy)

- MEDIUMSHIP OR CHANNELING (apparent communication with discarnate beings, sometimes accompanied by physical or quasi-physical phenomena)

The healthy skeptic will be pretty certain that most of the types of phenomena listed could not occur at all, and the few that seem to occur will eventually be susceptible to "natural" and "scientific" explanations. Yet the plain fact of the matter is that (like firewalking) all of these have been reported in a variety of societies, over dozens of centuries, and all have been investigated by careful and scientifically sophisticated observers. That is not to say that they have been "demonstrated" to the satisfaction of the scientific community—far from it. To the contrary, the data remain tantalizingly equivocal (for reasons we shall explore in the next chapter). But all the same, when we take into account the potentiality of whole cultures to see "realities" that other cultures don't see, the experimental research on, and anecdotal reports of, psychic phenomena cannot be totally dismissed.

As H. J. Eysenck, head of the Department of Psychology at Maudsley Hospital in London, summed it up more than thirty years ago: "Unless there is a gigantic conspiracy involving thirty university departments all over the world, and several hundred highly respected scientists in various fields, many of them originally hostile to the claims of the psychic researchers, the only conclusion the unbiased observer can come to must be that there are people who obtain knowledge existing in other people's minds, or in the outer world, by means yet unknown to science."

A recent cartoon shows a woman driver attempting to deal with a police officer who has accosted her for driving the wrong way down a one-way street. "Officer," she says, "did it ever occur to you that maybe the *sign* is wrong?" Like the one-way street sign, perhaps—if these anomalous phenomena persist in happening despite the fact that they seem to clash so directly with prevailing assumptions about the nature of scientific reality—it is our "official" concept of reality that is wrong.

In the M-1 metaphysical assumption frame this paradox is totally baffling, and leads to a fruitless search for "physical mechanisms." From the M-2 viewpoint the occurrence of the phenomena is not so disturbing, but it is not obvious what kind of research will lead to understanding of the consistently inconsistent nature of the data.

In the M-3 framework the erratic nature of psychic phenomena tends to be understood as related to the psychological phenomenon of resistance. No such phenomena are intrinsically impossible, but they do violate the order that is (in a sense) "agreed upon" in the collective mind. Thus while such phenomena may occur on occasion, there is deep-level unconscious resistance to exactly the kind of data the scientist seeks—data that would "scientifically demonstrate" the existence of these anomalous events.

Of all the challenges to positivism and reductionism, these exceptional capabilities are the most directly challenging, the most elusive, and the most controversial.

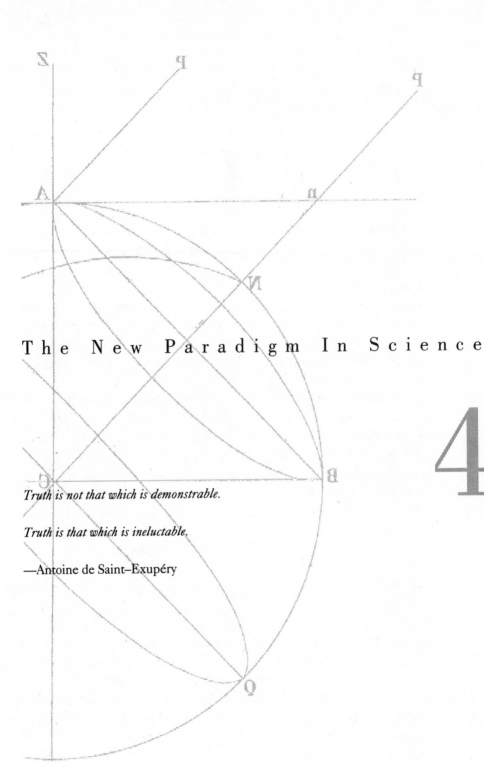

The New Paradigm In Science

Truth is not that which is demonstrable.

Truth is that which is ineluctable.

—Antoine de Saint–Exupéry

THE FUNDAMENTAL PUZZLE of Western science has been long recognized. If the world that science tells us about is reality, how does it happen that we don't feel more at home in it? If my most direct experience of reality is my own conscious awareness, why doesn't science have more of a place for consciousness? Indeed, there have been attempts in the past to bring consciousness into a more central place in the knowledge system. Some of these (for example, phenomenology, introspectionism, gestalt) failed to gain acceptance as meeting basic methodological criteria; others (such as Tibetan Buddhist psychology) come from other cultures and are only now receiving serious consideration.

Once we recognize that bias is inevitable in any society's knowledge system (two of the main sources being the tacit metaphysical assumptions and the bias toward culturally useful knowledge), the question of how to test that knowledge becomes central. Testing scientific knowledge is a more subtle matter than is sometimes assumed. Two criteria are commonly taken to be most characteristic of the scientific method, namely, *objectivity in investigative procedures* and *reliability through replicable experiments*.

THE DIFFICULT TASK OF BEING OPEN-MINDED

Let us consider objectivity. In the present context, the word means that one seeks to obtain a view of reality undistorted by personal feelings or prejudices. It thus implies not only research procedures that insulate the findings from the desires and expectations of the researcher, but also openness to new evidence that may force change in one's beliefs. Thus it is not just a characteristic of scientific methodology; it refers also to *a character trait of the investigator.*

56

There has been a tendency in teaching the history of scientific thought to represent the Scholastics of the Middle Ages as being congenitally closed to new thoughts. The scientist, on the other hand, is portrayed as ever curious after new facts and eager to have his or her theories demolished by the impact of new data—then reconstructed in ever more inclusive form. History records how the scientists Galileo and Bruno and Harvey were harassed and opposed by the established powers citing classical authority. We sometimes gloss over the harassment and opposition suffered by Semmelweis, Pasteur, Darwin, Freud, and numerous others, from their own scientific colleagues.

If one looks beneath the covers in the history of science, one sees no end of examples of ill treatment by scientists of other scientists whose theories or investigation didn't "fit in" with accepted conceptual frameworks. However, there is little point in criticizing these scientists who exhibit an all-too-human frailty. The conscious desire may well be to be open and objective; unconscious protectiveness may cause the behavior to be otherwise. We are not just referring to the scientist who has so much ego-involvement with his or her own theory that psychologically he or she can't afford to see conflicting evidence. Even more powerful and ubiquitous is the issue of being objective in the face of the unconscious assumptions shared by one's entire culture (or scientific subculture).

The early seventeenth century authorities may not have been very open-minded about unexpected indications of satellites revolving around Jupiter. We may assume, however, that they were quite willing to investigate, within the approved framework of methodology, a claim of dream prophecy, of miraculous healing, of the appearance of a figure resembling the Virgin Mary, or of a meditating monk seemingly rising off the ground and being suspended in the air. Thus in an important way often neglected, *objectivity is a function of the prevailing (partly unconscious) assumptions about the nature of reality.*

One thinks, for example, of the pronouncements of the committee appointed by the French Academy in 1772 to investigate reports of what are now called meteorites—those extraterrestrial bodies that appear as flaming objects streaking through the sky and crash to the ground as scorched hunks of metal and stone. (The committee included Antoine Lavoisier, the "father of modern chemistry.") The conclusion reached by the committee, after long deliberations and examination of much evidence, was that with which they started: There are no such things as hot stones that have fallen from the sky because there are no stones in the sky to fall! The prevailing interpretation of the Newtonian model of the solar system left no room for these extraneous bodies. Therefore, the reported phenomena must have other explanations—delusionary "visions," stones heated from being struck by lightning, stones borne aloft by whirlwinds or volcanic eruptions. Such was the prestige of the committee and so convincing its arguments that museums all over Western Europe threw away their meteorite specimens. (After all, there could be no such things!) As a result, there are very few preserved meteorite specimens that date prior to 1790.

More recently, the fate of scientists who presumed to take seriously the persistent reports of unidentified flying objects (UFOs) has been harassment and ridicule. The basic argument seems to be that it would be extremely difficult to account for such phenomena within accepted cosmological frameworks; hence the thousands of investigated phenomena must not have occurred, the striking photographs of UFOs must all have been faked, and the corroborating data must be the product of some kind of conspiracy to deceive.

The history of the physics of light is interesting in this regard. As far back as 1650, the Italian physicist Francesco Grimaldi had performed some experiments, shining light through a narrow slit and obtaining a pattern of light and dark bands that we would now term a diffraction pattern. The work excited only short-lived interest, because of the general acceptance of Newton's views regarding the particle nature of light. Thomas Young's epoch-making 1802 papers that described experiments on interference, suggesting a wave-type theory, were called by a member of the Royal Society "paltry and insubstantial papers . . . destitute of every species of merit." The abusive attack on Young marred his reputation for many years; feelings over the issue ran high. One critic warned that the wave theory "can have no other effect than to check the progress of science and renew all those wild phantoms of the imagination which . . . Newton put to flight from her temple."

In spite of such vehement opposition, the wave theory won a temporary victory. Discouragement and ridicule were now aimed at attempts, which started in the eighteenth century, to measure the pressure of light impinging on a solid body. The reason was because, as a priori reasoning argued, there was no conceivable way that nonmaterial waves could exert pressure. (Later on, as it turned out, the pressure of light was not only observed but fit into theory.) Maxwell's mathematical theories of electromagnetic waves initially met with widespread rejection because of the problem of imagining some sort of all-pervading "ether" to support the waves. To his dying day, Lord Kelvin never accepted Maxwell's hypotheses and insisted that Roentgen's discovery of X-rays (like light with extremely short wavelength) must be some sort of elaborate hoax—because a priori reasoning showed they couldn't exist. Meanwhile Einstein had proposed the photon or "light particle" theory of light, and its opponents were objecting that its acceptance would throw science back by centuries.

Bohr's complementarity principle finally furnished a resolution of the wave-particle controversy. In essence this principle asserts that the wave and particle descriptions represent complementary aspects of a reality that cannot be fully conceptualized in either metaphor alone. We are free to measure either the wavelength or the position of a photon as precisely as we choose. But the two quantities do not appear in the same conceptual model, and an attempt to think in terms of both at the same time leads to a paradoxical situation. For the principle of uncertainty states that the more precise our knowledge of the wavelength, the greater is our ignorance regarding the position, and vice versa. That is, what is "real" in one model is elusive, if not illusory, in the other. (Note the intriguing similarity, in this respect, of the relationship between consciousness and matter-energy.)

Fashions change with regard to what kinds of explanations are acceptable. The sedative effect of opium was explained in pre-Newtonian days by the assumption that opium has a "dormitive potency." In the late seventeenth century, with the prevailing faith that all facets of physical experience could ultimately be expressed in terms of elementary particles, the favorite explanation for opium's sedating and analgesic qualities had it that the round shape of the opium molecules soothes the nerves along which they move. In our own day we are more likely to be comfortable accounting for pain suppression in speaking of opium molecules affecting the sleep center of the brain, and of the mating of endorphin-like molecules in the opiate with receptors in the central nervous system. But the situation has not changed essentially. We have no adequate conceptualization of the nature of sleep, or of sedation, or of pain and its relief—because we have no adequate conceptualization of the role of consciousness in these processes.

During the eighteenth century the Royal Society suppressed evidence supporting the existence of various phenomena of witchcraft. Later, similar evidence was recognized and studied—but as manifestations of hypnotic powers. Hypnosis itself was largely rejected by the early scientific community as "animal magnetism." (The investigating commission that concluded in 1784 that no "magnetic fluid" exists included Benjamin Franklin and Lavoisier. Striking recoveries from illnesses were not denied, but, rather, attributed to "mere imagination.") The first comprehensive delineation of hypnotic effects was put forth in 1826, and included amnesia; analgesia; hallucinatory activity; improved recall ability; hypersuggestibility and compliance; telepathic communication; "sight without eyes" (clairvoyant remote viewing); clairvoyant ability to diagnose, prescribe for and prognosticate about illness; and ability to take on the illnesses of other people and cure them.

Hypnosis tended to be a relatively taboo area for university research until the mid-twentieth century. This was undoubtedly true in part because of this early association with extrasensory perception. The definition no longer includes or implies such phenomena, and they are seldom reported in laboratory research. This may mean that they never occurred at all, or it may mean that their occurrence is precluded by the contemporary researcher's disbelief. (It is somewhat ironic that one of the foremost nineteenth century researchers in extrasensory perception, F.W.H. Myers, complained that British research in telepathy was held up because of its association with the unsavory area of hypnosis!)

Around 1840 physicians John Elliotson in London and James Esdaile in Calcutta made extensive use of hypnotic suggestion to carry out painless major surgery, including leg amputations. Medical journals denied publication of the results on the grounds that there was no conceivable explanation for the claimed analgesic effects. Although hundreds of apparently painless major operations were performed, some in public demonstration, doctors and patients were accused of "deluding or colluding." Patients, it was claimed, must have been just pretending to feel no pain while they had legs amputated or abdominal operations performed without benefit of anesthetic!

We have earlier observed that parapsychology has been an extraordinarily controversial area throughout most of its century-long history. Attacks have ranged from quiet ridicule to open hostility. Critics tended to ignore the fact that data on the spontaneous occurrence of presumably paranormal phenomena had been carefully collected for decades prior to the initiation of serious efforts to conduct controlled experiments. They charged or hinted at faulty techniques in experimentation (failure to ensure against sensory cues, systematic errors perhaps unconsciously influenced by the experimenter's bias in favor of the ESP hypothesis, erroneous use of statistical methods), at gullibility, and at willful deception. By divide-and-demolish techniques, experimental findings were disposed of, one by one, on the multiple bases of chance, error, and fraud. At mid-century, neurophysiologist D. O. Hebb typified the prevailing scientific opinion in admitting, "I do not accept ESP for a moment because it does not make sense. My external criteria, both of physics and of physiology, say that ESP is not a fact despite the evidence that has been reported." (More succinctly to the point was the remark of a well-known contemporary scientist who, when confronted with some particularly convincing evidence of clairvoyant remote-viewing, snorted, "I wouldn't believe it even if it *were* true!")

We can easily see that some of the best scientists have had their difficulties with being objective. The problem is faced frontally in the case of dealing with self-reports of subjective experience, which is a key issue in consciousness research.

SCIENTIFIC OBJECTIVITY AND RELIABILITY

Consider a common form of research—testing the efficacy of a new analgesic by giving the drug to a large population of subjects and making a statistical analysis of the data. Pain is a subjective response affected by all sorts of subtle variables, such as the subject's desire to cooperate with the experimenter, placebo effect, deliberate or inadvertent suppression of pain by autosuggestion, individual uniqueness, and variability of the subject's responses from day to day. Even with all the sophistication of double-blind techniques, you would not expect, in research that so centrally involves self-reports of subjectively felt pain, to be able to apply rigid definitions of objectivity and of replicability. Nor would you expect that the merits of the research should be severely criticized because of this intrinsic difficulty.

In research more directly related to exploring the powers of mind, the problems with objectivity and replicability are more acute. Take two examples: research on imagery and suggestion as aids to cancer remission, and research on psychokinesis. In both cases there is a fair amount of careful work carried out by competent researchers; in both cases the results would strongly suggest the existence of a genuine phenomenon. Yet because of the absence of some sort of "mechanism" to account for the phenomenon, stringent demands are placed on the research findings—and by strict standards, they fail to pass the test. Researchers with positive beliefs about the phenomena tend to report positive results, and skeptics tend to get negative results—thus raising the question of objectivity. And the results are erratic even under what appear to be similar conditions.

The skeptical tend to interpret these characteristics of the research as evidence for the nonexistence of the phenomena; however, they can also be interpreted as indications of inappropriate demands for "objectivity" and "replicability" in an area of research where the usual meanings of the words don't fit. Once one postulates the possibility of the subject's mind affecting the environment at a distance, then it becomes apparent that the state of the experimenter's mind can also affect the results—so strict objectivity is an impossibility. Once we recognize that human beings make choices at unconscious as well as conscious levels (such as addiction—an unconscious choice overruling a conscious one; or guilt feeling—a message from part of the unconscious mind that it disapproves of a choice made consciously) then the phenomena must be reinterpreted. Unconscious as well as conscious choices are involved in either cancer healing or psychokinesis. The person may want one thing at a conscious level, yet unconsciously want its opposite. With this uncontrollable factor entering in, strict replicability is impossible.

Thus, rigid interpretations of objectivity and of reliability through replicability would appear to be inappropriate when the matter being researched involves consciousness and subjective experience. However, surely there are criteria something like these which are appropriate. For instance, the Buddhist ideal of *nonattachment* would come highly recommended as a substitute for objectivity. In the Buddhist tradition one's perception can be undistorted only when there is no attachment to theories, expectations, outcomes, desires, research grants, material rewards, and such like.

As to reliability, if we are working in an area in which strict replicability of controlled experiments is not to be expected (or even, as in astronomical research, replicability of measurements on systems that one can neither perturb nor control), still there must be some way in which we assess the trustworthiness of knowledge. It may have to be established on the basis of multiple imperfect tests. (For example, scientists have often chosen between two theories both of which seem to fit with the known facts, on the basis of one being more aesthetically elegant than another.)

MULTIPLE PERSONS IN A SINGLE BODY

Research on multiple personalities is an interesting area that illustrates some of the difficulties associated with self-report data. The conscious "ordinary" self is usually quite sure of being one mind in one body. The self that dreams knows another world, but is also sure, both in the dream state and when awake, that it is the same "I." However, there are persons—victims of "multiple personality disorder"—who appear to have two or more distinct personalities. (Dr Jekyll and Mr Hyde is the classic fictional example.) In actual cases the condition almost always seems to have its roots in severe child abuse, and is typically confusing and painful for the persons who suffer from it. Current research on this phenomenon is interesting from a number of standpoints, including some methodological puzzles. (See Putnam, 1989, for a more thorough discussion.)

In such a person (a "multiple"), different personalities (which in many cases have no awareness of one another) alternately control the physical body. Alternate personalities may be quite dissimilar in speech and thought patterns, mood, temperament, voice characteristics, apparent gender, physiognomy, posture and movement patterns, accessible memories, reported age and life history, and other individual and personality characteristics. Different personalities have often mastered different physical abilities, interpersonal skills, and intellectual subject areas. They may be able to speak different foreign languages. The impression that wholly different personalities are expressing themselves through a single body can be corroborated by correlating these various changes with the personality shifts as subjectively experienced by the psychiatrist or researcher.

The current surge of research interest in this topic has come about partly because of the discovery that in these cases of personality shift, physiological and biochemical changes may be observed as well. These can include brain wave patterns, chemical composition of bodily fluids, immune status, allergies, skin electrical responses, and others. This development leaves little doubt that in some important sense the alternate personality "really exists" as surely as does the usual personality. Research on multiples could potentially shed new light on a host of questions relating to consciousness.

The study of multiple personalities raises a different sort of methodological question. Most of conventional science seeks reductionistic explanations for phenomena. But "personality," like "health" and "love," is a holistic concept. How is truth sought in an area where one has to deal with a holistic situation that includes not only behavior and other measurable dimensions, but also the full spectrum of subjective experience? The most fruitful inquiry appears to involve explorations of these inner experiences, often quite profound and moving, in an atmosphere of mutual trust and rapport—not at all like the cold detachment of the controlled experiment.

Switching from one personality to another may be a voluntary act on the part of the multiple, or it may be spontaneous—often triggered by emotional response to a situation. Some alternate personalities appear to be destructive; they may be masochistic, or get the multiple in trouble through sociopathic behavior. Sometimes an alternate has a role as helper. One personality may exhibit unusual physical strength, and act as protector when the situation requires physical protection. Another may act as healer, and take over in emergencies with extraordinary knowledge about how to heal the body. An alternate may take over the body while the main personality is "sleeping," and prepare dinner, clean up the dishes, or perform other helpful acts. When one personality is stressed or tired, another may take over and function at a high level of effectiveness.

Under some conditions alternates may permanently "fuse" into a single personality, or alternate personalities may "leave." Both of these events can lead to more comfort for the patient and higher levels of effectiveness; in other words, they may be part of a "cure." But in the rare case a multiple doesn't want to be "cured"; having the body run by a well-functioning committee, so to speak, may be handier than being limited to one personality.

In the course of therapy one particular alternate may be encountered, which has been termed the "inner self helper." This unique personality is typically very cooperative with the therapist, even to the point of giving advice and pointing out mistakes. It seems to never display negative emotions such as hatred, anger, anxiety, fear, depression. It is typically cheerful and loving, with a good sense of humor. It seems to be both wise and compassionate. This "helper" personality appears to be potentially present in every known case, although it may not appear spontaneously. Unlike the other alternates, who typically report having been "born" during some traumatic period in the early childhood of the body, this particular one is likely to say, "I have always been." Queried about death, it reports that at death the body decays and the other personalities disintegrate, but "I remain." (It is interesting to compare this recent finding with the following quotation from the Upanishads [India, 1000 BCE]: "The atman, the Self, is never born and never dies. . . . It is beyond time, unborn, permanent, and eternal. It does not die when the body dies.")

The phenomenon of multiple personalities seems related to other kinds of dissociative states, some of which are not considered pathological but, rather, highly prized. Of course we all have alternate personalities in a sense; we have each experienced periods when we definitely feel the internalized parent to be in control, or the petulant child. One dissociative experience often considered to be beneficial is called out-of-body experience; it is sometimes associated with a near-death episode. Many persons have reported that such an experience has had a positive, transformative effect on their lives. Another example is the subjective experience of some sort of inner genius, such as the poet's muse or Socrates' "daemon," that may present an answer to a question, the solution to a problem, or a musical composition or the image of a work of art.

Sometimes one alternate personality may seem, both to the main personality and to an outside observer, to be knowledgeable and wise and beneficent, far beyond the capabilities and usual character of the host personality. Such an entity may claim to be a spirit guide, for instance. This is not dissimilar from the phenomenon of "channeling." The term channeling is usually used to connote a kind of communication that is external to the individual's "ordinary" conscious-unconscious mind system, and may seem in some respects to be quite superior to the ordinary mind. This "other" source may seem or claim to have been a person once alive on this Earth, or a being of some extraterrestrial sort not embodied in the usual physical sense. Other terms have been used for some forms of this phenomenon, at other times or under specific circumstances—these include "inspiration," "creativity," "deep intuition," "mediumship," "religious experience," and "revelation."

The history of science, mathematics, art, and intellectual achievement is replete with anecdotal episodes of this sort of communication seeming to come from somewhere other than the usual self. The revealed scriptures in many religious traditions are purported to have derived from such a source. Clearly the channeling experience, however interpreted, has profoundly affected the history of the human race. Yet science has had very little to say about the phenomenon, beyond admitting that most of its own conceptual advances seem to have arrived in this way. When something like this has been studied at all, it has been—like the studies of multiple personality—in the context of pathology.

As such research is pursued (as we can assume it will be, now that its potential importance has been widely recognized), it confronts us with a methodological question even more fundamental than those already raised. As deeper understanding of our own consciousness is sought, do we eventually encounter some questions that are indeed beyond science, beyond even some future extended form of science—although *not necessarily beyond ultimate human understanding?*

Suppose, for instance, that we were to conclude that in some cases of alternate personality, or channeling, there is contacted a source that appears to far exceed ordinary humans in intelligence, knowledge, and wisdom. Our tendency to ask of everything what it can be "used for" may in this case have to be curbed, for attempting to exploit such a source would be like the rat in the laboratory presuming to perform an experiment on the scientist. Our exuberant Western attitude that all of nature is here to be exploited for our ends may have to be replaced by a far more humble stance if we are to learn from the universe what it would teach us.

Creativity And Unconscious Knowing

It was mentioned earlier how we "know" in the unconscious mind much that is not ordinarily accessible to the conscious mind. This unconscious "knowing" is a far more pervasive aspect of experience than is ordinarily taken into account.

For example, research in biofeedback training discloses that we "know" unconsciously how to relax muscle tensions, change brain waves, alter heartbeat or blood pressure, change blood flow and skin temperature—but we aren't aware of this knowing until the feedback signal is provided. If I tape a small thermometer to read the temperature of the tip of my index finger, and focus my mind on how nice it would be if the temperature would rise five degrees, the temperature goes up! Unconsciously I know how to dilate the capillaries, increase the blood flow, and warm up the fingertip. Consciously I have no idea how to do this. I didn't know I knew, until provided with the feedback signal of the thermometer reading. Furthermore, once I get the "feel" of it I can dispense with the thermometer and warm the fingertip without it. (Children can do this with more facility than adults. It is not unusual for a young child, told to imagine the skin temperature very hot, to be able to raise it to 6 or 8 degrees above normal blood temperature!)

Unconsciously we "know" how to operate this remarkable organism called the physical body. We know how to produce peptic ulcers or alleviate them; to produce migraine headaches or be relieved of the pain; to heal wounds and restore damaged tissue, stopping with the appropriate quantity. We apparently know how to protect the soles of the feet so that they are unharmed while treading over burning coals. Unconsciously the pregnant woman knows how to "grow" the fetus and initiate the birth process.

With our unconscious minds we know how to carry on mental activity that we can't do or even understand with the conscious mind. An everyday example is recalling information stored in the memory— for instance, somebody's name. Straining at it doesn't help: Let's see, now, does it begin with a P or a B? Giving up for the moment, you "file a request" with another part of the mind to come up with the name. Sometime later, in the middle of a conversation on an unrelated topic, up pops the name! Unconsciously we know exactly how to search the memory files, identify the correct name from very scant clues, and bring the desired name up to conscious awareness. Consciously, we haven't the faintest idea how to accomplish this feat.

This may seem a very elementary example of what, when the task is more complex than memory, we call the creative process. The essence of creative problem-solving and intuitive decision guidance is much as it appears in this memory example. Creativity and intuition are terms we use to refer to those occasions when unconscious knowing is made accessible to the conscious mind. (So also are aesthetic experience and spiritual experience.) Sometimes there is a "request filed" for solution of a specific problem or answer to a question; sometimes the creative product simply arrives unbidden. But there is a part of the unconscious—a creative/intuitive mind— that knows how to find the solution or to produce the created product. And the key to creativity lies in opening up access to that mind, removing barriers, dissolving resistance.

In this drama of inner creativity there are at least three actors: the conscious mind, which wants to know; the creative/intuitive mind, which knows; and yet another part of the unconscious, which, for whatever reason, chooses to block or partially block access. (Not very long ago it would have been considered scientifically naive to speak in this way, but the experience of the fragmented mind with different parts "choosing" contradictory goals is one often described in contemporary literature on creativity.) One of the most powerful techniques for dissolving the resistance and releasing the creative abilities is that of affirmation (expression of self-fulfilling beliefs) and inner imagery.

AFFIRMATION AND INNER IMAGERY

Reprogramming the unconscious beliefs that block fuller awareness of our creative/intuitive capabilities depends upon a key characteristic of the unconscious mind, namely *that it responds to what is vividly imagined essentially as though it were real experience.* Thus, to revise the unconscious beliefs we need only vividly imagine new beliefs, and they tend to become "true." Because the unconscious beliefs have been reexperienced or reaffirmed repeatedly over a long period of time, the substitute beliefs and/or images must also be presented repetitiously over a period of time, preferably in a state of deep relaxation when the portals of the unconscious are most open. This basic principle is embodied in a variety of seminars and workshops and teaching techniques aimed at increasing effectiveness and releasing intuition and creativity.

There are many practical applications of the principle that what we affirm and program into the unconscious belief system we tend in subtle ways to bring about. When we establish and affirm an intention or a goal, imagining that it is already so, the unconscious mind is programmed to achieve that goal even in ways which the conscious part of the mind does not plan or understand. Athletic coaches, for instance, train athletes to image championship performance. Doctors train cancer patients to heal themselves by imagining the functioning of the immune system in ridding the body of the cancer cells. Business executives learn to affirm that desired goals are already achieved. The basic principle has long been a core idea in the esoteric inner-core understandings of the world's spiritual traditions. The most familiar formulation in the Christian tradition is found in Mark 11:24—"Whatever you ask for in prayer, believe that you have received it and it will be yours."

In practice, the process of changing the unconsciously held beliefs may not seem as simple as just represented. As earlier noted, we tend to manifest resistance when presented with information or experience that would threaten the unconscious belief system. A hypnotized person will present fantastic rationalizations to deny evidence that conflicts with the picture she or he has agreed to perceive, or to explain why behavior directed by a post-hypnotic suggestion (that is, behavior in response to a suggestion from the hypnotist that the subject does not remember, cued by a signal of which the subject is unaware) is really perfectly reasonable behavior. The phenomenon of denial is familiar in psychotherapy; the client will actually fail to see what is apparent to any onlooker, because to see it would be too threatening.

Psychologist Abraham Maslow wrote eloquently about this matter in a chapter in *Toward a Psychology of Being* entitled "On the need to know and the fear of knowing." He observed that we are all ambivalent when it comes to knowing ourselves. We may consciously intend to use affirmations to reprogram the unconscious, and then because of the inner resistance we "forget" to carry out the exercises. We want to know where we are deceiving ourselves, but at the same time we will go to great lengths to avoid finding out. We have been thoroughly taught in Western culture not to trust ourselves—not to trust that ultimately we *do* know what we most deeply desire, and how to resolve our inner conflicts. We have been taught that beneath the thin veneer of the socialized conscious mind lurk who-knows-what animal urges, repressed hostilities, and other evils. We have been taught not to risk exploring the unconscious mind—at least not without a psychiatrist seated alongside in case we should get into trouble. And so we fear to know the fearsome and unsavory about ourselves. But as Maslow points out, "we find another kind of resistance, a denying of our best side, of our talents, of our finest impulse, of our highest potentialities, of our creativeness. . . . It is precisely the god-like in ourselves that we are ambivalent about, fascinated by and fearful of, motivated to and defensive against."

THE LIMITS OF CREATIVITY

What then are the limits of the creative/intuitive mind? What is possible? We have already implied that the experienced limits are a function of the person's unconscious beliefs. If there is no reason in one's personal belief system to expect extraordinary performance from the creative unconscious mind, that assumption may limit the performance observed. Or inverting this observation, it is the oft-repeated testimony of successful executives and other creative people that the more one uses the creative/intuitive mind, the more faith one displays in turning to it with difficult decisions and problems, the better it seems to perform. And yet most people, dimly aware of its potentialities, deal with it as though it were marked FOR EMER-GENCY USE ONLY. Even much of the literature on creativity encourages us in this—for instance, the assertion is often made in literature on creativity that one must strain to try to solve the problem with the conscious mind first, and absorb a great deal of information about the problem, before the behind-the-scenes creative mind will go to work. It is felt to be somehow cheating if one doesn't struggle first to solve the problem with the rational analytical mind, and only in desperation turn to the unconscious servant. Thus those who presumably teach the "techniques" of creativity are in many cases unwittingly teaching *limitations* as well.

Now comes a key question. If indeed one comes to learn that a liberated creative/intuitive mind can outperform the conscious rational mind (at least in some ways), why not turn over to it all questions and problems? Resistance to this idea is likely to be immediate and resolute. For to assent to removing the ego-mind from its position of gatekeeper, governing what questions get asked of the creative unconscious, is to threaten its domination. To assent to accepting answers coming from the deep intuition is to assent to not guiding decisions by other means—plans, goals, ambitions, logical analyses, ethical rules, and so forth—all the ways in which the rational ego-mind maintains its control (and all the ways we were taught in school as the right way to think). Yet this idea of submission to the deep intuition appears to be exactly what many successful persons in a wide variety of fields have come to adopt.

So what are the ultimate limits to creativity? The answer is not known, but we get some clues from a concept we will call the "spectrum of creativity." Near the "low" end of the creativity spectrum are all those accomplishments of the unconscious mind that strike us as mundane and familiar, hardly deserving of the term—maneuvering the car down the freeway while the conscious mind is otherwise occupied, as an example. Farther along are the more recognized phenomena of creative problem solving, such as intuitive judgment and hunches and aesthetic creation. Some of these instances of creativity and creative problem solving are quite remarkable—as when a composer "hears" an entire musical composition in his or her "inner ear" and has only to copy it down, or an inventor intuits a complex solution to a problem. Still farther toward the "high" end of the spectrum are instances of "automatic writing," in which the manuscript seems to pass directly from unconscious mind to writing hand without passing through the conscious mind. Other more extreme examples of creativity seem to involve the person having information not available by ordinary means (such as diagnosis of illness at a distance without seeing or knowing the patient) or even producing effects not possible by our usual understandings of reality (for example, abnormally rapid healing). Way out at the "high" end we might think of the more unbelievable miracles, and of the "grand inspirations" of the scriptures of some of the "divinely inspired" religious traditions.

Each person has some familiarity with phenomena along this spectrum. Each draws a line somewhere and insists that beyond that point the reported phenomena are incredible. Different people, and different societies, place the credibility marker at different points on the spectrum.

What is being discovered in research on human consciousness is that the perceptual bias of Western industrial society (which includes its predilection for objective, reductionistic science) has been limiting in a way that until recently was largely unsuspected. The more fully the spectrum of creativity is explored, the more it appears that the demarcation line between "plausible" and "preposterous" is largely a marker of our own resistance. Perhaps it does not perform a useful function at all. That does not mean, of course, that we should believe everything we see or hear. But it does mean that we need not cling so tenaciously to our beliefs that certain things shouldn't happen. As the Danish philosopher Søren Kierkegaard once remarked, there are two ways to be fooled: One is to believe what isn't so; the other is to refuse to believe what is so.

Again it is helpful to view this situation from the vantage points of the three metaphysics defined earlier. From the M-1 standpoint (see page 29), science may someday be able to explain "ordinary creativity" in terms of something like rapid computer manipulations together with some sort of sensing device that can identify the right answer when the brain-computer cycles around to it. But for much of what lies out toward the "higher" end of the creativity spectrum this explanation seems very dubious indeed, and in fact it takes some straining to accommodate the concept of a "sensing device."

Viewed in M-2 or M-3, the situation can be accommodated with less strain. While creativity and intuition remain mysterious, there is at any rate no temptation to distort experience to fit preconceived limitations. And in the M-3 view in particular, *it is not clear that there are any limits to the human mind other than those we believe in.*

The 'Perennial Wisdom' In Religion

We have spoken earlier of the power of affirmation and inner imagery as taught in seminars and workshops that have been increasingly accepted by the business world as valuable for executive development. Although the techniques vary somewhat from case to case, in essence the principle is simple and straightforward. The person is taught to imagine success, create a vision, in whatever form may be meaningful to that person—and hence to bring about success. The imagining is to be done in a disciplined way, a number of times a day, every day for weeks or months. In this process, which is closely related to autohypnosis, it helps to be in a state of deep relaxation when the achievement of the goal is affirmed or imaged.

Much of the seminar is devoted to persuading the person to believe enough to give the process a fair trial. The individual is encouraged to not assume any limits to what kind of a goal can be achieved, or how. Limits there may be, but when you believe in limits you may make them real—whether or not they might be otherwise.

Applying the principle that the deep intuition is our best judge of what goal to select, some of these executive development workshops go a step farther. They encourage an interplay between two states or activities. One is affirming the desired goal and expecting its achievement to come about. The other is referring to the deeper mind to find out what one *really* wants.

The two can in fact be combined in a single affirmation something like the following: *I have but a single desire, to know the deepest (or highest, if you prefer) part of my Self, and to follow that.* I assume that what the deepest part of myself wants is what "I" want. I affirm that I have *no other* goals, ambitions, plans, and the like (that is, all the things I was taught to employ to "get ahead in life"), because those can be only concoctions of the ego-mind that deflect from what I really want.

There are two things to be noted here. One is that, as earlier noted, the business world is eminently practical. If this approach is used, it is because it works. It gets results. Never mind whether there is a theory to back it up; that can come later. The second observation is that there is a relationship between this key to effective living and age-old wisdom. Both parts of this approach are actually esoteric "secrets" that have been known for thousands of years, and are found in all the major spiritual traditions on the Earth.

These secrets were esoteric, or hidden, not because there was some inherent reason they had to be concealed from view, but because they tended to be antithetical or heretical to most societal belief systems. That is, to be known to practice them could be hazardous to your health (like being burned at the stake or tortured with one of those ingenious devices invented for carrying out the Inquisition). To put it another way: If you have discovered that it works out well to live your life based on an M-3 metaphysical assumption, but you happen to live in a rigidly authoritarian M-1 or M-2 society, be careful how you talk about your discovery!

We have already noted that the first part of this esoteric wisdom is expressed in Christian tradition in the proposition: "Whatever you pray for, believe that you receive it and you will." The second is also expressed in the form of prayer—not my will, but "Thy will be done." That certainly suggests that there is a relationship to religion to be explored.

One of the most important understandings of the last half century is of the conditions for a meaningful and effective life. This has arisen partly out of the experiences of psychotherapy and partly out of research in comparative religion. As the art of psychotherapy became increasingly free from its initial emphasis on pathology and shifted more to helping well persons discover how to function even more effectively, the discovery of untapped inner resources became a central focus. William James' *Varieties of Religious Experience* had long ago argued that the central core of religious experience appeared to be that the person identifies his real being with "the germinal higher part of himself" and then "becomes conscious that this higher part is co-terminous and continuous with a MORE of like quality, which is operative in the universe outside of him, and which he can keep in working touch with, and in a fashion get on board of and save himself when all his lower being has gone to pieces in the wreck." Transpersonal psychotherapy had uncovered a similar principle.

Meanwhile, in the field of comparative religion, a profound and related discovery had been made. Aldous Huxley was the first to announce it in a popular book, freed of weighty technical jargon, in 1945—in *The Perennial Philosophy*. It was this: When the various religions of the world and of history are studied, it is found they each fall into two types. First, each religion has one or more *exoteric* or public forms. These are what we usually think of when the term religion is used. They are characterized by their rituals, the architecture of their halls of worship, their revealed literature, and so on. But besides this, each spiritual tradition tends to have an *esoteric* or secret version, known only to an inner circle, and usually involving some sort of meditative discipline. The range of exoteric religions is fantastically diverse. However, all of the esoteric traditions are essentially the same—or, more precisely, appear to be based in some form of potentially universal spiritual experience. This common core has sometimes been referred to as the "perennial wisdom."

This esoteric "perennial wisdom" of the world's spiritual traditions is not a theory or a hypothesis to be articulated in ways familiar in scientific and philosophical treatises. Aldous Huxley says of it:

> Nothing in our everyday experience gives us much reason for supposing that the mind of the average sensual man has, as one of its constituents, something resembling, or identical with, the Reality substantial to the manifold world; and yet, when that mind is subjected to certain rather drastic treatments, the divine element, of which it is at least in part composed, becomes manifest, not only to the mind itself, but also, by its reflection in external behavior, to other minds. . . . It is only by making psychological and moral experiments that we can discover the intimate nature of mind and its potentialities. In the ordinary circumstances of average sensual life these potentialities of the mind remain latent and unmanifested. If we would realize them, we must fulfill certain conditions

and obey certain rules, which experience has shown empirically to be valid.

Among the "rather drastic treatments" Huxley refers to may be included various forms of yoga, meditative disciplines, ascetic vision quests, shamanic rituals, and the use of "entheogenic" sacramental substances such as soma and peyote.

This "perennial wisdom," being a distillation of the experience of many inner explorers over thousands of years, is without doubt an invaluable guide. It is also in principle compatible with any of the religious traditions since it is found in all of them; the long-standing conflict between the exoteric and the esoteric seems to have lost some of its hold. Although it may not have seemed so in the past, the "perennial wisdom" is also in principle compatible with science.

SCIENCE AND THE 'PERENNIAL WISDOM'

The modern world long assumed that there was a fundamental incompatibility between science and religion. For a time it appeared as a series of direct conflicts over such issues as the age of the Earth, the meaning of the fossil records, evolutionary theory, the Freudian re-interpretation of the human soul, and so forth. Religion always seemed to lose. Then as the world moved well into the twentieth century the conflict subsided, and people tended to live their religious lives apart from whatever they thought science was telling them about the nature of reality. The price paid for this schizophrenia was that neither science nor religion fully satisfied the person's desire to know with inner certainty. But now it becomes apparent that whereas there may indeed be conflict between positivistic science and dogmatic, exoteric religion, there is no necessary conflict at all between the esoteric "perennial wisdom" and a science based on an M-3 metaphysic.

We can try to make this a little more specific by considering some aspects of the "perennial wisdom" and indicating how science is already approaching them. But let us not be misunderstood. Science has not, is nowhere near, and presumably never will "prove" the inner understanding we are referring to by the term "perennial wisdom." The "perennial wisdom," in turn, is not, and presumably never will be, articulated in a form such that it can be tested in a scientific manner. It may be, however, exemplified in a life, and "proved" by living it. The best scientific knowledge available would seem at the least not to contradict it, and at most to tend to support it.

The French poet Saint-Exupéry said, "Truth is not that which is demonstrable. Truth is that which is ineluctable"—which cannot be escaped. Science deals with the demonstrable. The "perennial wisdom" insists that the ineluctable is found only through exploration of, and identification with, the deep Self.

We can point, in a general way, to this relationship between science and the "perennial wisdom" by considering six headings:

Consciousness

Of all the findings of modern psychology, one of the most firmly established and the one with the most pervasive implications is that only a small part of our total mental activity is conscious. The more vast portion is out of conscious awareness—in the unconscious. Ordinary conscious awareness may be thought of as a narrow "visible spectrum" between the subconscious (for example, instinctual drives, repressed memories, autonomic functioning) and the supraconscious (for example, creative imagination, intuitive judgment, aesthetic sense, spiritual sensibility).

Some of this out-of-consciousness activity is, so to speak, in the "deep unconscious" and we become aware of it only through inference. Some of it is at least partly accessible to conscious awareness under certain conditions (such as through hypnotic suggestion, dreaming, biofeedback training, meditation, autogenic training). Access to unconscious processes is facilitated by attention to feelings, emotions, and inner imagery.

All of the above is compatible with the "perennial wisdom," but that tradition goes further. It finds that there is a creative/intuitive/ spiritual mind that is not limited in ways we might expect the mind to be limited. Access to it, and indeed identification with this deep Center, can be facilitated by various meditative disciplines, again to an extent that is ultimately unlimited. Man's deepest ecological, humane, moral, and spiritual commitments are all rooted in this realm of human experience. As Ralph Waldo Emerson put it, when this other mind "breathes through his intellect, it is genius; when it breathes through his will, it is virtue; when it flows through his affection, it is love. And the blindness of the intellect begins when it would be something of itself."

Perception

Perception is greatly affected by unconscious beliefs, which in turn are shaped by suggestion, expectation, influence of authority, cultural beliefs, and so forth. This conclusion is supported by extensive and varied clinical and experimental research and anthropological studies. Seeing may be believing, but what is seen is not necessarily what is there. (One of the more startling examples of altered perception is when, through hypnotic suggestion, a person is led to perceive what isn't there.) In fact, when the influence of unconscious conditioning on perception is fully taken into account, the more accurate statement might be "Believing is seeing."

Here again the "perennial wisdom," while compatible with contemporary science, goes further. We are literally hypnotized from infancy by the cultural milieu in which we are immersed; we see the world the way we are enculturated to see it. A prime task of adult life is to become dehypnotized, "enlightened"—to see reality as it is and to "know thy Self." In this process we come to realize that we, in the out-of-consciousness collective mind, create the world of ordinary experience—which we then experience with the conscious mind.

Oneness

Whether or not one chooses to think in terms of "extrasensory communication," there is a kind of experience known to everyone in which individual consciousness communicates at a deep level with the consciousness of others. We refer to this experience with words like "rapport" and "love."

Research on telepathic communication, while not totally convincing to the skeptical, reinforces the impression that we sometimes know what is going on in other minds, without any of the usual physical sensory cues. In fact that knowledge may not be accessible to conscious awareness. (In one such experiment a flashing strobe light stimulus in one person's eyes produces an electrical component in the EEG pattern of another, distant and isolated, who has no physical indication of and no conscious awareness of the remote strobe light's flashing.)

In the "perennial wisdom," this awareness of rapport and of being joined is referred to in yet another sense. In higher states of consciousness there is an awareness of being one with the universe and all its creatures, of a knowing—a *gnosis*—related to that of the Creator. Because these kinds of insights are so different from the ordinary experience our language usually expresses, they are not easily conceptualized and verbally communicated. Myth, symbol, paradox, and poetic metaphor become more effective means of communicating these insights and experiences.

Resistance

We humans are well known to be ambivalent with respect to our desire to know ourselves. We will resist that knowledge that we most deeply desire.

We think we want to see reality as it is, to see truthfully. But our illusions are part of an unconsciously held belief system; any attack on those illusions is perceived (unconsciously) as a threat. Thus an effort to dispel illusion, although ultimately beneficial, may nevertheless generate resistance. We truly desire to discover and actualize our highest intuitive capacities, yet to the extent that removing illusion is essential to that discovery, we will resist that which we truly desire. (We may, in fact, resist it by using the most convincing "scientific" arguments and concepts.)

The ego self is threatened by the existence of the real Self and throws up a variety of smoke screens to block awareness of the true Center. In the end, for integration the ego self must become subservient to the real Self.

Creativity

The creative/intuitive capacities operate outside of conscious awareness in solving problems and providing answers to posed questions. Limits to the creative/intuitive mind arise from unconscious beliefs (such as "I am inadequate and unworthy"; "failure and ridicule are to be feared"). In general, its performance can be enhanced by intention, expectation, trust, and belief in the efficacy of the deep mind.

Trust in the creative/intuitive mind implies nonattachment to the goals of the rational/analytical mind.

The mystery of the creative/intuitive mind is underscored in the "perennial wisdom," which finds the deep intuition connected to the one Universal Mind. Thus there are indeed no limits to its capabilities save those the individual creates as part of the resistance to discovering one's godlike qualities. Furthermore, because of this connection to the All, problem solutions that come from the deep intuition will be to the benefit of all, not one solution at the expense of others.

Choice

Each of us, as we naturally stand, is fragmented. We make choices at unconscious as well as conscious levels, and they are not necessarily in alignment. Viewed in this light, the psychodynamic defense mechanisms can be thought of as unconscious choices. Repression is a choice to hide information from oneself; denial and resistance are choices not to perceive that which would imply change. Choices effected by the "authoritarian conscience," the introjected parent, Freud's superego, are likewise unconscious choices. On the other hand, choice may be guided by the supraconscious intuitive, aesthetic, or spiritual sense. Values are guides for choice that have been integrated into the personality or cultural pattern; in general, they have an unconscious component.

To anyone who is still at some stage of resistance to recognizing his or her inner abilities, the "perennial wisdom" appears to make an extreme, even startling leap when it comes to the matter of choice-guidance. When the other stages of awakening the inner senses are fully realized, the esoteric teachings enjoin us to turn over all choices to the deep intuition, the "authentic conscience." Only in this way does the person become totally integrated (a person of integrity), with the whole of one's being—subconscious, conscious, and supraconscious—directed toward the same ends. This fundamental decision implies having no other ambitions, seeking no other goals. Hence the admonition—"abandon all to have all."

These observations are not a demonstration of an incontrovertible conclusion. They do not argue that science will end up "proving" the "perennial wisdom."

Science does seem to be in the process of further substantiating that most of our mental activity is out of conscious awareness, that our "unconscious knowing" goes much farther than we might have imagined, and that our "unconscious choosing" has both tyrannical and liberating aspects. These findings are at least compatible with, and perhaps extrapolate to, the "perennial wisdom." That suggests that in the end science and religion are not at odds, but are complementary ways of knowing—both being essential to achieving the highest measure of what it means to be human.

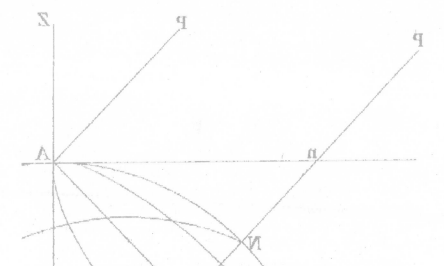

Legitimizing The Transpersonal

5

Human beings are not isolated,

they are not "monads without

windows" as Leibniz thought.

They may at times feel subjectively

isolated, but the extreme existentialistic

conception is not true, either

psychologically or spiritually.

—Abraham Maslow

MODERN SOCIETY HAS a peculiar characteristic—namely, that it teaches fear of death, and that fear underlies many other fears. If in fact we fundamentally evolved by mechanistic processes out of a material universe, and if life is basically a set of very complex physical and chemical processes regulated by coded messages in the DNA, then when those processes stop we die, and that is the end of us as physical organisms. If our consciousness, our cherished understandings and values, our individuality, our personhood, are simply creations of those processes, then when those processes stop we are no more. That is surely a fate to be feared, and indeed the fear of death permeates our society, disguised in a multitude of ways in which we seek "security."

But the "perennial wisdom" of the world's spiritual traditions has disagreed—has asserted that we are in an essentially meaningful universe in which the death of the physical body is but a prelude to something else. The mystical and contemplative traditions have often gone on to give more detail, although probably the insights of these traditions are very inadequately conveyed by any verbal description.

This issue of consciousness and survival is only one aspect of the shifting worldview; it is a useful one to explore, however, because it illuminates the strength of our prejudices. Serious attempts have been made to explore the concept of the continuation of personhood after physical death, and the evidence gathered has been disturbing to both positivist scientists and convinced religionists, because it fails to conform to their preconceptions. However, if that evidence is explored with humility and open-mindedness, it seems to point to features of an emerging "new story" quite different from the prevailing worldview.

THE ISSUE OF UNEMBODIED EXISTENCE

The medieval worldview was characterized by a continuum between this world and the next, such that the question of continuation didn't even come up. This continuum had been shattered by the scientific revolution, so that by the mid-nineteenth century there was a near-total discrepancy between a religious worldview within which the survival issue was presumably resolved and a scientific worldview within which the question was generally held to be irrelevant, or obviously answered in the negative. Interest in the survival question peaked around the turn of the century and waned to a mere trickle after World War I. There was a slow resurgence of interest beginning in the 1960s, and we seem set for a fresh look at the question in the last years of the twentieth century.

Much of the evidence for the survival hypothesis has centered around the phenomenon of mediumship, wherein a person in an altered state of consciousness appears to be able to receive communications from discarnate entities, and on occasion to evoke such physical manifestations as raps, table tipping, ouija board influencing, slate-writing, and the like. In earlier years, before the days of electronics, messages came in various ways. Some were oral utterances by the medium, taken down by a recorder. Others came in the form of automatic writing. A few were inscribed on closed hinged slates (of the type that used to be commonly used by schoolchildren) in which a slate pencil had been inserted, and the closed slates held by the researcher or placed under heavy objects to eliminate any possibility of fraud. (On careful examination, the particles of writing material appeared to have been deposited on the slate face, rather than rubbed off the slate pencil in the normal way. Of course, the idea that writing could take place without a writer to move the pencil was not accepted by skeptics, but there seem to have been adequate critical observers to give the reports credibility.)

Eventually all of this activity attracted the serious interest of such scholars as Sir Oliver Lodge and Frederic W. H. Myers in England and William James in the United States, and led to disciplined investigation and the creation of professional societies, the most prestigious being the Society for Psychical Research formed in 1882.

Myers' investigations in England were outstanding, and toward the end of his life in 1901 he summarized the evidence for survival in a landmark two-volume work *Human Personality and Its Survival of Bodily Death*. (This work is long out of print; however, an abridged version came out in 1992; the early research on survival is well described in Brian Inglis, 1992.) Myers and his fellow researchers were consistently frustrated by the difficulties of studying mediumistic communication. Thus he half-jokingly promised his fellow-workers that when he died he would devise an experiment that would leave people in no doubt as to his identity and survival. Beginning shortly after his death, and continuing for three decades, there were a remarkable series of communications purporting to come from him (with a few from his colleagues Edmund Gurney and Henry Sidgwick, who had also died by this time) which became known as the "cross-correspondences." These scripts came to a dozen mediums, living at various locations on three continents. They comprised fragments of messages, including fragments of classical quotations, which were clearly incomplete in themselves but when assembled at the SPR office in London fit together like pieces of a jigsaw puzzle.

Myers' attempt to bring afterdeath experience into the reach of science did not, it seems, stop with his death, nor even with the cross-correspondences. Over twenty years after his death, a sensitive in northern Ireland named Geraldine Cummins began to take down through automatic writing lengthy scripts attributed to the deceased Myers. These were published (with Cummins identified as author, but with a foreword explaining why she believed them to be transmissions from Myers) as two books: *The Road to Immortality* and *Beyond Human Personality*. (These books too are long out of print; they are summarized in Raynor Johnson, 1957.) They contain a fascinating report of his afterdeath experience and his mapping of the afterdeath possibilities, the latter being broadly similar to mappings that have appeared before and since from other sources.

Basically, death appears less as an extinction than as awakening to "where one is all along." We don't go somewhere at death; we are already there. In general, the center of awareness shifts at death from the physical to higher planes. Immediately after death individual experiences are as different, one person from another, as they are in earthly life. There may be a period of confusion and/or sleepy resting, or we may visit whatever was our idea of "heaven" while on the Earth. When the soul is ready, learning resumes; the journey to greater awareness continues. Our consciousness is of the same quality as that which pervades the universe, and our awareness of that universal consciousness is potentially without limit. Our sojourn on Earth has been, in Wordsworth's words, "a sleep and a forgetting"—a temporary unawareness of our true nature. Learning does not stop with the death of the body; the path to higher awareness is never-ending.

Recent Developments

All of the work with mediums over many decades faced the obvious problem that, whatever the original source of the communication, there was no way of telling how much it had been corrupted by bubbling up through the medium's unconscious mind. This problem plagued all of the researchers from Frederic Myers on, and was a source of continual frustration, even when there seemed to be something significantly evidential in the messages received.

As if in response to this problem, shortly after magnetic tape recorders became widely used, in the 1950s, messages began to appear on various tape recorders that purported to be from discarnate beings. This was "hard" evidence, presumably uncontaminated by the mind of some medium. Some of these messages were from persons who, prior to their death, were deeply involved with research on the survival issue. In still more recent times, as other technologies became available, these communications have extended to involve television screens, videotape recorders, and words and images scanned into computer disks; to include real-time two-way communication; and to include photograph-like images as well as verbal messages. All of this would seem on the face of it to constitute a totally preposterous claim, yet some of these communications, collected by researchers in at least six countries, comprise intriguing evidential significance. They even suggest that further progress will be made through the active collaboration of researchers on *both* sides of the curtain we call death. (Accounts of this work will be found in Pat Kubis and Mark Macy, 1995.)

There is other evidence of a different sort. Therapies based on recollection of past lives (Winafred Lucas, 1993, and Ian Stevenson,

1987) and on the possibility of spirit attachment (William Baldwin, 1993) are now well established although the conceivability of neither concept is considered to merit scientific credence, since they imply things like reincarnation and discarnate intelligences. (In weighing this lack of official endorsement, one should bear in mind that the concept of the unconscious mind had become a widely accepted basis for psychoanalysis and other psychotherapies a full half-century before it gained acceptance in strict scientific circles.)

Needless to say, all of this evidence tends to be summarily dismissed by the scientific community. However, the issue is so important that we need to understand what lies behind this dismissal. One can imagine how much of the fear in our society would disappear if a new view of death were to become real in our lives— if we came to realize that we couldn't nonexist if we wanted to.

Reductionist science is extremely powerful in modern society, but, as we have seen, there are numerous indications that it might be in error. Most scientists today would claim that there is no satisfactory scientific evidence to support a hypothesis of the continuation of personhood through the transition called death. That objection would be based largely on the presumption that unembodied intelligence is simply impossible; consciousness and memory cannot be imagined to exist in the absence of a physical brain. It is essential to recognize that *science in its present form is not in a position to deny that possibility.* That is because the present epistemology ("rules of evidence") of Western science rules out any consideration of consciousness as a causal reality. Thus it does not find in its understanding of causality anything resembling a self or a personality, endowed with reason, will, and a valid sense of value—*either* before or after death.

TOWARD A MORE COMPREHENSIVE SCIENCE

As we have seen, modern science adopted, at an early stage in its history, the stance of objectivism, positivism, and reductionism. For practical and political reasons that were quite valid at the time, the scientific enterprise became characterized by three assumptions that have become almost synonymous with "scientific method":

- The *objectivist* assumption, that there is an objective universe that can be explored by the methods of scientific inquiry and can be approximated, progressively more precisely, by quantitative models;

- The *positivist* assumption, that what is scientifically "real" must take as its basic data only that which is physically observable; and

- The *reductionist* assumption, that scientific explanation consists in explaining complex phenomena in terms of more elemental events (for example, gas temperature and pressure in terms of the motions of the molecules; human behavior in terms of stimulus and response).

These characteristics have seemed so integral to the scientific method that it is hard to imagine they would ever be displaced. Yet the data of exceptional abilities and the "inner empiricism" of the esoteric spiritual traditions challenge them in a way that may bring about a major revolutionary advance.

Science has a long history of defending the bulwarks against the persistent reports of phenomena and experiences that "don't fit in"—such as the spiritual and religious, the exceptionally creative and intuitive, the "miraculous" in healing and regeneration, the paranormal, seemingly teleologically motivated instinctual patterns, etc. But these defensive efforts have often seemed to be unfruitful and divisive.

One wonders if we have not become trapped in the quagmire of our own dogmas. Is there not a way to escape from these dilemmas without sacrificing any of the intellectual rigor, open spirit of inquiry, and public validation of knowledge that characterize science at its best?

Suppose, instead of the stance adopted because of history and circumstance, science were to adopt a different approach, namely, to *assume the validity of any type of human experience or extraordinary ability that is consistently reported down through the ages, or across cultures, and adapt science in such a way as to accommodate all of these.* This approach is basically that recommended by philosopher-scientist William

James in his essays on "radical empiricism" (Harman and de Quincey, 1994).

Let us explore some of the characteristics of such an extended science.

Holistic Models And Holarchical Causes

In contrast with conventional science, such a more comprehensive science will include more emphasis on holistic models and will center around some concept of hierarchically related causes. Let us illustrate this with some simple examples.

It may seem almost obvious that *the whole is qualitatively different from the sum of the parts.* A chemical compound displays qualities quite different from the qualities of any of its separate ingredients. An ecological system has characteristics one would not have suspected from simply examining its component organisms. A culture has characteristics that are not simply the sum of the behaviors of the individuals who compose it. The human body is not simply the sum of its organs and tissues.

Yet that basic principle has implications with regard to causative models that have not been appreciated through the history of science; that lack of appreciation has led to bitter dissents. *If characteristics emerge at higher system levels that are qualitatively different from those at lower levels, then the sciences appropriate to different system levels will be qualitatively different.* The science of cells is qualitatively different from the science of organisms, which in turn differs from the science of ecological systems.

A simple extension of this principle leads to the concept of a hierarchy—or better, a holarchy—of complementary and mutually noncontradictory "explanations" for the same phenomenon. (Arthur Koestler coined the terms "holon" and "holarchy." Everything is a holon, in the sense that it is a whole in one context, and a part in another. Thus an organ is a whole, composed of cells; yet it is a part of an organism. A holarchy is an order of increasing holons—that is, of increasing wholeness and integrative capacity. For more detail see Ken Wilber, 1995.) The factors that enter into an explanation at one level of system complexity may be meaningless at another level. Thus at one level of system holarchy a conscious decision to act may be part of the explanation, whereas at another level we can comprehend only nonvolitional, physical forces.

For example, suppose that I come down with a cold. At one level of explanation we may say that a virus "causes" the cold. But viruses, bacteria and a vast assortment of other microorganisms inhabit the space known as "my body" all the time. Some are beneficial, such as the bacteria in the intestines that are so essential to the digestive process. If we include in this accounting the body cells, I am "really" a vast ecological community of microorganisms that exist in a state of largely cooperative balance—most of the time. If this ecology gets out of balance, perhaps following my taking a chill, then I am said to have a particular disease, characterized by that imbalance. Put another way, the body's immune system functioning—which, after all, is the consequence of actions of a host of "friendly" microorganisms, T-cells and the like—is impaired, and that is why I have the cold. That is another level of explanation.

At yet another explanatory level we may observe that the reason the ecology of bodily microorganisms got out of balance was something called "stress." Stress is a psychological response to the environment such that various glandular secretions increase, and the body gets ready for "fight or flight." Repeated or continuous stress in situations in which fleeing is unseemly and physical fighting is impermissible can lead to malfunction of the immune system— hence susceptibility to colds.

These three explanations, each valid in its own way, are at different levels in some sort of holarchy. Moving from the first to the second to the third, there is a progressive increase in the amount of the universe included in the system under consideration. Furthermore, the causal agents are different at the different levels. At one level it may be the cold virus; at another, the condition of the body's immune system; at another, attitudes toward home and work that bring on the stress condition. These causal agents are progressively less physical and more abstract. Note that the abstract causes are not less "scientific" than the others; they merely occur at different levels in the holarchy.

At a less mature stage in its development, science had a tendency to consider the level of physical causation to be somehow more "real" than the more abstract levels (positivism). Thus, for example, there was considerable initial resistance to the idea of psychosomatic illness, or to the idea that positive emotions might have a salutary effect on the body's immune system. Furthermore, "scientific explanation" tended to imply interpretation at the level of physical causation (reductionism). Thus teleological causes (explanations involving purpose) were ruled out. A reaction of the arm to an external stimulus could be dealt with scientifically, but an arm movement for the purpose of reaching a desired object could not. The need is increasingly apparent to somehow extend science beyond the restrictions of this predilection for the physical level.

The Holarchical Structuring Of Science

Let us consider one such schema for structuring scientific knowledge in a holarchical way—not a new concept in the philosophy of science (see Popper, 1965), but one that seems never to have been really taken seriously by mainstream scientists.

Imagine a set of bookshelves, the shelves of which are labeled, upward from the bottom shelf: "Physical Sciences," "Life Sciences," "Human Sciences," and "Spiritual Sciences." The volumes on the "Physical Sciences" shelf deal with the physical sciences, more or less in their present form. In the volumes on the "Life Sciences" shelf we find expositions of the biological and health sciences. They describe biological and medical phenomena in terms compatible with the physical sciences. However, in the volumes on this shelf we encounter holistic concepts like "organism," and teleological concepts like "function," that are foreign to the discussions on the bottom shelf. Furthermore, living organisms differ from nonliving things in that they are basically self-creating; in the term coined by Francisco Varela, they have the property of *autopoiesis*. Their possibilities in this regard are somewhat limited by the next lower holon level; for instance, humans don't have the subsystems with which to fly. On the other hand, every holon gets its purpose or meaning from the next higher holon level; for example, the function of the organ is to serve the organism. (In our highly individuated and alienated Western culture, some human-holons are reluctant to recognize any higher holarchic level than themselves.)

At the third shelf level dealing with "Human Sciences," the laws of the biological sciences partially describe the phenomena. However, discussions of these "Human Sciences" contain even more holistic and abstract concepts like "personal health" and "personality" and "individual purpose." The fourth shelf labeled "Spiritual Sciences" (required if the deep subjective experience of untold mystics, prophets, artists, and poets, down through the ages, is to be honored) deals with the transpersonal. Here we find discussed still more abstract concepts, perhaps, such as "universal purpose." (The diagram hints at how the topics of healthcare and evolution might involve qualitatively different concepts when approached from the four levels.)

It is apparent that an extensive "level 1" science of the physical world already exists. In the life sciences and psychiatric theory there are fragments of a "level 2" science that repudiates the claims of some molecular biologists that eventually all behavior is explained by the genes. As for "level 3" science, humanistic psychology and sociology are even more fragmentary. At the fourth level we find attempts such as transpersonal psychology and Tibetan Buddhist psychology.

Behavioral conditioning may seem to fit comfortably at level 2, whereas volition, intention, comprehension, and paying attention are level 3 concepts; values and meaning may be thought of in terms of level 4 concepts. James Lovelock's "Gaia hypothesis" considers the Earth as a self-regulating organism; in its most widely accepted form it is a level 2 concept, but some would attribute consciousness to the planet, a level 4 hypothesis.

In systematic biology, a level 2 science, the quality of connoisseurship becomes important in species recognition. Empathy may be a desirable characteristic of the scientist at level 3. At level 4 one encounters the problem of a limited number of qualified observers (qualified in terms of their own inner development), and it has been extremely difficult to avoid the pitfalls of dogma and cult.

Further Characteristics Of A
Holarchically Structured Science

We need to note a number of further characteristics of such a holarchically extended science.

Questions asked. Questions not appropriate at one level of models *may nevertheless fit at another.* Thus teleological questions have no place in the level of reductionistic science of physical reality. At the next level, however, it is appropriate to ask about the function of the body's immune system, or of elaborate instinctive patterns in animal behavior. At the third level volition may be acceptable as a causal factor, and personality is a meaningful construct; one can inquire into the significance of personal acts and habit patterns. At the transpersonal or spiritual level questions about "other kinds of consciousness" achieved in meditative states, and guidance of choices by some kind of deep intuition, may be meaningful.

In the past, scientists have tended to insist that teleological questions and value-focused questions are not appropriate to science. Of course, they have always been asked in some areas, such as the health sciences. A question about the function of some part of the body's regulatory system is teleological, and certainly a question about what leads toward health is value-focused.

To those who still ask whether these kinds of questions are appropriate to science, one can reply with the question, "If not science, then what?" There is no other authority in modern society with the prestige of science to ask these important questions.

Models and metaphors. The models and metaphors used at one explanatory level may be obviously inappropriate at another. The holistic metaphors appropriate to considering human personality are "nonphysical" and do not appear at the physical level; on the other hand, atomistic explanations of organic processes at the physical level leave out the essence of what is being studied at the higher levels.

It should be noted that there need be no claim to exclusivity in terms of which level is ultimately "real." Physicists led the way in the recognition that reality is too rich to be fully expressed in any model, theory, metaphor, or equation. Wave models do not invalidate particle models, and vice versa; the two metaphors are *complementary*, not contradictory. Similarly, an explanation of human behavior in terms of the philosophy of life adopted does not contradict, but rather complements, an explanation in terms of repressed desires and conditioned responses.

A scientist may behave professionally as though the physical level describes what is "real." Another scientist (or for that matter, the same one) may lead his or her personal life as though only the transpersonal level of mind and spirit points to the ultimately real. There is no contradiction involved, and the individual does not become a schizoid personality for holding both views at the same time. Indeed, a person may be a better scientist for not having to fight so strongly to defend the positivism and reductionism appropriate to the physical level.

Of course there are aberrations to be avoided, arising from adopting too extreme a position. The extreme positivist, reductionist position leads to having to deny the reality of the most immediate experience, such as that of attention and volition. The extreme transpersonal position can result in a person who is ineffective through not being "grounded."

Methodology. The methodology used is that appropriate to a given level and may be quite different for a different explanatory level. The rigidly controlled experiment, and the expectation of strict reliability of experimental results, are appropriate to the physical level and, to a more limited extent, the organismic. Even at these levels there may be intrusions of observer effect that are understandable from higher levels but "anomalous" at the lower.

The idea that the scientific observer cannot be "objective" in the sense of isolating himself or herself completely from the phenomena observed applies at all levels to some extent, and particularly at the higher ones. What the scientist perceives is a function of unconscious conditioning and previous suggestions picked up from the environment. Furthermore, as the universe is perceived from the higher levels, the contents and processes of the experimenter's mind can affect the experiment in ways not understandable from the lower explanatory levels.

These kinds of considerations become especially relevant whenever "consciousness as causal reality" is a significant factor in the phenomena being observed. They suggest that strict interpretations of objectivity and of reliability through replicability are inappropriate in research on subjective experience; and that surely, if they are, there must be other criteria something like these that *are* appropriate. Perhaps as the scientific exploration of these areas becomes more mature, something like the Buddhist ideal of "nonattachment" will indeed replace the concept of strict objectivity, which, as is well known, no longer seems to fit even the relatively dependable area of the physical sciences. And something like "trustworthiness" (perhaps established on the basis of multiple imperfect tests) may replace strict reliability through replicability.

Consider as an example the research on multiple personalities discussed earlier. Is it really true that, incredible as it may seem at first thought, the same body may be inhabited by more than one personality? This holistic concept can hardly be explored at all without interacting with the person(s); thus objectivity in any strict sense is inappropriate. However, the ideal of nonattachment to preconceived notions of what can and cannot be is clearly pertinent. Not too long ago, the concept of an alternative personality expressing itself through the same body depended almost entirely on the psychiatrist's impressions. The concept has gained credibility in recent years because of the discovery, as we have seen, that when the personality shifts, various measures of bodily functioning also change (the striking example being a person who is allergic to something with one personality not being allergic with another!).

One other methodological point is important to note. In carrying out research that involves higher explanatory levels, the observer is not unchanged by his or her scientific activities. One cannot explore altered states of consciousness without being sensitized and otherwise changed in the process.

It is also the case that a willingness to be transformed is an essential characteristic of the scientist of the higher explanatory levels. The cultural anthropologist who would see clearly another culture than her or his own must allow that experience to change her or him so that the new culture is seen through new eyes, not eyes conditioned by the scientist's own culture. The psychotherapist who would see the client clearly must have worked through his or her own neuroses which would otherwise warp perception. The scientist who would study at the level we have called "spiritual science" has to be willing to go through the changes that will make him or her a competent observer.

Data admitted. It seems clear that the new science will in some way have to deal with subjective reports of deep inner experience. When this has been put forward in the past (as "introspectionism"), the idea was rejected by the main body of scientists. Perhaps it will come forward now in more sophisticated form.

At the level of "physical reality" admissible data are primarily in the form of quantifiable physical observation. At the organism level somewhat more holistic kinds of observations become important, such as instinctive behavior patterns, or the functioning of the digestive system. Self-reports of inner, subjective experience become relevant at the personal level, and essentially comprise the sole source of data at the transpersonal level.

'Upward-looking' and 'downward-looking' explanations. Reductionism has been so characteristic of most science that one almost automatically thinks of scientific explanation in those terms. We understand (scientifically) a phenomenon when we can describe it in terms of more elemental phenomena. Prestige is given to an explanation of behavior of a living organism in terms of responses to external stimuli, biochemical tensions, DNA composition and structure, and so on—in other words, downward-looking explanation.

Yet it is clear that scientists also use (often reluctantly) *upward-looking explanation*—explanation in terms of concepts at a higher level (Sperry, 1987). For example, when the immune system attacks a particular virus it is not understood as just a complex chemical reaction; it can really be understood only in terms of the function of the immune system being to protect the organism from harm (a level 2 concept). In regeneration of a lobster claw after amputation, the complex building process can be understood only in terms of some kind of morphogenetic image of the nature of a whole lobster claw. To understand altruistic behavior it is necessary to invoke at least level 3, and possibly level 4, concepts. Teleological explanation (in terms of purpose or goal) is only one form of upward-looking explanation.

It is as though in the diagram shown on the next page the physical sciences shelf and the downward-looking arrow have been in boldface throughout most of the history of science. Only in very recent years are

97

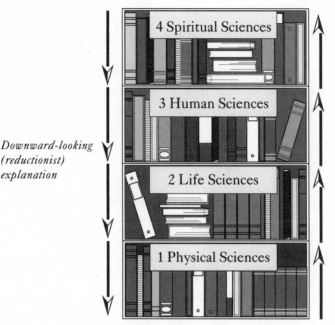

Downward-looking (reductionist) explanation

Upward-looking (teleological) explanation

Complementary Modes
Of Explanation

we ready to consider seriously the complete knowledge system implied by the rest of the diagram.

At the same time that we recognize the validity of both downward-looking and upward-looking explanations, we need to note that the basic hunger for meaning, for making sense out of our lives, which is so characteristic of the human condition, tends to be more satisfied by the upward-looking explanations. They may or may not be more fundamental by some rational argument, but they feel more fundamental.

The reframing of unfruitful controversy. One of the most important results of coming to think about science in this holarchically structured way is that many of the scientific controversies of the past simply disappear when we reframe them in terms of such levels of explanations. The behaviorist issue is clearly a matter of a certain group of scientists insisting that they will not deal with what is not at the level of physical measurability. The perennial "free will versus determinism" debate is resolved simply by recognizing that these are two complementary concepts that fit on different levels. Dualistic approaches amount to considering only two levels, rather than at least four. Miraculous healings, such as those meeting the stringent criteria set by the International Medical Commission at Lourdes, France, may in the end be considered to fit at the transpersonal level and to not contravene the usefulness of the physical and organismic levels of explanation for many other purposes.

One of these perennial controversies has been over interpretation of the phenomena of *morphogenesis*. Morphogenesis (literally, the birth of form) is particularly evident in healing, regeneration (restoration of a mutilated organism), and embryonic growth. An extreme form of regeneration is found in some simple animals, like hydra or planaria, where a tiny fragment of the organism can regenerate a complete individual. In embryonic growth, multiplication of a single cell eventually results in the formation of a complete organism, with many diverse cells performing widely differentiated functions. In order to explain the phenomena, the concept of a vital force, peculiar to living organisms, that directs form and development has been introduced. "Vitalism," as this idea has been termed, has in general been very controversial in the scientific community. The term "morphogenetic field" has been used since the 1920s to describe the organizing principle whereby the many cells are guided to combine, with differentiated functions, to produce a living organism of particular form. (The same term was later adapted and extended by Rupert Sheldrake to account for complex instinctual behaviors in animals.) But there seems to be no satisfactory way of explaining morphogenesis at the physical level; some higher-level concept appears to be required.

A somewhat similar controversy is present with regard to evolution (complicated by the fact that fundamentalist Christianity and the US Supreme Court are also in the act). The prevailing neo-Darwinist theory tends to account for the evolution of high-order species through random mutation and natural selection. This, however, leaves many puzzles, not the least of which is that posed by structures (such as the two eyes for binocular vision) that would appear to have no survival value in any intermediate stage, so that it is hard to imagine their evolution taking place in any sort of incremental way—and equally hard to imagine through a sudden transformational leap.

One of the most puzzling aspects of evolution is the evidence from the fossil record that the progress of evolution has not been a monotonous progression from simple to more complex organisms, through random mutation and natural selection. Rather, there are long periods during which relatively few new forms appear, and a few much narrower periods (such as the early Cambrian, as described by Stephen Jay Gould in *Wonderful Life*, 1990) during which there is a veritable explosion of new forms, many of which seem to have suddenly sprung into existence as though Nature were saying, "Let's try out this new organism and see how it fares." Somewhat as we humans create new things and try them out to see how they work, so we can imagine at another level new phyla and orders being "created" by formative mind to "see how they work out" with regard to a particular environmental challenge. This sounds like simplistic anthropomorphism, but it need not be. It is at least as plausible as the official dogma that all those remarkably complex and wondrous organisms, with all their amazing instinctual patterns (including some, like migratory instincts, for which biologists search in vain for some purely physical mechanism), were the chance result of random mutations and natural selection alone.

It seems possible that a more adequate theory of the evolutionary process will eventually include both the neo-Darwinist sort of mechanism and some higher-level morphogenetic directing force, something like a universal (or at least planetary) mind. But not all such controversy is so easily removed. For example, astrology has been sustained for thousands of years by empirical generalizations based on the predictions of horoscopes; if there is ever to be a robust theory of astrological influence it will obviously have to be at a transpersonal level. Again, the seventeenth century destruction of belief in phenomena related to witchcraft, shamanism, animism, and the like was in the face of overwhelming evidence supporting existence of the phenomena; new kinds of acceptable explanations may well appear in time, but they will have to be at a personal (for example, as phenomena of hypnosis) or transpersonal level.

Particular mention should be made of the principle of parsimony—the idea that a simpler and more aesthetically elegant conceptualization should be preferred to a more elaborate or complex one, when both accommodate the known facts. This principle would seem to have been often misapplied in the past, when it has been used to disallow explanations at the higher levels in favor of straining to reinterpret (or disallow) data to fit the explanation into the physical level.

Explanatory concepts at one level may be very useful in complementing the primary explanations of phenomena at some different level. The conceptualizations at the physical level, for example, may add rich detail to psychosomatic processes where the basic explanation appears to be at a higher level. The highly sophisticated transpersonal conceptualizations of the Tibetan Buddhist psychologies, on the other hand, may contribute important insights into processes at the personal and organismic levels.

SCIENTIFIC CAUSALITY: A PHILOSOPHICAL COMMENT

It seems desirable to include a brief discussion of a philosophical issue that is key to understanding the predicament of the modern world. (Those readers who find themselves allergic to words over five syllables may wish to skip to the next section.)

It is a fascinating historical fact that (a) philosophers of science have been concerned with the issues of scientific causality for many decades, and (b) practicing scientists have paid little attention. More than one scientist has quoted, with some tinge of self-satisfaction, the anonymous remark that "philosophy of science is about as useful to scientists as ornithology is to birds."

Scientists typically assume (or behave as if they do) that the philosophical premises underlying science are not at issue—that they are part of the definition of science. But many debates that appear to be about scientific matters in fact center around implicit ontological and epistemological issues.

Ontological questions have to do with the nature of reality; epistemological ones with how we acquire knowledge about reality. (As one writer expressed it, when the soprano sings "I know that my redeemer liveth," the ontological question is: Who is your redeemer? The epistemological question is: How do you come to know?) Both are presumably more fundamental than empirical questions based on sensory experience, which can be resolved by empirical investigations. The practical significance of both questions is that any society's knowledge system, modern science included, is based on some ontological and epistemological assumptions. The issue is, how are these established and how is their adequacy evaluated?

Students of science, at least in the earlier part of this century, were typically given the impression of a vast structure within which the fund of knowledge is continually increasing in size and quality and the more fundamental laws are increasingly certain. It comes as a shock, then, to discover that in fact some of the most basic assumptions regarding scientific causality are very much in question—perhaps more so than at any time in the past three centuries. It may be less shocking in the context of a brief history of the changing concepts of causality and its centrality in science.

Brief Historical Background

From the time of Aristotle, his fourfold typology of causality has been influential in Western thinking. We may illustrate these four types by examining the "cause" of the images on a television screen:

- Material cause (for example, the television receiver)

- Efficient cause (for example the electric currents and voltages; the incoming electromagnetic signal)

- Formal cause (for example the program concepts in the mind of the producer)

- Final cause (for example the ultimate purpose of selling the sponsor's product).

In Aristotle's terms, modern science is about material and efficient cause; it is not about formal and final cause. There has been essential agreement on that point for the past three and a half centuries, although not without argument along the way. For instance, Harvey's discoveries concerning the motion of the heart and blood implied functional utility (final cause); Boyle claimed this was appropriate to science whereas Descartes insisted not. It is with regard to the biological sciences that the causality question has been most often raised. Is biology in the end a molecular science? Probably most practicing scientists would say yes, but there is much reason to doubt, as we have seen.

The dominant worldview of the sixteenth century assumed a deep unity between nature and *gnosis* (knowledge which, although hidden, is accessible to imaginative thought and feeling). What emerged in the seventeenth century was a science based on a profound division between mind and the nature it contemplates, so that an "ontological gulf" exists between consciousness and its object. In this view the real is truly an object that stands over against the thinking mind, appearing *to* it but not *in* it. This dramatic change in perception emerged from a fierce and fateful struggle for legitimacy and power between the members of groups championing radically different programs of development and reform in Europe at the end of the sixteenth and the beginning of the seventeenth century.

One of these programs was a movement for radical change and reform centering around the Renaissance nature philosophy of a group of fifteenth and sixteenth century scholars, somewhat associated with the Medici court in Florence. Francesco Giorgi was a Franciscan friar whose *De harmonia mundi* of 1525 was based on the themes of the thirteenth century philosopher and mystic Ramon Lull. Others in this group were Johannes Reuchlin, John Dee, and Giordano Bruno.

Within this philosophy, all of reality was a single coordinated domain, every region of which was related to every other region. Thus to know the region called "nature" entailed knowing the whole sphere of Being within which nature was embedded. Mind and nature were thus undergoing a continuous cooperative transformation. But to achieve this knowledge and insight, the seeker had to make a spiritual commitment so as to experience *gnosis*, knowledge that transforms both self and other—mind and nature then simultaneously changing to states of greater harmony and unity. In alchemy, this dual transformation was described as a golden illumination of the mind or soul of the practitioner of the art, at the same time that gold was emerging in the crucible. Thus nature was undergoing transmutation simultaneously with the spiritual illumination of the seeker. Neither could occur without the other.

The growth of Catholic power in Iberia led to the expulsion of the Jews in 1492 and of the Moors in 1505. Reuchlin was caught up in the wave of anti-Semitism because of his espousal of Jewish scholarship and cabalistic teaching. His reform program was destined to lose out to a competing program which turned out, in fact, to be the nascent empirical science.

The Parisian monk and mathematician Mersenne saw Giorgi's gnostic nature philosophy as a threat to a very different proposal for reform, one that he deeply felt to be the path of intellectual and political rectitude and stability. (Descartes studied mathematics for two years with Mersenne, an experience that presumably had some influence on his philosophy. Mersenne was a key figure in the early development of science, acting as what might in modern parlance be called a "networker" among Descartes, Desargues, Fermat, Pascal, Galileo, and others. In this role he was instrumental in spreading Descartes' concepts of scientific method.)

Whereas Reuchlin was a reformer, seeking a mystical solution of religious problems, his contemporary Luther sought a political solution. The fragmentation that followed Luther's attempts at reform in religion was matched by an equivalent fragmentation of scientific knowledge that followed upon the establishment by Mersenne and Bacon of a science from which the astral linkings of Giorgi's universal harmony were banished. Their concept of what might be termed a "science of separateness" won out, and the more holistic concept of science went into hiding.

The science that Mersenne helped to shape in the seventeenth century and which has come down to us as the dominant tradition of Western scientific and philosophical thought is based upon dualisms that split the unified world of the Renaissance magi into separate domains of power. This science, for an assortment of pragmatic, historical, and psychological reasons, is based on a number of metaphysical assumptions that came to characterize the endeavor by early in the eighteenth century. The most basic of these assumptions is that of separateness: separability of observer from observed; of human from nature; of mind from matter; of science from religion; separateness of "fundamental particles"; separability of the parts of a system or organism to understand how it "really" works; separateness of scientific disciplines; of investigators, competing over who was first discoverer. This assumption leads to the hubris that humankind can pursue its own objectives as though the Earth and the other creatures were here for its benefit, to the myth of the "objective observer," to reductionist explanations, and to the ethic of competition.

Modern scientific thinking is often assumed to have begun with Descartes. In his *Discourse on Method* (originally entitled "Project of a Universal Science Destined to Raise Our Nature to Its Highest Degree of Perfection"), he outlined the new method of inquiry. The basic tenet of Descartes' philosophy is a dualistic position: The universe is composed of two distinct kinds of substance: mind, the essence of which is thought, and matter, the essence of which is extension in three dimensions. This dichotomy creates the "mind-body problem," which is the question of how these two such dissimilar substances can interact—how mind can know matter and affect matter.

The method of Bacon, Galileo, Descartes, Newton, and Leibniz was characterized by "radical impersonalism." Bacon was deeply suspicious of the active, imaginative mind, advocating the superiority of the disciplined mind as the surer way to scientific truth. The focus of these early scientists on rigorous discursive reasoning eventuated in a universe whose atomic constituents were only extrinsically correlated with one another, obeyed generic laws of interaction that made no provision for the individual characteristics, and was held together by a mysterious yet clearly nonanthropomorphic force: gravity. In contrast, the world-picture of Renaissance nature philosophy had been of a Cosmos composed of intrinsically correlated elements, holarchically ordered in accordance with anthropomorphic values, and held together by a force called "love."

Thus the most fundamental aspect of the seventeenth century scientific revolution was a basic shift in the dominant picture of reality. The cosmic vision of wholeness was replaced by a perception of separateness. Activities became rationally organized around impersonal and utilitarian values rather than around ceremonial and traditional ones. There was a shift from action that is prescribed to action by choice. This secularization of values marked the beginning of modern times. It brought a differentiation of institutions and social division of labor. Change became expected or desired and was increasingly institutionalized. There was increasing orientation toward the individual and toward pluralism in values.

After the seventeenth century, the emphasis was increasingly on "scientific" explanations in terms of efficient cause. The ancient Babylonians had been such good astronomers that the accuracy of their observations was unsurpassed until the late nineteenth century. The Greeks accomplished little by way of astronomical observation, and depended mainly on the Babylonian data. But the Greeks are considered the more "scientific" because they asked questions about *cause*. Most of the Greek astronomical theories were later discarded, but they asked the questions scientifically. They were trying to understand the physical events that produced observable phenomena.

Final causation and teleological explanations were specifically excluded from the realm of scientific explanation. Descartes' mind-body dualism became common sense, and mechanistic explanations were assumed to be adequate for scientific purposes. The fact that conscious intention results in action was left for philosophers to ponder over as the "mind-body" problem or the "free will versus determinism" debate.

Thomas Hobbes' definition of a cause tended to be unchallenged: "the sum or aggregate of all such accidents, both in the agents and the patient, as concur to the producing of the effect propounded; all which existing together, it cannot be understood but that the effect existeth with them; or that it can possibly exist if any one of them be absent." Every phenomenon must have a cause. The entire cause, being sufficient to produce the effect, produces it necessarily.

Isaac Newton held that it is the task of the scientist to discover the mathematical laws of phenomena, but the ultimate natures of things, or the ultimate causes upon which these depend, may be made the subject of endless hypotheses among which it is impossible to decide by any available evidence. "We are to admit no more causes of natural things than such as are both true and sufficient to explain the appearances," he said.

David Hume's views on causation in *Treatise of Human Nature* (1739) brought about some quiet consternation. He observed that all the human mind ever knows is its own perceptions. Analysis of our idea of causation reveals the idea of contiguity, and the idea of succession—of cause and effect. These two ideas are readily trace-able to the external impressions in which they originate. But our idea of *necessary connection*, which is also an intrinsic constituent of our idea of causality, is not similarly traceable to an external impression. In no case is any connection observable between cause and effect, only their contiguity and succession. What connection there is, therefore, is purely subjective—a habit of mind, with no provable existence. Causation is nothing but regular conjunction of phenomena, accord-ing to Hume. But John Stuart Mill, in *A System of Logic* (1843), still maintained that the cause of anything is "the antecedent which it invariably follows" (not the same as "the antecedent which it invari-ably has followed in past experience."). And scientists (they were called that after Whewell introduced the term in the early nineteenth century) continued to believe, nonetheless, that they were uncover-ing the true causes of phenomena.

Certainly the idea of cause has never been a simple one, clearly and uniquely defined. Discussions of the question of causality seem invariably to be connected with the question: "What is reality?" Scientists typically assert that they are working with "models" of reality, and that the theories or conceptual frameworks with which they work have value because they prove to be useful, not because they are in some ultimate sense "true." Thus they use the word "cause" to be almost synonymous with "explanation" within a theoretical structure that has proven capability toward prediction and control. Nevertheless, in some of the conflicts that arise over such scientific concepts as the Freudian and Darwinian examples, or over such contested areas as parapsychology, it becomes clear that some, at least, of the disputants are equating "scientifically explained" with "really true."

The process by which one scientific outlook becomes out-moded and another rises to prominence has never been fully orderly and rational, and has sometimes been violently disputatious. For example, there was a spirited debate in the seventeenth and eigh-teenth centuries between Cartesians and Newtonians over the legiti-macy of the appeal, in Newton's theory of gravitation, to action at a distance. This was later resolved by introducing the device of a gravitational field, assumed to fill the space between the attracting bodies and to provide the necessary link. Later on, the concepts of electric and magnetic fields served a similar purpose. Since these hypothetical fields are known only indirectly, in terms of their effects, one could say that they serve mainly a psychological function, to enable persons better to visualize nonlocal causation. When electric and magnetic phenomena were linked, still later, through the concepts of electromagnetism, a nonmaterial substance, called "ether," was postulated to fill all space and to be the medium that supported electromagnetic fields. Although scientists have since done away with the hypothetical ether, the concern with nonlocal causality is still bothersome.

Around the end of the nineteenth century, embryology was torn by a prolonged battle between vitalists and mechanists over the appropriate kind of explanation for developmental phenomena. Sides were taken with all the fervor one finds accompanying religious strife. The mechanists held that all of physical reality—including all questions about the development of biological organisms—must ultimately be explainable in terms of fundamental scientific laws that hold equally for inorganic and organic realms. The vitalists insisted that living organisms are different, that some sort of creative principle, some *élan vital*, must be present in all organisms and responsible for development and evolution. Vitalism is certainly out of favor, and from surface appearances the vitalists would seem to be in retreat, but even casual questioning reveals that in the confidential thoughts of many a sophisticated biological scientist, vitalism is alive and well. But if it won't die, how can the questions it tries to address be more satisfactorily answered?

Plato had taken the position that Reality is not to be found in the physical world (the world of *sensibilia*) at all, but rather in the nonphysical world of *intelligibilia*, a world that housed mathematical entities and other nonphysical objects of thought. Only by turning away from the sensible world and by contemplating the nonsensible objects of intellection could real understanding be achieved. Interaction with the physical world might yield opinion or mere belief, but it could never yield knowledge of Reality. Pure contemplation was the proper occupation of the rational soul, itself a nonphysical substance capable of existence independent of the physical body.

From the Renaissance to the latter half of the twentieth century there was steady erosion of Plato's influence, largely because empirical science progressively proved itself to be outstandingly successful and Plato's views appeared to be antithetical to empiricism.

Kant had attempted to revise the pure empiricist view. He held that all knowledge is mediated by the mind, which imposes a structure and an organization on the input. Thus our knowledge of inner objects and processes is no more immediate than our knowledge of outer objects and processes. This means that there is nothing epistemologically unique or sacrosanct about introspectively based beliefs; they are not on an entirely different footing from beliefs about the outer world, and they have neither more nor less need for justification.

Bacon had divided natural philosophy into two parts, with physics handling the material and efficient causes and metaphysics handling the formal and final causes; Kant was more optimistic about the ultimate power of physical science. He felt that physical science could be extended by the principle of final causes "without interfering with the principle of the mechanism of physical causality." A neo-Kantian theme held out the possibility that the framework of concepts for understanding our inner life could be improved by science in much the same way that our beliefs about the outer world are improved by science.

Philosopher David Hume had shown that it is never possible to prove that a general statement is true. Karl Popper maintained that one could not even show that it was likely to be true. He argued that falsifiability is the proper basis on which one can corroborate (but not confirm) theoretical statements. Charles Sanders Peirce, whose philosophy of pragmatism was influential in America, thought the idea of Unknowable Reality was metaphysical tomfoolery, and took instead the view that the only reality is the reality that science discovers, and that the *truth* about nature is what science *at the limit of inquiry* will say about nature (scientific realism).

Many battles continue within science, and about science, over what is ontologically "true." Meanwhile, the main body of scientific work goes on, satisfied to know what is scientifically *useful* in explanatory power, and in assisting to predict and control. The basic tasks of science are generally taken to be twofold: first, to construct and confirm scientific hypotheses, laws, and theories; and second, to explain, causally, phenomena in nature, and to predict their occurrence. The traditional methodology for the former is hypothetico-deductive; that is, a hypothesis that has been put forth inductively is tested by deducing what would follow *if* the hypothesis were true, and confirming this empirically. The methodology for scientific explanation is deductive-nomological; that is, the explanation for a phenomenon is constructed in terms of presumably well-confirmed scientific laws.

The philosophy of *logical empiricism* (or logical positivism) was especially influential in science (particularly in America) during the period 1940-1970. It expanded the concept of science and developed theories about the structure and system of knowledge in general. This "received view" of scientific theories, based in logical empiricism, was clearly formulated by the 1920s and was influential for the next half century. Central to this view is the rule that all concepts must be operationally defined. Relationships are mathematically formulated. Theoretical terms are admissible only if they admit of explicit phenomenal or observational definition. Scientific explanations are to be found by following *reductionistic* analysis. In this view a *positivistic* assumption prevailed; that is, science deals with that which is physically observable, and such nonphysical concepts as purpose or consciousness have no place in scientific analysis. Logical empiricists tended to accept a verificationist theory of meaning, which assumed the illegitimacy of positing or recognizing mental events except insofar as they could be explicitly linked to observable behaviors. Thus the only appropriate human science was *behavioristic*. Although these assumptions had gone through various modifications since the initial formulations of the scientific method by Descartes and Bacon, the meaning of a scientific explanation was generally assumed to have settled down well before mid-century.

Yet even as this influence of logical empiricism was approaching its peak, a questioning of some of its most fundamental assertions had already begun. By the 1980s, the concept of causality contained within the "received view" was widely agreed to be inadequate, although there is as yet no consensus regarding its replacement. Philosopher W.V.O. Quine asserted that we must give up the idea that we can use experience *either to confirm or to falsify* particular scientific hypotheses. Evidence does not itself determine our evaluation of hypotheses. When experience contradicts science, the science must be changed, but this can be done in a number of different ways. There is no logic for determining exactly what to change in one's theory: Any hypothesis can always be "protected" and the falsity shifted to other statements elsewhere in the overall theoretical network. Thus it is possible for competent and rational scientists to disagree even after a great deal of data has been accumulated.

The atmosphere in the 1990s appears to be somewhat more relaxed than in earlier days, which may reflect a certain maturity of science. Karl Popper's insistence that theories are never proved, but only falsified or not, seemed at one point an important insight; in today's science to talk of "verification" or "falsification" of theory sounds naive and simplistic. When a sophisticated theory is undergoing active development, it is commonplace to suppose that the present version of the theory is defective in some respects. Observation and experiment are used to discover shortcomings in the theory, to determine how to improve the theory, to discover how to eliminate distortions in the explanations of reality that the theory affords, and to guide the further development of the theory. There is general clarity that reality is too rich to be fully represented in the sorts of models and metaphors that are the stuff of science. Thus scientists tend to ask, not is a theory "proven," but "does it adequately represent the phenomena for specified purposes?"

Nevertheless, the temptation remains to extrapolate scientific formulations to become cosmologies to live by. The regularities of the laboratory are extrapolated to apply to the entire universe; the concept of time that holds up well in scientific measurements is extrapolated to become a pronouncement about the absolute nature of things. The general public is guilty of this extrapolation, but so to some extent are some scientists. Questions such as "Do the laws of physics hold outside the universe? Before the 'Big Bang'?" are, like some children's questions about God, simply not raised by grownups. It is an article of faith that proper scientific laws hold for all time, and everywhere—that although the universe *evolved*, scientific laws did not.

As is the case with all faiths, the best way to hold them is (a) to wholeheartedly live by them, and yet (b) be willing at any time to reexamine them in the light of new experience. In many areas of science, particularly the consciousness-related sciences, the older concepts of scientific causality seem inadequate or do not appear to have been fruitful. Most scientists today would assert that science has moved away from the strict determinism, reductionism, positivism, and behaviorism of a half century ago. But when they do so, they appear to have little idea what we might be moving *toward*.

With the decline of religious authority, science has become the only generally recognized cognitive authority in the modern world. That being the case, it is imperative that the ontological and epistemological assumptions underlying science be a subject not just for scientific and philosophical but for civil debate as well.

If modern science had started out in a holistic way, it would not strain so hard to insist that instinctive behavior in animals can be explained by chance and natural selection alone, or that cell differentiation in development must be explained in terms of present forces rather than some future pattern, or that this is a deterministic universe in which free will is a delusionary concept. On the other hand, had science been holistic from the start, it would clearly not have made the rapid progress it did with regard to the prediction-and-control kind of knowledge.

Perhaps the mistake of modern society has been to assume that, ultimately, reductionistic "scientific" causes should explain everything. One should not expect reductionistic scientific causality to comprise an adequate worldview—ever. The context of reductionistic science is the desire to gain control through manipulation of the physical environment. Within that context its description of "causes" works amazingly well. Our problems arise when we change the context and attempt to elevate that kind of science to the level of a worldview. That is when we generate conflicts like "free will versus determinism" and "science versus religion."

The question of whether we could have a more adequate science with a different epistemology remains.

TOWARD A MORE ADEQUATE EPISTEMOLOGY

A recent effort to identify a suitable epistemology for the study of consciousness in the broadest sense (that is, level 3 and level 4 science) resulted in the following nine proposed characteristics (see Harman and de Quincey, 1994):

1. The epistemology will be *"radically empirical"* (in the sense urged by William James) in that it will be *phenomenological* or experiential in a broad sense (that is, it will include subjective experience as primary data, rather than being essentially limited to physical-sense data) and it will address the totality of human experience (in other words, no reported phenomena will be written off because they "violate known scientific laws"). Thus, consciousness is not a "thing" to be studied by an observer who is somehow apart from it; consciousness involves the interaction of the observer and the observed, or, if you like, the *experience* of observing.

2. It will aim at being *objective* in the sense of being open and free from hidden bias, while dealing with both "external" and "internal" (subjective) experience as origins of data.

3. It will insist on *open inquiry* and *public (intersubjective) validation* of knowledge; at the same time, it will recognize that these goals may, at any given time, be met only incompletely, particularly when seeking knowledge that includes deeper understanding of inner experience.

4. It will place *emphasis upon the unity of experience.* It will thus be congenial to a holistic view in which the parts are understood through the whole, while not excluding a reductionistic approach that seeks to understand the whole through the parts. Hence it will recognize the importance of subjective and cultural meanings in all human experience, including experiences—such as some religious or interpersonal experiences—that seem particularly rich in meaning even though they may be ineffable. In a holistic view, such meaningful experiences will not be explained away by reducing them to combinations of simpler experiences or to physiological/biochemical events. Rather, in a holistic approach, the meanings of experiences may be understood by discovering their interconnections with other meaningful experiences.

5. It will recognize that science deals with *models and metaphors representing certain aspects of experienced reality,* and that any model or metaphor may be permissible if it is useful in helping to order

knowledge, even though it may seem to conflict with another model that is also useful. (The classic example is the history of wave and particle models in physics.)

6. It will thus recognize *the partial nature of all scientific concepts of causality.* (For example, the "upward causation" of physiomotor action resulting from a brain state does not necessarily invalidate the "downward causation" implied in the subjective feeling of volition.) In other words, it will implicitly question the assumption that a nomothetic science—one characterized by inviolable "scientific laws"—can in the end adequately deal with causality.

7. It will be *participatory* in recognizing that understanding comes, not alone from being detached, objective, analytical, coldly clinical, but also from cooperating with or identifying with the observed, and experiencing it subjectively. This implies a real partnership between the researcher and the phenomenon, individual, or culture being researched—an attitude of "exploring together" and sharing understandings (see Skolimowski, 1994).

8. It will involve recognition of the inescapable role of *the personal characteristics of the observer*, including the processes and contents of the unconscious mind. The corollary follows, that to be a competent investigator, the researcher must be *willing to risk being profoundly changed* through the process of exploration.

9. *Because of this potential transformation of observers*, an epistemology that is acceptable now to the scientific community may in time have to be replaced by another that is more satisfactory by new criteria, for which it has laid the intellectual and experiential foundations.

The virtue of this approach is in its open-endedness. The above nine characteristics do not seem revolutionary in their import. In fact, they may seem simply to reflect changes that are already going on in various areas of science, under such rubrics as "qualitative methodology," "participatory methodology," "phenomenological inquiry," and so on. However, they implicitly recognize the continual two-way interaction between culture and science, and the fact that as the personal characteristics of scientific investigators change (because they are living in a changing culture), what is an acceptable episte-mology will also change.

In other words, these nine characteristics imply that scientific inquiry is a dynamic cultural process that changes as it proceeds, not merely in accumulation of more knowledge and more adequate theories, or even in "changing paradigms," but more profoundly through a re-assessment of the metaphysical assumptions that have guided it so far—re-assessment in the light of a changed historical and evolutionary context.

CONSIDERING THE POSSIBILITY OF DIFFERENT ONTOLOGICAL ASSUMPTIONS

If indeed something like the above epistemology were to be adopted as the scientific community attempts to construct a true science of consciousness, it would seem that serious attention would have to be paid to those inner explorations that have gone on for thousands of years within the world's spiritual traditions—to the "perennial wisdom." In a recent paper, Ken Wilber (1993) explores the ontological implications: "Reality, according to the perennial philosophy, is composed of different grades or levels, reaching from the lowest and most dense and least conscious to the highest and most subtle and most conscious. At one end of this continuum of being or spectrum of consciousness is what we in the West would call 'matter' or the insentient and the non-conscious, and at the other end is 'spirit' or 'godhead' or the 'superconscious' (which is also said to be the all-pervading ground of the entire sequence). . . . The central claim of the perennial philosophy is that *men and women can grow and develop (or evolve) all the way up the hierarchy to Spirit itself*, therein to realize a 'supreme identity' with Godhead."

A central understanding of this "perennial wisdom" is that the world of material things is somehow embedded in a *living* universe, which in turn is within a realm of consciousness, or Spirit. Similarly, a cell is within an organ, which is within a body, which is within a society . . . and so on. Things are not—cannot be—separate; every-thing is a part of this "great chain of being."

As Wilber observes, Western science became restricted to the matter end of the continuum only, and to "upward" causation only.

With that restriction came a faith that in the end, a nomothetic science can adequately represent reality—a faith that phenomena are governed by inviolable, quantified "scientific laws." From that restriction came both the power of modern science (basically, to create manipulative technology) and the limitation of its epistemology. From it also stem all sorts of classical "problems"—the "mind-body problem," "action at a distance," "free will versus determinism," "science versus spirit," and so forth.

This restriction of science to only a portion of "the great chain of being" was useful and justifiable for a particular period in history. The only mistake we made was to become so impressed with the powers of prediction-and-control science that we were tempted to believe that that kind of science could lead us to an understanding of the whole. What must be done now, according to Wilber, is to retain the open-minded scientific spirit, and the tradition of open, public validation of knowledge (that is, abjuring any scientific priesthood), but to open up the field of inquiry to the entire continuum and to downward as well as upward causation. Whether that will be soon done within science is a good question. However, because of the cultural shift that appears to be taking place, attaching increased importance to the transcendental, there may be growing public insistence that some such development take place.

A Concluding Comment

The importance of the issues raised here can hardly be overestimated. It can be indicated by one simple observation. We in modern society give tremendous prestige and power to our official, publicly validated knowledge system, namely science. It is unique in this position; none of the coexisting knowledge systems—not any system of philosophy or theology, nor philosophy or theology as a whole—is in a comparable position. Thus it is critically important—to an unparalleled degree—that our science is adequate. *It is impossible to create a well-working society on a knowledge base that is fundamentally inadequate, seriously incomplete, and mistaken in basic assumptions.* Yet that is precisely what the modern world has been trying to do.

If one takes seriously the implication that Western science is an artifact of Western society, based on implicit assumptions compatible with that society's basic reality outlook, it follows that the primary impetus for a fundamental change in its underlying assumptions will come not from scientists, but from the surrounding culture. Indeed, we see much evidence over the past quarter century that such a force may be gathering. Thus the relevance of this critique is as much to the public at large as to the scientist.

With this in mind, I have deliberately kept this argument simple for the most part, and minimized the amount of supportive detail and qualifications. The basic concept is a simple one, and can be understood by non-scientists. The cost of past dogma-versus-dogma conflicts, within and outside science, has been too high. We can no longer afford it. The most urgent need in the modern world, in this time of growing crisis, is arguably to deal with the "taboo" epistemological issue in science. This could result in something like the holarchically arranged explanatory levels suggested above. It would certainly seem preferable to continued conflict over the evolution issue, the parapsychology issue, the vitalism issue, the holism/reductionism issue, the science-versus-religion issue, and so on ad infinitum.

Thus we end this chapter with a conclusion that has the most profound implications for all societies: There appears indeed to be no conflict between a mature science and a mature religion. Indeed, we must seriously question whether we have a mature science as long as such conflict appears to exist.

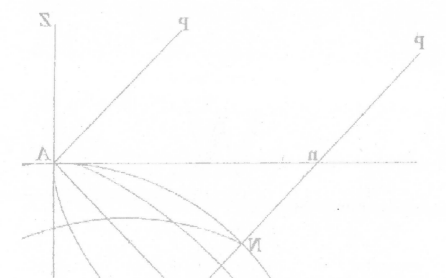

Transforming The World Macroproblem

6

We stand on the brink of a new age:

The age of an open world and of a self

capable of playing its part in that larger

sphere. Every goal [humanity] reaches

provides a new starting point, and

the sum of all [humanity's] days is

just a beginning.

—Lewis Mumford

W HY IS THIS CHANGE in underlying metaphysic taking place now, in the last quarter of the twentieth century? Partly, no doubt, it is because science has become more mature. The recognition that science has had an intrinsic bias is not as threatening as it would have been a half century or more ago. It is much easier to accept that inner, subjective experience has been a neglected area that requires some new approach to handle it.

For one thing, the physicists have long since made it clear that science deals with *models* of reality; hence it is not so surprising to find that any given model does not adequately represent all aspects of reality. Niels Bohr's introduction of the concept of *complementarity* into quantum physics was an important step in this maturing process: Wave models and particle models of light turned out to be complementary rather than contradictory, in that each represented certain observable aspects of the mystery of light. So too might matter-energy models and mind-spirit-consciousness models turn out to express complementary aspects of the mystery of life.

Quantum physics has brought some additional surprises. From a "thought experiment" devised by three physicists and referred to as the "Einstein-Podolsky-Rosen paradox," later verified in the laboratory, it appears that if two particles have been intimately associated and are then separated in space, they are "connected" nonetheless. If one of them is perturbed in certain ways, the other one is affected *instantaneously*. (The connectedness, in other words, does not depend on a signal traveling at the speed of light or slower.)

Related to this experiment is a mathematical demonstration called Bell's theorem, which says essentially that everything in the universe is connected. More specifically, it falsifies the "principle of local causes," which holds that a phenomenon can be explained in terms of causes in the immediate space-time vicinity. That is, the results of an experiment conducted here and now would not be expected to be affected by what is happening at some spot in the universe remote in space or time or both. (For example, the images in my mind would not be expected to be affected by the fact that on the other side of the continent a loved one has just been involved in a serious automobile accident.) Bell's theorem denies this "common-sense" assumption. Physicist David Bohm theorizes more generally that we can never understand reality in terms of particles and fields alone; we must ultimately perceive the "unbroken wholeness" in a nonreductionistic way.

In sum, the ultimate triumph of reductionistic physics is to demonstrate the *necessity* of a new paradigm that goes beyond reductionistic science. (Much confusion exists on this point. Both in management theory and the understanding of healing, the prestige of quantum physics, complexity theory, and so forth is often called upon to validate creative, intuitive, and healing aspects of mind that would not require validation had they not been first invalidated by the bias of Western science. This faulty logic may be simply a transition phenomenon.)

Other factors that are not directly related to developments in science are influencing the shift in paradigm as well. One of the most important of these is that with increased education and understanding, in the last half century the omnipresence of the "perennial wisdom" in the world's spiritual traditions has become apparent and widely accepted. (Before that, most Western explorations of religious traditions other than Christianity and Judaism had been as anthropological or historical curiosities, not as records of human experience from which we might learn.) Not only has it now become clear that the "perennial wisdom" is compatible with the world's spiritual traditions, since it is at the heart of each, but the supposed conflict with science is turning out to be not as real as had been earlier assumed.

In addition to these reasons, the contemporary reassessment of basic assumptions is also a consequence of the growing suspicion that without some sort of fundamental change, modern industrial society appears to be unable to resolve the socio-political and ecological dilemmas that beset us. Not only does each decade seem to be more problem-laden than the last, the problems seem more and more intertwined, and the tradeoffs get progressively less and less favorable. The change required is not simply a shift from one form of industrial society to another (such as capitalism to socialism), but rather a major change in the basic assumptions underlying both versions of industrial society.

To get a fresh perspective on this latter observation, let us perform a little thought experiment.

A DIFFERENT PERSPECTIVE

Imagine that you are an anthropologist from another civilization—let's say on another planet—visiting the Earth for the first time. You soon sense, especially as you talk with the children, that there is a lot of insecurity about the future. In particular, the continuing presence of many thousands of nuclear weapons, as well as unknown amounts of chemical and biological weapons, forces awareness—at least at an unconscious level—that the world appears ready to self-destruct. What is the reason for all that insecurity? you inquire. The answer: The quest for national *security*!

You note that the insecurity in vast regions of the world takes another form. World distribution of food, income, and wealth is extremely uneven—far more uneven than is the distribution in any single country, even those with the most notoriously unjust political orders. Yet there appears to be no workable proposal to correct this situation. Instead, economic and demographic forces seem inexorably to cause the maldistribution to grow steadily worse. The rich "North" partakes of a feast that the world's limited resources can sustain only with increasing difficulty, while the teeming populations of the impoverished "South" remain trapped in a remorseless cycle of deprivation that revolves around poverty, illiteracy, and high birthrates. The threat of ultimate "wars of redistribution" grows ever more imminent.

You discover something else fundamentally strange about the structure of the most powerful societies on the planet—they place in paramount position, as guard of the most precious values of the society, *economic* institutions, rather than those institutions that have to do with wisdom, knowledge, learning, religion! You see no obvious reason to believe that economic logic and economic values will ever lead to wise social decisions. Curiouser and curiouser!

For example, you find that virtuous behavior is defined by the leading institutions to be economic consumption, so much so that citizens, especially in the United States of America, refer to one another as fellow "consumers." Frugality, once a central virtue, is subtly discouraged as being bad for the economy!

Why is so much consumption required? you inquire. To use up the production, you are informed. (The global arms trade is good for that, too.) The economic indicators, such as the GNP, which measure how well the society is doing, are essentially measures of how rapidly resources are being used up—converted to economic product. The more economic product, the "healthier" the economy and, by implication, the society.

Is that good, you ask, on a finite planet to place a premium on the maximum rate of using up resources? It is necessary in order to create jobs, you hear in response, and to create purchasing power so that there will be a market for all that economic product. You reflect again on that historical document *Alice in Wonderland* in which it was cited one had to run pretty hard just to stay in the same place. But these jobs—will they, you inquire, be devoted to ennobling activities: fostering wholesome human development, beautifying the environment, caring for the natural world, promoting virtue? Well, no, you're told, that sort of thing

Curious: Tens of thousands of nuclear weapons for national security; economic logic used to make social decisions; knowledge based on a science which ignores courage and virtue—the M-1 mindset brought great benefit in the past but now creates problems faster than it solves them.

tends to be a drain on the economy, because those things are performed in the public sector. The jobs will produce goods and services for the marketplace—products like computer games, and guided missiles, and off-road vehicles, and services to financial speculators, and leisure industries, and new shopping centers . . . I see.

Economic production is taken to be the primary basis for the individual's relating to society. The overwhelming proportion of recognized social roles involve having a job in the production economy, being married to someone who has a job, or training to get a job. With modern means of industrial production, many of these roles have ceased to be meaningful and satisfying. Furthermore, as planetary limits to further material growth are approached, and as economic rationality pushes for further automation and robotization of production, the number of jobs will fall increasingly short of the number who want them. Does the society at this point ask itself what meaningful and constructive activities can now be engaged in because economic production does not require the full efforts of all? No, it engages instead in frenzied activities to *increase consumption*!

How does this society make its important decisions? you ask. The choices that will affect the lives of future generations, of people all around the globe? *Through economic analysis* is the answer. Individual leaders may bring in personal values in arriving at their initial decisions, but the bureaucratic way is to defend decisions with cost-benefit or similar economic analysis. And how does the well-being of future generations enter into such decision making? Economists *discount the future* at a rate of 10 percent or more, so the consequences for future generations don't really enter into present decisions. (Many years ago, before the ethic changed, there once was a tradition that the farmer should leave the land for the next generation *better* than the farmer found it. Such sentimental notions fly in the face of "sound" financial management, which puts the emphasis on mining the soil and underground water to improve next quarter's bottom line.)

You ask further into the kinds of decisions evoked by this prevailing economic rationality. It appears that, regrettable as it may seem, society in the United States can no longer afford really good education for every child. It can no longer afford to protect citizens in the city streets at night. It cannot even afford to give all citizens the healthcare they need. On the other hand, extravagant packaging and advertising, wasteful consumption, and unnecessary transportation *all* add to the GNP. (Take, for example, the energy required for food production—energy for fertilizer, tractor fuel, long-distance hauling, packaging, freezing, thawing, cooking, and so forth. In the end there is many times as much fossil fuel energy as solar energy represented in the food on one's table. That is a situation which may be "economically sound," but surely in the long term is ecologically foolish.)

The dwellers in this society are proud of their society of "abundance." Yet you can't help noticing that this abundance and affluence have brought about new forms of *scarcity*—scarcity of natural resources, of fresh air and water, of arable land, of the waste-absorbing capacities of the natural environment, of resilience of the planet's life-support systems, of spirit-renewing wilderness. These are partly a consequence of the forms of technology employed (such as fossil fuel burning in preference to solar energy sources; non-biodegradable materials; hazardous chemicals; agricultural practices employing vast quantities of artificial fertilizers and pesticides). The "new scarcities" are of course also related to population growth, which in turn is a consequence of improved sanitation and public health measures.

You note another peculiarity: Here is a society whose predominant knowledge system (science) ignores altruism, courage, virtue, eternal values, and which earns its paramount position through its success in enabling manipulation of the physical environment. In fact, this society boasts of its ability to "control nature"—which seems to you, as an alien visitor, to be the ultimate in confused thinking since you thought human beings were an intrinsic part of "nature."

It is not necessary to go on. Time was when the most serious problems of humankind had to do with satisfying basic needs and dealing with the hazards of the natural environment. The most serious problems of modern society arise from the *successes* of the industrial society paradigm. The horrors of modern warfare, worldwide environmental spoliation, interference with life-supporting ecological systems, progressive resource depletion, widespread poverty and hunger, prevalence of hazardous substances, stress-related disease, and the possibility of detrimental climate changes stemming from carbon dioxide buildup in the atmosphere are all interconnected components of what we might call the one world macroproblem. They are consequences of a mind-set and the behaviors and institutions associated with it—the industrial-society paradigm, which brought great benefits in the past but now creates problems faster than it solves them. The world macroproblem will be satisfactorily resolved only through fundamental change of that mind-set.

ORIGINS OF THE WORLD MACROPROBLEM

There is no need here to describe the world macroproblem in detail. Let us briefly summarize the interrelationships among three of its chief aspects: widespread poverty and hunger, environmental degradation, and the weapons dilemma.

The weapons dilemma is that there are now, and there will be in the foreseeable future, enough long-range missiles with nuclear warheads, at various places in the world, and enough chemical and biological weapons, to imperil human civilization if not human existence on the planet. Among the countries that now have or will soon have access to nuclear and biological weapons there are some for whom the present world order offers little hope. For most of the vast majority of the Earth's population the goal of becoming a rich high-consumption society (which seems to be the best model the industrialized world has to offer) is forever beyond their reach—for reasons of planetary resource and environmental constraints, among others. Even if the birth rates drop far more dramatically than now seems possible, the Earth's population will continue to increase for decades, and the rich industrialized world—a shrinking fraction of the whole—will be viewed with increasing envy and hostility by the rest.

The World Lacks A Vision
Of A Viable Global Future

The industrialized world, having lost any consensus on ultimate meanings and values, steers itself mainly by economic and financial signals serving as pseudo-values. Part of the developing world is scrambling to catch up with the West; other parts are seeking some attractive alternative to scrapping their own cultural roots and adopting the alien culture of the West. Many of the Third World countries are caught up in a global arms race to which there appears to be no end; some are spending more on technically sophisticated arms than on health, education, and social services combined. And some stagger under debt loads such that oppressive interest payments impair their ability to improve their lot.

The global environmental condition worsens steadily, notwithstanding temporary or localized reversals of the general trend of deterioration. Much of this is associated with the economic activities of the industrialized countries—acid rain, toxic chemical concentrations, diminishing and deteriorating water supplies, local environmental degradation. But much of it also is a consequence of the desperate quest of the poor for food, firewood, grazing land, and shelter; it has often been said that poverty is the planet's greatest polluter.

Throughout the world, economic, social, and international policy is being implicitly based on some image of the global future—some picture of how human advancement will take place in diverse societies, as well as how we will husband or exploit the Earth's resources and life-support systems. Practically all of that policy is founded on concepts of global development that seem inexorably to lead toward continuing widespread misery and conflict—because of the gross disparities between the rich and the poor; because of forces pushing peasants off the land and into urban slums; because of the wrenching apart of societies by the temptations and imperatives of modernization; because of deforestation and water pollution and soil destruction and desertification and a hundred other kinds of environmental spoliation; because of sudden wealth stemming from natural resources that are coveted by the industrialized world; because of irreversible changes in plant and animal species, soil composition, and climate. If these trends do not change, continuing conflicts seem inevitable. With modern sophisticated weaponry they can be perilous indeed.

This macroproblem has its origins in basic assumptions, starting with the prevailing reality view. Since modern culture ascribes no "reality" to inner experience, transcendent values have no power and materialistic values prevail. Thus it seems reasonable for society to be characterized by economic rationalization of an ever-increasing fraction of social behavior and organization. Industrialization of production of goods and services gradually extends to more and more of human activities; increasingly, they all become included in the economy. One result is monetization and commercialization (all things coming to be measurable by and purchasable in units of currency). The economic rationalization of knowledge leads to the "knowledge industry": to science justified by the technology it produces, and to education justified by the jobs it prepares for. Economic rationality becomes predominant in social and political decision making, even when the decisions it leads to are unwise by other standards (such as the well-being of future generations). Technological solutions are attempted for problems that are basically socio-political in nature. The worth of persons (to say nothing of our nonhuman fellow creatures on the Earth) is assessed by their value in the economy. Humankind's relationship to the Earth is essentially an exploitative one.

From such reasoning and values the components of the macroproblem spring, as is quite apparent to our imagined visiting anthropologist. This is not a totally new or recent observation. The inevitable consequence of trying to run a society from an M-1 metaphysic (see page 29) was apparent to some scholars long ago. One of them was the distinguished Harvard sociologist Pitirim Sorokin.

Sorokin had examined the rise and fall of civilizations in his four-volume work *Social and Cultural Dynamics*, written between the two world wars, which he later summarized in *The Crisis of Our Age* (1941). His conclusion, based on an impressive study of cultural and social indicators for as far back as he could find any records, was that Western society, like some before it, has gone so far in the dominance of "sensate" values that it must almost inevitably swing back, probably to a better balance of inner-directed and outer-directed values. This, however, involves change at the deeper level of basic beliefs—or, to use the in-vogue term, change in the dominant paradigm. Sorokin described the signs of an impending "transformation," which he probably did not expect quite as soon as it seems to be arriving.

The British historian Arnold Toynbee also anticipated an early end to the industrial era as we have known it. In *A Study of History*, written in the 1930s and 1940s, he made an even more exhaustive study of the evolution and devolution of civilizations. He has been widely interpreted as being pessimistic about the future of industrial society. However, he also spoke of the possible "transfiguration" of modern society into some kind of respiritualized form.

Lewis Mumford was perhaps the most unquenchably optimistic of the lot. Forty years ago, in a little book called *The Transformations of Man* (1956), he described the previous transformations of Western civilization, fewer than a half dozen. He then went on to outline a coming transformation, the signs of which were invisible to all but a very few:

> Every [human] transformation . . . has rested on a new metaphysical and ideological base; or rather, upon deeper stirrings and intuitions whose rationalized expression takes the form of a new picture of the cosmos and the nature of man. . . . We stand on the brink of [such] a new age: the age of an open world and of a self capable of playing its part in that larger sphere. An age of renewal, when work and leisure and learning and love will unite to produce a fresh form for every stage of life, and a higher trajectory for life as a whole. . . . In carrying [human] . . . self-transformation to this further stage, world culture may bring about a fresh release of spiritual energy that will unveil new potentialities, no more visible in the human self today than radium was in the physical world a century ago, though always present. . . . Who can set bounds to man's emergence or to his power of surpassing his provisional achievements? So far we have found no limits to the imagination, nor yet to the sources on which it may draw. Every goal [humanity] . . . reaches provides a new starting point, and the sum of all [humanity's] . . . days is just a beginning.

More contemporary arguments arriving at similar conclusions can be found in a number of recent books. Alvin Toffler's *The Third Wave* (1980) summarizes:

> Despite what today's parties and candidates may preach, the infighting among them amounts to little more than a dispute over who will squeeze the most advantage from

what remains of the declining industrial system. . . . While short-range political skirmishes exhaust our energy and attention, a far more profound battle is already taking place beneath the surface. On one side are the partisans of the industrial past; on the other, growing millions who recognize that the most urgent problems of the world— food, energy, arms control, population, poverty, resources, ecology, climate, the problems of the aged, the breakdown of urban community, the need for productive, rewarding work—can no longer be resolved within the framework of the industrial order.

The subtitle of Theodore Roszak's *Person-Planet* (1978) summarizes a similar argument: "The Creative Disintegration of Industrial Society" (and the creation of the new). Similar discussions will be found in Fritjof Capra's *The Turning Point* (1984) and Marilyn Ferguson's *The Aquarian Conspiracy* (1980). David Korten's *When Corporations Rule the World* (1995) is perhaps most penetrating in its analysis of why the present course of global society is not sustainable in the long term, the conclusion being that radical change is imperative. These various essays emphasize different aspects of a common theme, namely, the necessary transformation of industrial society over the next few decades (a tremendous speedup over any such revolutionary change in the past, largely because of modern travel and communication binding the world into a more tightly interconnected whole).

CLUES FROM SOCIAL MOVEMENTS

What are the salient characteristics of this new postmodern age? We can obtain some clues from seeing what people seem to be asking for, as they interrupt the smooth course of their lives to devote energy to an assortment of social movements.

Starting in the decade of the 1960s, a host of social movements came into being or took new form from older movements. There was a peace movement, related to but not the same as the peace movements of the 1920s and 1930s; there was a women's movement, which extended the women's suffrage movement into claims of other rights beyond the vote, and eventually became a powerful force for changed value emphases and a balance of masculine and feminine perspectives; an environmental movement growing out of the old conservation movements, maturing into an eco-feminist force for profound cultural change; a civil rights movement which was in a way an extension of the earlier abolitionist, populist, and labor movements, and did much to increase awareness of subtle oppression by seemingly legitimate institutions; and so on. One heard a good deal about "radicalization"; certain demonstrations and other activities were carried on, not so much to win a tactical objective as to bring about a "radicalization" of minds, a lessening of the hold of the accepted belief system of the culture.

This radicalization or change of perception was primarily in two forms. One involved altering one's perceptions with regard to what were claimed to be oppressive, regimenting, depersonalizing, alienating, stupefying, stultifying characteristics of modern social institutions. Confrontations with authorities were deliberately set up, for instance, to invoke the "mind-changing" quality of such confrontation. The other form of radicalization was that associated with the sudden interest in yoga, meditation, Eastern philosophical-religious systems, transpersonal psychologies, psychedelic chemicals, and the like. This involved changing self-perception, specifically in recognizing one's essential spiritual nature.

By the mid-1990s the picture had changed somewhat. The ecological movement, peace movement, and women's movement are now more clearly recognized to be different drops in a single wave of transformative change. While there is some student involvement, the issues have come to have appeal for many more mature citizens as well. The word "radicalization" is seldom used, and "changing consciousness" has taken its place. This change in consciousness is partly toward perceiving how the whole pattern, the underlying paradigm, of Western industrial society leads inexorably to the kinds of problems and global dilemmas we now face, and toward realizing that the dilemmas have their satisfactory resolution only through change in the dominant paradigm. It is partly toward recognizing that we unwittingly "buy into" belief systems (in which the Earth and its creatures exist to be exploited, "premodern" cultures are to be superseded, people with nonwhite skins are inferior, women have a subordinate role, nuclear weapons bring "security," profligate consumption is "good for the economy," and so on); and that a major step is taken when realization comes that what our society takes for granted is not necessarily true—that it is not necessary to "buy into" the beliefs. It is also partly toward the empowering realization that all institutions in society, no matter how powerful, obtain their legitimacy from the perceptions of people—and hence that people have the power to change institutions by challenging the legitimacy of prevailing institutional behaviors.

Even the most powerful institution can change or crumble when there is a strong challenge to its legitimacy (as we have seen in Eastern Europe in the autumn of 1989, and the USSR Communist Party in August 1991). The basis for such a legitimacy challenge is typically a combination of one or more of the following: The old order is not functioning effectively to achieve agreed-upon goals, it is not functioning in accordance with consensually approved values, or it was never duly constituted in the first place. What passes relatively unnoticed is that the modern growth-based capitalist economy fails on all three counts. It is not achieving societal goals, as described above; economic values are an inadequate guide for an institution which so powerfully affects all aspects of society; and the corporation was never originally chartered to have such freedoms as it currently enjoys.

Aided no doubt by awareness that the world is steadily working less well, a contagion of reperception has been spreading around the world for at least the past thirty years, infecting first the educated middle class but then moving on to exclude no age, race, or socioeconomic class. Evidences abound in the forms of survey data, social movements, Green political parties, book sales, workshops and seminars, and numerous other social indicators. The fraction of the total US adult population involved in a radical reperception has been variously estimated at from 10 to 40 percent, most of whom have made the shift within the last two decades. These persons espouse values that are significantly different from the values during the high economic growth of the 1950s and early 1960s. Similar changes are evident in northern Europe, Canada, Australia, and to a lesser extent elsewhere in the industrialized world, including the Eastern European countries. A complementary reperception can be found among a smaller "alternative development" group in the Third World. One of the most interesting examples to watch is South Africa, where the commitment to profound but nondisruptive change seems especially notable.

To characterize this reperception we may identify five aspects: search for wholeness, search for community and relationship, search for identity, search for meaning, and sense of empowerment.

Search For Wholeness

The world has become fragmented, as has the individual. A technological ethic of "man controlling nature" has contributed to the separation of humans from the matrix of life around them. With the rise of capitalism the economy has become separate from, and dominant over, the rest of society. The steady deterioration of the environment and violence to natural ecological systems is one consequence. A sense of alienation is another. One's work has become a job, and the job is separate from the rest of life. Religion too tends to be something separate, based on different premises than seemed to prevail in the most powerful of society's institutions.

In a variety of ways—an ecological movement, a holistic health movement, emphasis on quality of work life, an appropriate technology movement—the perception is presently being expressed that life is whole and that there is something wrong with a society that breaks it into fragments.

Having been educated to be specialists and to view the complex whole in "manageable" segments, we are now faced with a multifaceted global crisis that will not be resolved by some technological or managerial "fix." Rather, it is claimed, the resolution will come out of some whole-system view. Just as at the individual level a holistic view of health involves the whole person—body, mind, and spirit—so at the planetary level the problem will prove to be solvable only through a holistic approach.

A key aspect of this wholeness is awareness of the finiteness and multiple-interconnectedness of the planetary ecosystem, the inextricable interdependence of all human communities and dependence on the planetary life-support system. An outlook that has come to be termed "deep ecology" goes beyond the contemporary scientific framework to a subtle awareness of the oneness of all life, the interdependence of its multifold manifestations, and the irrepressibility of its tendencies toward evolution and transformation.

Search For Community And Relationship

Both urbanization and modern economic realities—most jobs being away from home and neighborhood—has brought about a loss of community. Bigness and concentration of power are among the chief contributors to the feelings of alienation and depersonalization in modern society. A response is taking the form of a rise in the informal economy; intentional communities; an assortment of human relations workshops, group therapies, and other endeavors to relate more deeply with fellow human beings; re-ruralization, decentralization; crafts; and appropriate technology movements. By the latter is meant technology that is human-scale and ecologically compatible, and in general "kind" to human beings and the planet. It includes technologies that enhance rather than diminish the human being; "soft-path" renewable-resource energy technologies and practices; regenerative organic agriculture, with practices of replenishing the soil and natural pest control; holistic healthcare emphasizing prevention and wholesome relationship to one's own body.

There is also a developing sense of a global community and an appreciation of the richness of the planet's cultural diversity. The tendency of the world industrial economy to obliterate competing cultures is felt to require correction; a global ecology of cultures is the more desirable state, rather than a world covered by Western industrial monoculture.

Search For Identity

In reaction to the depersonalizing aspects of modern society there has been in the industrialized societies a widespread seeking for personal identity, often through psychotherapies and weekend workshops, but often simply in an individual Wanderjahr. An aberration of this tendency manifested as the "Me Generation" phenomenon of the 1970s.

Beginning around the 1960s, various groups began to resist the homogenization to which modern society is prone, with its mass markets and mass media. Some of these are ethnic groups asserting their differences—the Quebecois, the Basques, the Chicanos, the Croatians. Others are indigenous peoples such as the Native Americans and Australian Aborigines, re-affirming the values of cultures that go much farther back. Other groups are different in other ways, but asserting their right to be themselves and not feel or be treated as inferior—the handicapped, the aged, homosexuals.

The two largest of such groups are women and the Third World. The women's movement had its early emphasis on liberation and equal rights. In its more recent form, however, it emphasizes sensitivity to the destructive aspects of patriarchal society and masculine competitive, aggressive, exploitative values—seeking a balance of these with feminine nurturing, cherishing, cooperative, conserving values and appreciation of the feminine perspective.

The Third World groups are struggling to release themselves from their self-perception as inferior, a consequence of generations of Western domination and colonization. While recognizing the material and managerial accomplishments of Western societies, they are affirming or reaffirming the values of their own cultural heritage. Thus whereas for a generation after World War II "development" had been assumed to mean economic development in the mold of the Western industrial powers, since the 1970s there has been a quest for "alternative development" more compatible with the peoples' own cultural roots.

Search For Meaning

This aspect of the reperception saw Western industrial society in a crisis of meaning and values. No need is so compelling as the need we all feel for our lives to make sense, to have meaning. We will tolerate almost any degree of austerity or risk in this indomitable quest for meaning; we may even choose suicide if we fail. After the "great debunking" of religion by reductionistic, positivistic science, and with the discovery that economic production, consumption and even technological achievement are unfulfilling, modern society felt a vacuum in the area of basic values and central meaning.

The incompleteness of positivistic science and its inability to deal with the whole of human experience was challenged by a rapidly developing interest in Eastern philosophical and religious outlooks, and a vast array of explorations of the world of inner experience— from yoga and meditative disciplines to confrontation therapies and psychedelic drug experiences. Within science a similar opening up of interests occurred, manifesting in humanistic and transpersonal psychology, exploration of altered states of consciousness, and so forth.

There are today multifold signs of a respiritualization of Western society, with emphasis on self-realization, transcendent meaning, and inner growth leading to wisdom and compassion. The picture is complicated because one of the most visible phenomena is the growth of Christian evangelical-fundamentalists—a group who appear to have little in common with the followers of some of the Asian gurus passing through. Some of these people are indeed attempting to bring back the past confidence of the "old-time religion"; however, talking in depth with many of them one detects a quiet but spreading commitment to an M-3 kind of metaphysical perception, and an awareness that that was always present in esoteric Christianity, however opposed to it mainstream theology appears to have been.

Sense Of Empowerment

One of the most striking changes in the past two decades has been the extent to which people are awakening and feeling empowered to take responsibility for their own lives and for changing society as necessary. This has happened in both industrialized and developing countries. There have been numerous technological issues (particularly since the "technology assessment" movement around 1969) where the people clearly asserted that because of potential consequences around the globe, and effects on generations to come, the issues were too important to be left to the experts. Examples were the SST and ABM, nuclear power, biotechnology. When the people in the US were sufficiently aroused, they effectively halted the Vietnam War. Increasing numbers of people around the world are raising questions about the legitimacy of national policies that imply war as a feasible option.

We just observed that the two "majority groups," women and the Third World, are awakening to the sense of their real, potential power. No economic, political, or military power can compare with the power of a change of mind—in particular, a challenge or withdrawal of legitimacy.

VALUE EMPHASES OF THE TRANS-MODERN WORLD

Assuming for the moment that the main thesis of this book is correct—that at the present time we are somewhere in the middle of a shift in prevailing metaphysical assumptions from M-1 to M-3— what does that imply about trans-modern (or trans-industrial) society? Probably at least the following five value emphases are implied:

- Humans in harmony with nature
- Humans in harmony with one another
- Individual self-realization
- Decentralization and an ecology of cultures
- Globalization of global issues

Humans In Harmony With Nature

In the M-3 perception of reality we are one with nature and in harmony with the life processes. Any disharmony is a consequence of faulty perception, and is correctable.

This basic harmony contrasts sharply with the exploitative attitude toward nature that has been a hallmark of industrial society. So-called primitive societies typically have had more cooperative, less exploitative relationships with nature. In some cases (for example, among many American Indian tribes) there has always been a clear tradition of caring for the Earth. Thus there is much precedent for the ecological ethic that now seems dictated by increasingly serious environmental problems.

The shift toward being more in harmony with nature is coming about only partly through the threat of what will happen to us if we don't change. It is more fundamentally a simple corollary of the M-3 assumptions.

Humans In Harmony With One Another

If we are all connected, and in some sense all one, then any disharmony I may feel in human relationships is also a matter of my own perception. The emerging vision emphasizes community in the small view, and global cooperation in the large. Institutions will be more person-centered, and nondiscriminatory with regard to gender, race, and culture.

One of the most important shaping forces is the rebalancing of masculine and feminine influences. The most powerful of the forces shaping the modern world—reductionist science and manipulative technology, competitive enterprise, the aggressive nation-state—were strongly biased toward masculine and patriarchal perspectives. Implicit in the M-3 assumptions is an emphasis on wholeness, involving a creative balance between masculine and feminine qualities—between aggressiveness and nurturing, competition and cooperation, rationality and intuition. Riane Eisler, in *The Chalice and the Blade* (1987), speaks of the change as being from a "dominator" model of society (which has predominated in the West for around 5,000 years) to a "partnership" model.

On the world scale there has to be a "great leveling" of rich and poor societies—not in wealth alone, but in equity and equality of opportunity. The Western concept of economic development toward a "consumer society" will give way in favor of "liberatory development" emphasizing liberation of spirit and energy, self-reliance, preservation of cultural diversity and identity, and reassertion of group history. There will be a progressive casting off of the mental yoke of fatalism, self-denigration, and submission to external authority—and increasing emphasis on human productiveness, autonomy, and global cooperation. For these conditions to be possible in the individual societies, there has to be a reshaping of the international order in a manner compatible with the legitimate goals of developed and developing countries.

Individual Self-Realization

The new order is to be one that fosters movement from self-subordination (to superiors in a hierarchy, to institutions, to "advanced" or powerful nations) toward self-realization. Especially in the workplace and in the development of Third World countries is this emphasis on self-actualization of central importance.

The basic idea involved here is summarized in psychologist Abraham Maslow's concept of "deficiency needs" and "self-actualization" or "being" needs. It appears that persons whose "deficiency" needs (for food, shelter, warmth, sex, belongingness, esteem) are reasonably well satisfied are then motivated by "being" needs. This was well expressed in a counterculture slogan of the late 1960s: "We don't want to have more—we want to *be* more."

Manifestations of this emphasis in the industrialized countries are to be found especially in the various "liberation" movements (of women, minorities, the elderly) and intentional communities, and in the worker self-government and "industrial democracy" movements of northern Europe. In the Third World the emphasis is seen most clearly as an insistence on rejecting the traditional acceptance of poverty and exploitation (by landlords, rich ruling classes, imperialists). In both cases the emphasis is on awakening to the realization that one has been imprisoned by "buying into" a set of beliefs that, once this is realized, one need not accept.

Decentralization And An Ecology Of Cultures

There is implicit in the new vision a repudiation of the centralist tendencies of both capitalist and socialist management and production, as well as of the continued urbanization tendencies of both industrialized and developing societies. Espoused instead is decentralization—of population concentration, of community, of agriculture, of management and control, of technology, of economic production, of mass culture.

The issue of decentralization is particularly apparent in the "appropriate technology" movement with its emphasis on human-scale technology under human control.

The value of cultural diversity will be deeply appreciated. Somewhat as an ecological community has resilience that a single-species community lacks, so the world population is more resilient when it comprises an ecology of cultures whose diversity is a source of enrichment to all.

Globalization Of Global Issues

Coexisting with the decentralization characteristic, and not in conflict with it, is the global management of those affairs that, by their very nature, are concerns of the entire population of the Earth. These include use and care of the oceans and atmosphere, sharing and tempered consumption of nonrenewable and some renewable resources, control of weapons of mass destruction, and control of diffusion of hazardous chemicals.

SYMBOL OF A NEW RELATIONSHIP WITH THE EARTH

One of the critical arenas in which change is both imperative and ongoing is that of attitudes toward the planet Earth. Since it is obvious that modern man's abuse of the Earth is related to the prevailing image of our relationship to the planet, it is interesting to examine a recently announced scientific concept of the Earth as being in important respects alive. This is the "Gaia hypothesis" which, it must be admitted, has thus far had more effect on the conference circuit than in the halls of science.

James E. Lovelock, a British biologist and atmospheric chemist, is largely responsible for the modern form of the idea that we human beings are not just living motes on a vast mineral ball, but that *the Earth itself is a living organism*. The core notion is that the Earth regulates itself very much like the human body or other living organisms. Somehow, temperature, oxygen levels and other aspects of the composition of the atmosphere and the oceans, soil acidity, and other key environmental conditions are kept within the narrow tolerances necessary to sustain life. Those regulatory processes involve, in turn, the biota—the sum of all living things including plants, animals, and microorganisms. The Earth thus exhibits the behavior (except for a reproductive ability) of a single organism—of a living creature. Lovelock's name for that organism is *Gaia*, the name the ancient Greeks gave to their Earth goddess.

Could a planet—almost all of it rock and that mostly incandescent or molten—really be alive? Lovelock suggests comparison with a giant redwood tree: It is alive, yet 99 percent of it is dead wood. Like the Earth it has only a skin of living tissue spread thinly at the surface.

If the Earth is a living organism, does it also exhibit *consciousness?* That is a question not to be answered quickly, but, as implied above, not to be dismissed either.

Lovelock was hired as a consultant in the early 1960s by the National Aeronautics and Space Administration to help determine if there is life on Mars. While others were busy designing landing craft to go see, Lovelock took a different approach. He reasoned that in the absence of life, the gases in the atmosphere should react in such a way that the whole reaches a state of equilibrium. The presence of life on Earth disturbs this equilibrium, because the Earth's plants, animals, and bacteria are continually injecting gases and energy into the air. As is well known, for example, plants give off oxygen and use up carbon dioxide while animals do the reverse; thus the Earth's atmosphere contains far more oxygen and far less carbon dioxide than it would if the Earth were not covered with its particular life forms. (Mars, on the other hand, gives no such indication of life.)

The amount of oxygen in the atmosphere near the Earth's surface remains virtually constant at around 21 percent by volume, "just right" for the life forms that have evolved. The life forms themselves appear to regulate the amount of oxygen so that it stays "just right." If the proportion should drop even a few percent, many organisms would die; however, the excess of plant life that would result would tend to raise the oxygen content again. On the other hand, if somehow the oxygen content were to rise to 25 percent, fires would burn out of control. That would no doubt reduce the plant life and hence the rate of replenishment of oxygen, so the proportion would tend to go down.

The temperature, too, is apparently regulated by the biota to just what they need. The Earth's average surface temperature has remained between 10 degrees and 20 degrees Centigrade, even through the Ice Ages, and the biota seem to have had something to do with this. Lovelock explains how, using a computer-based model called "Daisyworld." Imagine, for simplicity, a world in which the only life forms are white daisies. Within the temperature range of 10 to 20 degrees, the higher the temperature, the more daisies. But since more daisies means more of the world's surface is covered with white flowers, more sunlight is reflected, causing the temperature to lower. Thus an equilibrium temperature is approached. Adding other life forms into the model (such as rabbits to eat the daisies, and foxes to control the rabbit population) results in a similar phenomenon. Daisyworld exhibits a temperature-regulating behavior (homeostasis) similar to the temperature regulation of the human body.

As another example, the humid tropical forests of the Earth alter the climate in the immediate vicinity, both in terms of temperature and rainfall. Like Daisyworld, they create the local climate they require in order to flourish. But they also remove carbon dioxide from the atmosphere. As they are cut down, that contributes to the rising carbon dioxide level in the atmosphere (which is also increasing due to massive burning of fossil fuels). Through the "greenhouse effect," the blanket of carbon dioxide is causing worldwide temperatures to rise. Thus the fate of the tropical forests affects climate on a global basis.

The *connectedness* of our decisions and our actions to the whole Earth is one key message of the Gaia hypothesis. But another, equally important one is the role of *cooperation* of all organisms in the evolutionary process.

For example, take the matter of dimethyl sulphide. This chemical is manufactured in tremendous quantities by phytoplankton, microscopic marine algae. It is useful to them because it reduces the harmful effects of drying when they are left on the beach by the ebbing tide. But it also plays an important part in returning sulphur from the oceans to the land, and a key role in cloud formation over the open seas—part of the "planetary refrigeration system." It seems that another chemical also manufactured by algae, methyl iodide, is part of a similar process for recycling the essential element iodine.

Now, do these, and countless other ways in which various parts of the total Earth system are necessary to each other, imply some sort of consciousness guiding the evolution of life on Earth? In a science dominated by the M-1 assumptions the answer is simply that the question is absurd.

That extension of the Gaia idea is, on the other hand, implicit in the traditions of American Indians. For example, Black Elk quotes the following prayer of the Ogalala Sioux: "O Mother Earth, You are the earthly source of all existence. The fruits which You bear are the source of life for the Earth peoples. You are always watching over Your fruits as does a mother. May the steps which we take in life upon You be sacred and not weak."

Some of the modern exponents of the Gaia hypothesis tend to speak of collective humanity as the "nervous system" of the biosphere, the organ through which it becomes conscious. Presumably this is because of the special properties of the human brain.

Yet clearly the sense in which the ancients and the American Indians experienced the consciousness of Gaia is something else again. That consciousness was presumably present before there were either humans or any other of what we think of as living forms.

To be sure, there is no scientific basis for postulating such an Earth consciousness. On the other hand, it is inherent in the way in which science developed that if the Earth did, in fact, possess consciousness, it is quite likely that science would have overlooked it.

A restricted form of the Gaia hypothesis, including the organism-like self-regulatory behavior of the Earth, seems almost certainly to have made its way into respectable science. Even in that form, it strongly suggests that humans had better pay heed to the extent to which their activities impair or impinge on the regulatory processes.

As to the Earth's being an organism with consciousness, the jury is still out as far as mainstream science is concerned. Yet this concept, with its profound ethical and ecological implications, does not seem all that strange in the M-3 worldview.

THE GREEKS HAD A WORD FOR IT

Where do all these indicators point? Are there any examples of societies that have been based in an M-3 sort of metaphysical perspective?

There's one, at least, of special interest—ancient Greece. Lewis Mumford had pointed to the Greek concept of "paideia" as the nearest thing to a model of the society to come. Robert Hutchins, in *The Learning Society* (1968), had chosen the same ideal—a society in which learning, fulfillment, and becoming human are the primary goals and "all its institutions [are] directed to this end. This is what the Athenians did. . . . They made their society one designed to bring all its members to the fullest development of their highest powers. . . . Education was not a segregated activity, conducted for certain hours, in certain places, at a certain time of life. It was the aim of the society. . . . The Athenian was educated by the culture, by *Paideia*." Paideia was the educating matrix of the society; its highest and central theme, according to its foremost scholar Werner Jaeger, was the individual's "search for the Divine Center."

We do not live in the time of the ancient Greeks, and we will not simply repeat their pattern. Our postmodern society may have cybernetic machines instead of slaves, and it may very likely have a deliberate concern with shaping the future that would have been alien to the Greek culture. It may borrow elements from other cultures as well, such as the relationship to the Earth from the North American Indians. But in one central feature it is likely to emulate the Greeks: the idea that self-development and the promotion of lifelong learning is the "central project" of a society that does not have to expend a large fraction of its effort simply supplying the necessities of life.

THE NEW BUSINESS OF BUSINESS

These indications of shifts in values, attitudes, and perceptions have an impact on all sectors of society. One of these, the business sector, deserves our special attention.

If there is anything at all to the proposition that a fundamental transformation is already underway, we should see signs in the business community. For one thing, business is all-pervasive in modern society and reflects any major change in any portion of it. Moreover, business makes it its business to be sensitive to changes in its environment, and to respond to them promptly. The modern business corporation is probably the most adaptive institution humankind has ever devised.

One such sign is the growing acceptability in business of the terms *intuition* and *creativity*, and the implications thereof. One dictionary definition of intuition is "the power or faculty of attaining to direct knowledge or cognition without evident rational thought and inference." The idea of arriving at insight without a recognizable thought process flies in the face of the ideal of "rational man." (In fact, until recently, it was usually spoken of as "feminine intuition.") Only recently have business journals such as *Fortune* or *Harvard Business Review* begun to publish articles referring to the use of hunches and intuition in business decision making. Management development courses in recent years have been increasingly overt about using such techniques as affirmation and inner imagery to remove barriers to creativity and intuition.

Studies of high-performing people in many fields show that successful, effective people tend to visualize the results they want in their lives and work, and to affirm to themselves that they will accomplish these goals. They create a clear and conscious intention to achieve certain outcomes and then allow that frequently affirmed intention to guide their actions. Rather than planning what they will do and how they will go about it, they start by creating an intensely alive mental representation of the end state. That representation then works through the individual's intuition and unconscious mental processes as he or she makes the multitude of everyday decisions that bring the goal ever nearer.

Charles Kiefer and Peter Senge, in a chapter in *Transforming Work* (1984), note the appearance of a new type of management based on new assumptions about the nature of human beings and complex social systems. People are viewed as fundamentally good, honest, and purposeful, and wanting to make a constructive contribution in the world. The locus of the desire to contribute is internal, not external; it arises from the person's consciousness of his or her relationship to the whole rather than from a desire for the approbation of others. In this view, the fundamental shortcoming of traditional management is its failure to design social systems in which these characteristics of the individual can develop. The new-style managers tend to appreciate the futility of trying to control complex systems from the top down. They focus instead on arranging conditions that foster the individuals' actualizing their own latent creativity, and on evolving highly autonomous business units in which local initiative and control can operate to the fullest extent possible.

The organizations employing this new management style are characterized by:

- A strong and deep sense of purposefulness and a vision of the future

- A high degree of alignment of members at all levels involving commitment to the shared vision

- A shared sense of ownership and personal responsibility for performance

- Decentralized and flexible organizational structures

- An environment that emphasizes growth and empowerment of the individual as the key to corporate success.

The great leaders of the past have tended to be either autocratic or charismatic; the new management style is empowering. Perry Pascarella, executive editor of *Industry Week*, writes in *The New Achievers* (1984):

A quiet revolution is taking place . . . in the business corporation. . . . Although we have been hearing more and more about corporate efforts in human resource develop-ment in recent years, we may miss the essential truth about what is happening: Individuals are awakening to the pos-sibility of personal growth and finding opportunities to attain it. The team building we hear about is secondary to the development of the individual. . . . Management is heading toward a new state of mind—a new perception of its own role and that of the organization. It is slowly moving from seeking power to empowering others, from controlling people to enabling them to be creative. . . . As managers make a fundamental shift in values . . . the corporation [undergoes] a radical reorientation to a greater worldview.

The organization that aspires to be excellent, and to gather to itself and retain excellent people, is finding in this new climate that it must seek to create an internal environment that fosters develop-ment of persons. Such organizations typically have a strong sense of corporate vision that has been communally developed, and a strong alignment around that vision.

Leaders in world business are the first true planetary citizens. They have worldwide capability and responsibility; their domains transcend national boundaries. Their decisions affect not just economies, but societies; not just the direct concerns of business, but world problems of poverty, environment, and security. Up to now there has been no adequate guiding ethic. Although these executives and their organizations comprise a worldwide economic network, binding the planet together in a common fate, there has been within that network no tradition of and no institutionalization of a philosophy capable of wisely guiding its shaping force.

As we see in this and the succeeding chapter, such a new ethos for business may be in the process of forming. Interestingly, it appears to be forming around an M-3 kind of assumption about reality.

The economic activities of the world business system have been a contributing element in the world macroproblem. But by the same token, world business will be a key actor in the ultimate resolution of the macroproblem. It crosses national boundaries with much more ease than do political institutions, and the business corporation is a far more flexible and adaptive organization than the bureaucratic structures of governments and international public-sector institutions.

In the next chapter we will explore four additional aspects of the macroproblem: the problem of chronic unemployment and underemployment; the problems of global development (including poverty, hunger, and environmental deterioration); the area of values and politics; and the perplexing problem of seeking national and international security in a nuclear age. These four examinations will make more specific the general assertion made earlier, that when the underlying assumptions change, everything changes. Perhaps not just by accident, everything seems to be changing in a hopeful direction.

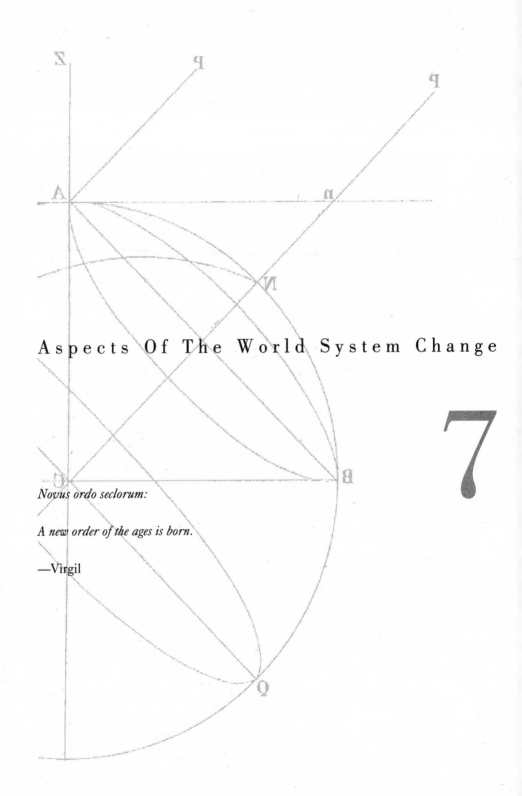

Aspects Of The World System Change

7

Novus ordo seclorum:

A new order of the ages is born.

—Virgil

I

T IS CRUCIAL TO UNDERSTAND that a shift at such a fundamental level of belief as we have been considering implies basic change in economic, corporate, financial, political, research, educational, and healthcare institutions—in all the most powerful institutions of society. As the pressure for these changes becomes more and more evident, it is likely to be accompanied by a good deal of fear. Fear and anxiety are the root cause of the social disruption and widespread misery that have most often accompanied such revolutionary changes in the past. The greater the level of understanding about what is happening, the less anxiety will be present.

FOUR CHALLENGES TO THE PRESENT ORDER

Around the world one detects murmurings that industrialized and "developing" countries alike have need for a new social order; that in fact, the situation calls for a worldwide systemic change. This sense comes from at least four challenges:

1. *The challenge of environmental sustainability:* The present social and economic order does not appear to be sustainable in the long term, in terms of effects on the Earth's ecological and life-support systems.

2. *The equity and justice challenge:* Power tends to concentrate—those who have economic, technological, and political power are in the best position to gain more, so that without some effective countervailing force, democratic tendencies are thwarted, both within countries and between countries.

3. *Increasing marginalization of people and cultures:* All the world is urged toward Western industrial monoculture, and a widening

150

fraction of the population is treated as superfluous to the needs of the global economy.

4. *The worldview challenge:* At a more fundamental level, the worldview that prevails in the most powerful institutions (strongly influenced by science) is increasingly challenged as being flawed, misleading, and destructive of humane values and meanings.

It is important to recognize that these challenges are in some sense the consequence of *modern society's successes in achieving the goals of the existing order.* That fact in itself suggests how profound the required changes may be.

Around the world, society is presently in a period of transition. The old order is showing obvious signs of decline, such as the militarization of societies around the globe; the recognized drift toward anarchy; underemployment and homelessness; widespread alienation and inner-city violence; general breaking of the social contract between society and worker; inability to halt the environmental destruction taking place on a broad front; the inherent ineffectiveness of the "war against drugs"; and a growing schism between the rich, consuming North and the populous, poverty-stricken South.

The shape of the new is not yet discernible, although we seem to see elements of it in an assortment of new kinds of entrepreneurial enterprises, new forms of community, alternative economies, and other social innovations that embody values and principles congenial to a new paradigm.

One subject that has received insufficient attention is the constructive role of business in this time of radical transformation. Business and the economy have become the dominant institution on the planet. By virtue of that fact alone, business must share in responsibility for the present and future well-being of the whole. But business has no tradition of such a responsibility. To the contrary, the tradition of business tends to be summed up in "the business of business is business"—with a little social responsibility added on to satisfy some of the stakeholders. What is required at this point in history is far more—a genuine stewardship of human societies and the planet. This implies a change in thinking that is by no means easily accomplished.

It will be helpful to explore briefly the four challenges above.

The Sustainability Challenge

No crisis in the history of civilized humanity compares with the challenge that the entire way of life of the modern world is not sustainable on a finite planet in the long term. It makes little difference whether by "long term" we mean half a century or two centuries. Once we become aware of the conclusion, the crisis is the same. Nothing short of fundamental transformation of all our powerful institutions, and underlying that, of modern thought and prejudice, will alter the ultimate catastrophe.

That's the bad news. The good news is that, perhaps through the unconscious wisdom of ordinary people, the transformation has already started. The depth of the transformation will startle us all.

Environmental sustainability is a minimal goal. We may aspire to more, but national and global society must at the very least become long-term sustainable before the next century is over—hopefully, long before. Individual organizations and communities must adopt ways that are sustainable, but that is not enough. It is impossible to have a truly sustainable corporation or city in an unsustainable global system, so we must talk about the whole. It is the whole of the interconnected, modern and modernizing, global society that is fundamentally unsustainable.

We are all aware of the worsening environmental dilemmas; it is revealing to think of these not as problems for which we must seek solutions but as *symptoms* of some more fundamental underlying systemic condition. It is that underlying condition that must be dealt with; otherwise, the "solutions" to apparent problems will simply continue to lead to other problems.

The analogy with treating symptoms of bodily illness is obvious. We would easily see the absurdity in the situation of a man who implores his physician to heal him, but subject to the conditions that the doctor not interfere with his drinking, smoking, eating, or sexual habits or his stress-producing attitudes toward work. Yet we are equally illogical when we admit the seriousness of the unsustainability of the modern world's present course, and insist that the cure be sought without disturbing our conviction of the necessity of economic growth and productivity increase; our concept of development as becoming industrialized "consumer society"; our concepts of "reasonable" financial return on investment; our attitude toward nature as provider of "resources" and ultimate dumping ground for our wastes; and our measuring our fellow dwellers on the planet, the fantastic diversity of plants and animals, in terms of their usefulness to the economy.

It is by now widely recognized that there is a strong correlation between such problems as environmental degradation, species extinction, soil depletion, deforestation, and desertification, and characteristics of the world economy—in particular, amount of economic product, and poverty. Some of the environmental problems are strongly linked to industrial processes, or to the amount and kind of economic consumption; these are often tolerated because remedying them would reduce profits, entail economic costs, or have a negative effect on jobs. Other environmental problems result from the demands made on the environment by those in a state of chronic poverty (mainly in the form of overgrazing; slash-and-burn agriculture; destruction of vegetation, with consequent soil erosion, in the quest for firewood; and surface water contamination). They can only be ameliorated in the long term through doing something about the poverty.

The best approaches to environmental policy attempt to take these facts into account. Nevertheless, all of the kinds of actions that have been seriously considered by the major national governments turn out to be insufficient in a more holistic picture. In other words, they still amount to little more than relieving symptoms.

The Equity And Justice Challenge

One of the most portentous developments on the face of the globe today is the awakening of the "sleeping giant" known as the developing world. Those multitudes who had, for so long, accepted the role of privation, inferiority, and servility are less and less willing to do so.

For the two decades following World War II this awakening took a dual form, as both a demand for political liberation and a yearning for economic development. It gradually became clear that the former by no means ensured the latter, and liberation was not simply a matter of shifting from political colony to member of the United Nations. The goal of economic liberation, involving needs satisfaction and equitable distribution of riches, was announced in the form of demands for a "New International Economic Order" (NIEO). In a series of documents relating to the NIEO, emanating from the International Labour Organization and other United Nations agencies, a set of universally felt needs has been defined, including not only basic human needs ("enough" food, shelter, healthcare, education, employment, and security of the person), but also dealing with such intangibles as dignity, justice, and solidarity. To greater or lesser extent, national governments undertake to insure that satisfaction of these needs is guaranteed to their citizens. However, a point of view is emerging that these principles that have been accepted and applied within the great majority of individual nations should now be extended to the entire family of humankind.

This demand amounts to much more than a mere adjustment of the existing economic institutions for more equitable distribution. It implies no less than a restructuring of international society around a newly recognized fundamental right. It is a demand as profound in its implications as was the concept of democratic government, two centuries ago.

This "fairness revolution" is related to the concept of rule by legal system, replacing more arbitrary and authoritarian forms of government. Practically all the nations of the world have been moving, to some extent at least, in this direction. The Rule of Law is expressly assumed as an essential precondition in the 1950 European Convention for the Protection of Human Rights and Fundamental Freedoms. The United Nations' 1948 Universal Declaration of Human Rights declares that "it is essential if man is not compelled to have recourse, as a last resort, to rebellion against tyranny and oppression, that human rights should be protected by the Rule of Law." The first prime minister of India, Jawaharlal Nehru, saw the Rule of Law as "synonymous with the maintenance of civilized existence." But however much the more powerful nations may be committed to the Rule of Law and to democratic institutions within their boundaries, not even the United States seems (by its actions) to believe strongly in the Rule of Law for the world.

Throughout history there have been numerous conditions—religious or political authoritarianism and tyranny; subjugation on the basis of class, race, or sex; extreme disparities of economic power or privilege; abuse and mutilation of women; cruel and unusual punishment—which may have for a long time been accepted as *misfortunes*, as regrettable circumstances that are unlikely to change. When a change in perception occurs such that these same conditions are perceived not as misfortunes but as *injustices*, as wrongs that must be righted, then the motive force is present for a fundamental change or revolution. Such a change in perception (from misfortune to injustice) results in a challenge to the legitimacy of the old order and an insistence on the new. Since the power of any institution depends in the long run on the public's perception of its legitimacy, a challenging of legitimacy is an extremely powerful social force for change.

Momentous decisions affecting the well-being of persons and cultures are made, not alone by governments, but also by the market. While the market is driven by individualistic self-interest, its proper function depends absolutely on a community that shares such values as honesty, trust, freedom, initiative, altruism, mercy, and thrift. Such values were once instilled from the religious foundations of the culture, through the family, and through religious, educational, and other institutions of society. In the modern world, that social fabric is now so weakened that little consensus remains. The authority of these virtues is rapidly being reduced to the level of personal tastes—a direct consequence of the positivistic individualistic philosophy of value on which modern economic theory is based. But without these restraining values the social fabric on which effective market function depends will gradually disintegrate. The market has a strong tendency to deplete moral capital, because it recognizes and values only behavior directed to short-term economic gain. In the end, the theoretical premise of economics that people are motivated only by individual interest becomes a self-fulfilling prophecy, destroying the integrity that is necessary to market efficiency. A market economy cannot function without a moral foundation; there must be an underlying assumption of integrity. The contemporary depletion of moral capital is also a factor in the equity challenge.

One may be able to convince oneself that "I, at least, am behaving ethically, even if others are not." But if one is at all aware, that still leaves the person complicit in the broader dilemma—namely, that even when institutions, particularly corporations, "follow the rules" of a competitive, materialist, capitalist economy, their actions seem to result in unethical consequences. Certainly there is nothing ethical about our leaving future generations saddled with debt and living in a near-lethally polluted environment. If the "normal" activities of the world's business and financial institutions are resulting in a systematic and persistent widening of the gap between the empowered rich and the disfranchised poor, those activities can hardly be termed ethical. Thus the real ethical dilemma arises, not so much from unethical persons, or even obviously unethical actions on the part of corporate management, but from "hidden" unethical consequences coming about from whole-system characteristics. In this sense, ethical considerations are inseparable from viewing things in a more whole-system way and recognizing the need for fundamental change.

Employment—Our Most Basic Dilemma

Modern society faces a dilemma that is so fundamental no politician dares bring it up, since there is no conceivable governmental action that could resolve it. No society can afford, politically and humanely, to have an increasing fraction of its population effectively marginalized and disfranchised. But neither can it afford—from an environmental standpoint, or from the standpoint of the tearing apart of the social fabric—the economic growth that would be necessary to provide jobs for all in the conventional sense, and the inequities that have come to accompany that growth. Where it may appear that a society could afford the latter, it is only because it has managed to push the environmental and fairness problems off onto some other group of people. This dilemma, more than any other aspect of our current situation, indicates how fundamental a system change is now required.

One of the most important functions of any society is to provide each individual with an opportunity to contribute to the society and to be affirmed and appreciated in return. The modern world has more or less equated society with the economy, and contribution with having a job in the mainstream economy. In the economy-dominated high-technology world, as the outspoken anthropologist Margaret Mead once put it bluntly, "The unadorned truth is that we do not need now, and will not need later, much of the marginal labor—the very young, the very old, the very uneducated, and the very stupid."

The accepted way to deal with this is for the economy to continually grow—for the economic product to increase exponentially with time. But because of the strong correlation between economic product and environmental deterioration (including pollution, toxic chemical concentrations, forest depletion, desertification, ozone layer thinning, and global warming), the goals of economic growth and desirable environment fundamentally conflict. To be sure, the "pollution index"—the ratio of environmental impact per unit of economic product—can be decreased by changes in technology, consumption habits, transportation and packaging, and so on. But if the economic product is to grow exponentially with time— which has been an article of faith for over half a century—then just to keep the annual environmental impact constant, the pollution index must decrease exponentially with time *forever*. Since there is no way that could happen, it follows that the only way environmental deterioration could be contained is to halt or reverse economic growth. However, economic growth is deemed necessary to create employment, and the social and political consequences of deliberately reduced growth are such that even a debate about it is almost a political impossibility.

The fruits of growth are far less fairly distributed than was the case a generation or more ago. In a modern industrial democracy the natural tendency for power to accumulate is held in check by traditions of equality of opportunity and of socioeconomic mobility, reinforced by a variety of regulating measures—antitrust laws, fair trade agreements, graduated income tax, checks and balances in government, collective bargaining arrangements, regulatory commissions, and so forth. But these mechanisms have proven inadequate to combat the forces bringing about an increasingly inequitable distribution. This failure is partly due to the growth of giant trans-national corporations with such enormous economic power and geographic spread that they are relatively immune to normal processes of community control.

Even more seriously, the industrial-era paradigm contains no rationale or incentive for more equitable distribution of the Earth's resources between the industrialized North and the poverty-stricken South. The seeds of worldwide conflict lie in the enormous and growing disparity between the world's rich and poor peoples. On no grounds are the industrial paradigm and late twentieth century capitalism more bitterly challenged. Because of the ubiquity of highly effective weapons of both precision and mass destruction, and the increased sophistication of terrorism and sabotage, that conflict will leave no group safely ensconced behind their bulwarks of "national security."

In other ways as well, the modern paradigm fails to provide goals that will enlist the deepest loyalties and commitments of the citizenry. Material economic growth and affluence are not enough to bring forth the best in people.

The fundamental question as we look ahead is not how we can stimulate more demand for goods and services and information, nor is it how we can create more jobs in the mainstream economy. The key question is a much more fundamental one. It is basically a question of meaning: *What is the central purpose of technologically advanced societies when it no longer makes sense for that central purpose to be economic production—because that is no longer a challenge and because in the long run focusing on economic production does not lead to a viable global future?* The question is fundamentally spiritual, not economic.

The roots of this dilemma go very deep. The fundamental concepts of business and labor, of employment and welfare theory, of liberal and Marxist analysis, are all based in *production-focused society*. It may have seemed to make sense in the past to think of economic production as the de facto goal of society; to think of an ever-increasing fraction of overall human activity being treated as commodities in the mainstream economy; to assume that the individual's primary relationship to society is through a job; to have social thinking dominated by concepts of scarcity, commercial secrecy, competition, and money exchange. However that is not the case in the future when one of our main "problems" is our capacity to over-produce.

The Worldview Challenge

For the past three decades there have been ample indications of a change in values emphasis, and indeed of a shifting underlying picture of reality, among an expanding fraction of the populace. Similar changes have been noted in most of the modernized countries in the world. It would be premature to attempt to say with certainty what this means; that will be the task of some future historical analyst. However, among the elements of this paradigm change that seem evident are the following three:

1. *Increased emphasis on the connectedness of everything to everything—* not only the "things" of the outer world, but also our inner, subjective experience. This element tends to be increasingly central in the ecological, feminist, holistic health, "new spirituality," and other social movements.

2. *A shift in the locus of authority from external to internal.* Whether in religion, politics, or science, we see growing disenchantment with external authorities and increasing reliance on intuitive, inner wisdom and authority. Perhaps this shift is most apparent in emphasis on intuition and the assumption of inner divinity in transpersonal psychology and other forms of the "new spirituality."

3. *A shift in the perception of cause from external to internal.* The weak meaning of a statement like "We create our own reality" is that the way we perceive the world around us (and ourselves) is affected by the contents of our unconscious and preconscious minds. The stronger meaning of such statements (and the assertion that there are no coincidences, and that behind apparently accidental events may lie hidden meanings and patterns) is that we are indeed co-creators of that world and that ultimate cause is to be sought not in the physical, but in mind, or consciousness.

The contrast between these three elements and the objectivist, positivist, and reductionist assumptions of modern science is striking. The scientific worldview has so effectively led to abilities to predict, control, and devise new manipulative technologies that it seems unthinkable that it might be found seriously in error. However, Western science entails a bias that sheds doubt on the completeness of the reality picture it presents. That bias comes from its *omission of consciousness as a causal factor* in the explanations of phenomena.

Both because of the emergence of a cultural shift in the direction of the transcendent, and because the adequacy of the worldview of prediction-and-control-focused science to guide individual and societal choices appears increasingly questionable, a shift in dominant worldview is more and more plausible.

THE 'CENTRAL MYTH' OF MODERN SOCIETY

Like every society that has ever existed on the planet, modern society has a "central myth"—a basic accounting for things around which all our powerful institutions have formed and our behaviors tend to orient. What is happening around the world is that modern society is outgrowing its "central myth."

The "central myth" of modern society is strongly influenced by Western science. In essence, it goes something like this:

> In the beginning was the Big Bang. Following that were something like 15 billion years of evolution of stars and planets; the coming together of certain chemicals to create life on planet Earth; the further evolution of more complex life forms, and their sorting out through natural selection; the resulting formation of increasingly complex neuronal networks culminating in the human brain with its fantastic capabilities. Thus the essential characteristics of human nature are to be understood as the consequence of an evolutionary succession of random events (from the origin of life to later mutations) and natural selections, and hence accidental—without purpose or meaning. The essence of ourselves is to be found in a material substance, the DNA with which we are born. Since our basic drives appear to be for survival, pleasure, and procreation, it is only natural

that the economy should have become the paramount institution of modern society, around which everything else revolves, and that economic logic and values should be the primary guides to our individual and collective decision making. It is only natural that we should treat the Earth and our fellow creatures as "resources," to be used in the service of the economy, and that we should view controlling nature through technology as one of modern society's most impressive achievements.

This "central myth" infuses and informs our education, healthcare policy, legal justice system, business, and other social institutions. If it were to be found fundamentally in error, the implications are far-reaching.

What the latter part of the twentieth century appears to be about is that a rapidly widening group of individuals are finding the "central myth" to be fundamentally in error and seriously misleading. We are engaged in a search for a "new story."

To better understand how fundamental a change is involved, let us look a little more deeply into four specific areas where this change is taking or will take place. These are the areas of work, money, development, and national security.

THE NECESSITY FOR REDEFINING WORK

There may be no aspect of the future about which people are typically more confused than the role of work in the life of the individual and in society. The reason in part is that we have failed to recognize the full implications of the social and economic changes that have been taking place.

Our present conceptions about work were formed in an era when the primary societal function of work was the production of necessary or desired goods and services, and in which one could foresee no end to the social desirability of increasing the economic productivity of the individual laborer through technological advance. Yet today these assumptions lead to a fundamental dilemma. On the one hand, if labor productivity in a country does not continually increase, the industry of that country tends to become noncompetitive in the international market. On the other hand, if productivity does increase, the economic product must increase (by definition) to maintain the same number of jobs. As various resource, environmental, political, and social constraints tend to limit economic growth, chronic unemployment becomes an intrinsic characteristic of the future. Since that is an unpleasant thought to contemplate, countries and individuals have tended to use tortuous logic and subtly evasive actions to avoid confronting it.

This problem of "superfluous people"—those marginal human beings not fortunate enough to be employed—grows more serious as society becomes more highly industrialized (or "postindustrialized"). Recognition of this chronic nature of unemployment goes back at least as far as 1930, when British economist John Maynard Keynes warned in his *Essays and Persuasions*:

> If the economic problem [the struggle for subsistence] is solved, mankind will be deprived of its traditional purpose.... Thus for the first time since his creation man will be faced with his real, his permanent problem—how to use his freedom from pressing economic cares.... There is no country and no people, I think, who can look forward to the age of leisure and abundance without a dread.... It is a fearful problem for the ordinary person, with no special talents to occupy himself, especially if he no longer has roots to the soil or in custom or in the beloved conventions of a traditional society.

Because understanding the changing role of work is so important, let us take the time to look fairly deeply into the history of work in the United States. While the story would be somewhat different in another country, what has happened in the United States has been influential in other industrial countries.

History Of Work In The United States

The fundamental social doctrine of eighteenth century colonial America strongly emphasized the dignity of labor. It stressed the virtue of diligent application to one's task and promised that earnest industry would be unfailing in its rewards. The values of diligence, sobriety, and thrift, characteristic of the rising middle class in England, were transported to America and became a dominant influence in the colonies. Accomplishment tended to be measured in material progress—the transformation of nature and development of useful arts and knowledge.

Personal aggrandizement was considered more or less incidental, and there were injunctions against waste, extravagance, and ostentation. Labor was scarce, returns from the individual's work were high, and opportunities to move to higher status were abundant. It was assumed that the idle poor brought poverty upon themselves; poverty was made so disgraceful that a man would labor to the extent of his capacity to avoid such a stigma. If not everybody prospered, the great majority of honest, hard-working men made their own way and improved their lot. Additional rewards of the virtue of work were found in the good opinion of others and the sense of having fulfilled one's "calling."

By the nineteenth century, a greater emphasis on self-improvement had developed. The self-made man, less moved by piety and virtue, still owed his advancement to the cultivation of God-given talents and habits of industry, sobriety, moderation, self-discipline, and avoidance of debt. Aiming to surpass the previous generation and provide for the next, he deferred gratification and lived for the future, patiently saving and accumulating. Wealth became more of an end in itself; compulsive industry, discipline, and self-denial were the means to that end. The public schools, available to all, inculcated industrial discipline, self-reliance, orderly habits, punctuality, workmanship, versatility, and obedience. They offered vocational training and served for industrial recruitment, selection, and certification.

The early twentieth century evidenced more stress on the will to win. The advent of mass production had brought an ever-growing hierarchy of supervisors and managers, and increasingly large staffs for engineering, management, distribution, and sales. Ambitious young men had to compete with their peers for the attention and approval of their superiors in order to advance in the corporate structure. Advancement was assumed to depend on willpower, self-confidence, energy, and initiative. The new ethos was one of salesmanship, boosterism, pursuit of wealth, and success as an end in itself. There was no apparent reason to question the role of work in either the individual's life or in society. It was self-evident that the individual worked to support himself and his family. As for society, the assumption that the role of work is industrial production, shared by economists from Adam Smith to Karl Marx, was widely accepted.

The great Depression of the 1930s signaled the end of labor scarcity and the beginning of a persistent fear of job shortages and chronic unemployment. That anxiety was put aside during World War II, but resurfaced as the war drew near to an end, and worries were expressed about the coming unemployment situation "when peace breaks out."

Part of the supposed solution to this problem was found in a Keynesian reasoning based on several new principles:

- Mass consumption is necessary to enable all members of a society to enjoy a high material standard of living; mass consumption is also necessary to support mass production in an industrial economy.

- Mass consumption cannot exist or continue unless there is a mass distribution of purchasing power.

- Full employment is necessary to create this mass distribution of purchasing power, and bring about prosperity and well-being for all.

- It is an appropriate function of government to promote full employment through promoting mass consumption and economic growth, and to insure that any who are left out of this participation in the mainline economy are adequately taken care of with social security measures.

Thus around 1950 the United States became a mass-consumption society—"throwaway society" it was termed then. People learned to consume and waste; to "use it and throw it away." They learned that frugality was no longer a prime virtue; rather, it was bad for the economy. Consuming became the new ethic; people began to call one another "consumers." They learned about "planned obsolescence," about needing to replace things with new models, either because the old ones fell apart or because the new model was more fashionable.

Another boost to the economy came from the Cold War and the global arms race. Particularly during the period just after World War I, Americans generally considered sales of arms to other nations to be highly unethical and immoral. By the late 1950s ethics had given way to practicality, and US sales representatives, in and out of uniform, were urging nations around the world that they needed more high-technology US-produced weapons.

From 1946 on there were several attempts to legislate full employment into existence. The social costs of unemployment were recognized as being very high. To be unemployed in modern industrial society is to suffer a severe blow to one's self-esteem. Much evidence links employment to psychological health, and unemployment to emotional disorders, alcoholism, disease, drug use, and crime. If it were possible to create ample, satisfactory work opportunities for all, it was believed that many of the social problems would disappear. But despite the heroic pronouncements of the "Great Society" era of the 1960s, the unemployment threat steadily worsened.

Current concepts of the "Information Society" are in part a reaction to that veiled threat. What do you do when the productiveness of the economy has risen to where the needs of society can be met employing only a fraction of the potential work force? Answer: Become obsessed with consumption, to try to use up the product and keep the machinery running. What do you do when technology has advanced to where anything you can train a human to do, you can train a computer (robot) to do; and furthermore the computer will probably do it better, faster, and cheaper? Answer: Become obsessed with economic growth to create new jobs for humans to do. And what will create that consumption, and that growth? Answer: Information! We can all develop an insatiable appetite for information, to be passed around at an exponentially increasing rate. Demand for information-related services can be made to increase at such a rate that we need not fear the further job-displacement effects of the computers. Never mind that mindless consumption of information services in order to create jobs may not be the choice of thinking people, any more than was boundless consumption of food as a response to increasing agricultural productivity. (Perhaps instead of Information Society we should call it "Makework Society.")

Chronic Unemployment And Underemployment

There is reluctant but growing admission in the United States (and in Northern Europe) that despite mass consumption and global arms races (and despite the advent of the "Information Society"), the long-term future of industrial society is characterized by chronic unemployment and underemployment (working at less than one's full productive capacity). The reasons are basically two: (1) in the long run, economic growth may not continue to generate enough jobs to accommodate the expanding work force; and (2) the quality of available jobs may not be compatible with the rising educational levels of the work force.

The problematic character of economic growth arises primarily from the tension between growth and the cluster of problems associated with resources and the environment. These problems could be eased if economic growth were modified to lessen resource utilization, since the economy displays a built-in correlation between economic product and resource utilization. But a slacking of growth increases unemployment. Thus despite a commitment to growth and full employment, environmental constraints and resource limitations will tend to keep the economy from generating enough satisfactory jobs to meet the demand.

Economic and demographic trends partially obscured this problem through the 1980s, especially in the United States. Earlier in the decade the labor force in the US was increasing at a rate of something like two million persons per year (2 percent growth rate). Both the postwar baby boom effect and the effect of the rapid entry of women into the labor force began dropping off, so there is a temporary reduction in labor force growth rate. Thus there is a temporary easing of the national unemployment problem, but the long-term prospects are another story.

Despite the fact that the unemployment/underemployment dilemma seems intrinsic to the industrial paradigm, economists and social scientists are divided on how fundamental the problem will appear in the future. This lack of agreement probably reflects, in part, different perceptions of the extent to which the problem already exists. One gains perspective by imagining what would happen to unemployment rates in the US if by some miraculous means sustained global peace were to become a reality and the portion of economic activity now involved with national security were no longer needed. Already we can hear the panic reactions whenever there is talk of canceling a defense contract or space project or shutting down an airbase. The true extent of the unemployment problem is further reflected in inflated age and education criteria for job entry, delays imposed on job elimination or automation of routine operations, subtle forms of featherbedding, and pressures on older employees to retire early.

Underemployment too is a major source of alienation and workplace problems. As the educational level of the work force rises, discontent and alienation spread among highly educated workers forced to take jobs previously performed by workers with less schooling. Education is no longer a sure route to increased status, power, and income. Neither does it insure work that is intrinsically challenging and that offers opportunities for creativity and self-expression.

People of high educational achievement tend to expect that their work should use their talents and develop their potential. But disappointment awaits many of those who anticipate managerial, technical, and professional positions, with middle-class income and status to match, that include opportunities for growth, challenge, and self-fulfillment. Increasing numbers of well-educated workers must accept jobs—white-collar as well as blue-collar—that are routine, stultifying, and unchallenging. A significant fraction of the jobs in industrialized society are neither intrinsically challenging nor obviously related to inspiring social challenges.

The nature of underemployment is revealed by the ancient story of two stonecutters who were engaged in similar activity. Asked what they were doing, one answered, "I'm squaring up this block of stone." The other replied, "I'm building a cathedral." The first may have been underemployed; the second was not. Clearly what counts is not so much what work people do, but what they perceive they are doing it for.

The frontiersman, the old-time craftsman, the farmer blessed with a fine piece of land, all would have scoffed at the idea that they were underemployed. But once mechanized agriculture appeared on the scene, one could no longer spend the day behind a horse and plow

167

in the same spirit as before. Once a robotized assembly line can mass-produce an item, the challenge to make the same item by hand is destroyed.

"Meaningful work" is not necessarily work that is exciting and challenging every moment; it may, rather, be work that is part of a larger endeavor that is infused with meaning. If the society has a "central project" in which people believe—for example, conquering a geographical or technological frontier, or building a new society or a new world democratic order—then even routine tasks take on meaning.

Unemployment In A Different Perspective

Let us now look at all of this with fresh eyes. There is no doubt that, by and large, the history of industrial society has been a fantastic success story. In only a few centuries Western Europe leapt from the relatively low capability and motivation to manipulate the physical environment that characterized traditional society to a technological capability so high that almost anything one can imagine wanting to do seems achievable. The "wave" of industrial society spread around the planet, affecting in time virtually every society on the globe—seducing with its glitter those it did not take over by force.

During those centuries a central focus on economic production seemed to make sense. Providing new tools, making persons' labor count for more, converting more and more of the Earth's resources into economic products, exercising increasing "control" over the natural environment through technology, drawing more and more of people's activities into the monetized economy (both as jobs and as "consumed" services)—all appeared to result in a raised material standard of living, and hence to increased human well-being.

But then we get to the hypothetical situation Keynes identified. What if a society advances technologically until it looks as though economic production of all the goods and services the society can imagine needing or desiring (or all that the resources and environment can stand) can be done with ease, using only a small fraction of the population?

The main answer so far appears to be to continue attempts to create jobs by stimulating economic growth. There won't be enough jobs, so those left out can be taken care of by transfer payments. In effect, the old ethic of "work in order to eat" seems to be changing to "the fortunate may work; the remainder will be kept as pets— supported, with little more demanded of them than that they be housebroken." One needs only to look at the northwestern part of England to get an advance glimpse of what this society will be like.

Another approach is talked about here and there—to treat work as a scarce commodity to be rationed. That concept is at the heart of various extant proposals and programs embodying work-sharing plans, limitations on the work week, and so forth. (This approach doesn't seem terribly sensible, when you think of all the room for creative work in the world.)

But both of the above approaches overlook how basic this shift really is. As we noted above, the real question is whether the assumption of production-focused society is fundamentally obsolete.

Informal and underground economies are serving many people today who can't make it into the mainstream. Cooperative sharing fits some situations better than money exchange. "Information society" is not going to solve the problems; the current unenforceability of copyright and patent laws shows the fallacy of considering information to behave like other "commodities" such as tomatoes and automobiles. Furthermore, we are clearly experiencing a breakdown of the leadership and government forms that are based on the assumption that information will be available only to the few.

If one views the situation again from the vantage point of an anthropologist from outer space, one sees clearly that an entirely new mode of thinking needs to be adopted, wherein the widespread elimination of human work that machines can be trained to do is taken as a stimulus to rethink and reexamine the basic assumptions of production-focused society. Society needs to take on a new "central project" now that keeping economic production in that position no longer makes sense. The assumption that income distribution should be linked strongly to jobs in the mainline economy needs to be reassessed.

Society's New 'Central Project'

The required new thinking, compatible with emergent value emphases, can be simply stated: In a technologically advanced society in which production of sufficient goods and services can be handled with ease, *employment exists primarily for self-development, and is only secondarily concerned with the production of goods and services.* This concept of work represents a profound shift in our perceptions with implications that reverberate throughout the entire structure of industrial society. It is hard to imagine it prevailing in a society dominated by an M-1 metaphysic (see page 29) and confused about meanings and values. If the whole society shifts to an M-3 perspective, the picture is a much more promising one.

We referred earlier to the Greek concept of paideia. In the Greek "learning society" the primary function of society and of all its institutions was assumed to be to promote learning in the broadest possible definition. Paideia was education looked upon as a lifelong transformation of the human personality, in which every aspect of life plays a part. It did not limit itself to the conscious learning processes, or to inducting the young into the social heritage of the community. Paideia meant the task of making life itself an art form, with the person the work of art. In theory, at least, the achievement of the human whole—and of the wholly human—took precedence over every specialized activity or narrower purpose.

The motivations and values implicit in the M-3 assumptions fit very well with this Greek concept of a "learning society." They clearly do not fit with mindless consumption, material acquisition, and endless economic growth.

In the "learning society" the occupational focus of most people is learning and developing in the broadest sense. This focus includes a wide diversity of activities such as formal education, research, exploration, self-discovery, various specialized roles, and participation in the community of concerned citizens to choose a better future. These activities contribute to human betterment and fulfillment. They are humane, nonpolluting, and nonstultifying. They can absorb unlimited numbers of persons not required for other sorts of work.

"Learning society" implies reversal of a number of aspects of the long-term industrialization trend. It almost certainly involves something like the "intermediate technology" or "appropriate technology" concepts of E. F. Schumacher and others. These terms refer to technology that is resource conserving, environmentally benign, frugal in the use of energy, relatively labor intensive, and understandable and usable at the individual or community level. Such technology tends to complement a strong ecological ethic; strong identification with nature, fellow human beings, and future generations; a lifestyle characterized by voluntary frugality ("doing more with less"); appreciation of the simple life and simple virtues; and the kind of work that fosters these attitudes.

It is premature to try to speculate in more detail what are some of the specific changes that this shift in thinking entails. As we saw in the last chapter, this basic concept is already being discussed in contemporary management; a number of small innovative corporations can be found that are deeply committed to the principle. What it eventually implies for the overall economy is less clear, but the change will not be a small one.

MONEY, BANKING, AND DEBT

As an important practical example of the effect of this shift in worldview, consider the money and banking system of the US (and most other major countries). Since the dominant, scientifically influenced worldview admits no reality to inner experience, transcendental values have no power and materialism prevails. One of the consequences of this has been that over the last half century or so, proscriptions against usury, debt, and gambling have dropped by the wayside. Hence there was little in the way of complaint or caveat when, in the early 1970s, all the major currencies of the world shifted from gold-based to debt-based money.

To understand what this means we have to go back to the invention of the bank. The term goes back to the Old Italian word for bench, *banca*, the moneychanger's table. When gold was the legal tender of the day, a person's gold was typically deposited with the local goldsmith for safekeeping. The goldsmith issued a certificate of deposit, which was then used as money. If ten people deposited their gold with the goldsmith, it was unlikely that they would all try to redeem their deposit certificates at the same time. Thus the clever goldsmith could issue additional certificates *on gold he did not have*, and these would pass as money also. The practice was of dubious ethical merit, but complaints were few and the practice continued. In fact, it became the basis for the modern banking system.

Contrary to the usual assumption, the government of the United States does not issue money. Yes, it prints currency, which it furnishes to the Federal Reserve System for the member banks to issue. Congress created the Federal Reserve System in 1913, with the intent of reducing both the likelihood of inflation by taking away from the federal government the ability to create money, and the likelihood of depression by regulating the banking industry. (The Act was strongly opposed by many bankers at the time.) The Federal Reserve System is basically a privately owned cartel, originally chartered "to serve the public interest," and now a key link in a global network of central banks that controls commerce world-wide. It is independent of the government and controlled by a small number of international financiers.

New money is created from debt in the following way. The federal government needs money, in excess of revenues from taxes and other sources, for payment of employees and suppliers. To this end it issues a bond to the Federal Reserve, which credits the government's account with the face value of the bond. Out of this account the government pays its creditors, who deposit their money in regular banks. These banks lend money out of these accounts (keeping a small percentage in reserve to take care of depositor demands), thus in effect creating more money. This in turn ends up in banks, which lend out most of it, creating still more money, and so on. All of this money is debt-created. Only a tiny fraction of it is in the form of paper currency; most of it is electronic signals in a computer network.

There are a number of problems with this system. With the development of electronic transactions, banks can realize an enormous number of money movements without any real liquidity base. With electronic bank clearing it is very difficult to ascertain whether banks are keeping up with the usual standards of liquidity and solvency. Furthermore, even though debt creates money, because of the interest on the debt the money supply has to increase faster than the debt. The effect of this in the long term is intrinsic inflation.

Each increase of the debt volume increases the need for any economic entity, whether company or consumer, to increase the amount of its working capital. Capital is needed for a variety of purposes, including carrying on the entity's activities during the period between the time goods or services are provided and the time payment for them is received. Business has come to assume that it is perfectly normal to have to borrow capital in order to participate in the economy. The last half century or so has been characterized by acceptance of indebtedness as a natural and pervasive state of affairs—for individuals, corporations, municipalities, and governments. There seems little doubt that this change and the characteristics of the money and banking system are closely interrelated.

High debt levels and high expected rates of return on investments (including interest rates) create other problems. With a high rate of discounting the future, decisions are made that may be financially smart in the short term but are environmentally and socially disastrous in the longer term. Furthermore, the high debt and interest levels mean there is a tremendous amount of debt servicing circulating around in the economy. From 30 to 50 percent of the purchase price of almost anything is hidden interest payments. Since everybody pays out this hidden debt servicing, and a limited number of individuals or households have surplus money to lend out, this amounts to a mechanism that systematically, day after day, transfers wealth from those who have little to those who already have much. Social problems like the homeless and the underclass are directly related to our money and banking system.

Another facet of this complex picture has recently exploded into prominence: the "global casino." Whereas the speculative economy had historically been very small compared with the goods-and-services economy, in the past two decades it has come to dwarf it. Only a few percent of the electronic currency sloshing around the globe has anything whatever to do with goods and services and human well-being; practically all the rest is, by one euphemism or another, part of the action in the global casino.

This, too, is intimately connected with the money and banking system. Think of the economy as having two parts—a production environment (where goods and services are created and exchanged) and a financial environment (where pieces of paper and electronic computer signals are exchanged). Interest payments on debt incurred in the production environment end up in the financial environment. If the money were to be re-invested in the production environment, that would be fine, but the possibility of higher rates of return in the financial environment is enticing. What seems to be happening is a steady "leakage" of working capital out of production into speculation, or "non-working capital."

One of the effects this has is destruction of community. You put your savings where you can get the greatest return. The net result is that capital is steadily sent out of the community, and outside the production environment (since profit margins in the production world are far smaller than the profit margins that can be made by trading paper in the financial markets).

As more and more people come to understand the insidious effects of our present ideas about money, banking, and debt, the legitimacy of the present way of creating debt-based money is bound to come into question. The exact form of the resulting change is impossible to predict. Whatever it is, it will be related to the reassertion of transcendental values over economic values.

REDEFINING GLOBAL DEVELOPMENT

Among the forces shaping the future, surely one of the most potent and long-range is the awakening of the "sleeping giant" usually referred to as the "developing world." The developing world comprises approximately three-quarters of the world's population (about half of them living in China and India), and the fraction is projected to increase to around four-fifths by the end of the century. Most of the countries that make up the developing world were, prior to World War II, either colonies of, or strongly dominated by, the industrialized powers. But those who have for so long accepted the role of privation, inferiority, and servility are less and less willing to do so.

For the two decades following World War II, development was more or less taken to be synonymous with economic development— that is, with "modernization" and industrialization. In other words, the prevailing assumption—in developed and developing countries alike—was that it is the destiny of all peoples on the Earth to follow the path of the United States and the other industrialized countries (with perhaps some differentiation along the capitalism-socialism dimension). That is to say, they would assimilate Western culture (with some small remnant of the original culture left, of course, to encourage tourism and promote products of native crafts).

We have earlier noted that people who spend their lives in different cultures literally experience different realities. Those who grow up in industrialized societies perceive reality in a very different way from an Australian Aborigine or a Bedouin or a Hopi. A Native American once characterized the Amerindian outlook as: (a) everything in the universe is alive; and (b) we are all relatives. Such a perception would be totally foreign to most educated Americans or Europeans. Similarly, the typical American would find it difficult to realize that the implicit goal in US society of ever-increasing consumption of goods and services might be viewed by an outsider as totally insane, or that the assumption that the "natural resources" of the Earth exist to be exploited is madness.

Thus the implicit objective of modernization has been rejection of the reality of the traditional culture and substitution of a foreign perception. However, the realities of some of the traditional cultures are proving to be more resilient than expected. Increasingly, cultural leaders in the developing countries have come to see that optimal development of people in the broadest sense is not necessarily fostered by abandoning their own cultural roots and adopting the alien culture of Western industrial society. Thus there has been growing insistence on a different international economic order and on exploring development paths other than "modernization."

In a speech the day before his death, E. F. Schumacher, author of *Small Is Beautiful* (1974), said of development aid that it is "a process where you collect money from the poor people in the rich countries, to give it to the rich people in the poor countries." Development, he said, could not center around bringing the technologies of the highly industrialized countries to the developing countries. "This kind of industry has no future. Nature cannot stand it, the resource endowment of the world cannot stand it, and the human being cannot stand it."

If these attitudes continue to strengthen, as seems likely, the thrust of global development will not continue to be, as at present, toward Western industrial monoculture around the globe. Rather, it will be toward an ecology of diverse cultures, each with its own interpretation of human development, societal goals, and ultimate meaning—and toward a world system that tends to support rather than diminish, thwart, and bias against this diversity. The momentum and influence of the single industrial world economy is so great, however, that any such change in the development thrust is tantamount to major change in the world's economic and financial institutions.

The potential impact of world attitude shifts on the future of the world economy is often ignored. For example, since the world economy runs on energy, dwindling fossil fuel reserves is a matter of concern: World public attitudes will be decisive as to whether augmenting and eventually replacing fossil fuels by some form of nuclear power leads to an acceptable future, or whether some form of "soft energy path" must be found instead.

World public opinion will be similarly critical with regard to how drastic measures will be demanded for dealing with serious environmental deterioration and with increasing problems of hazardous substances, toxic wastes, and agrochemical runoff. Pressures of economic competition would seem to dictate rapid deployment of robots and artificial intelligence in industrial production and service industries; the spectre of rising world unemployment may spawn opposing reactions. Spreading public perception that negative long-term consequences of the activities of large corporations may outweigh benefits has already implied a significant challenge to the legitimacy of present corporate behaviors.

How powerful these changes in world attitude may eventually become is difficult to foretell. In a series of documents from the International Labour Organization and other United Nations agencies relating to Third World demands for a "New International Economic Order," a set of universally felt human needs has been defined as being in essence:

- Basic human needs ("enough" food, shelter, healthcare, education, employment, and security of the person)

- A sense of the dignity of being human

- A sense of becoming (a chance to achieve a better life)

- A sense of justice or equity

- A sense of achievement, of being involved with something worth achieving

- A sense of solidarity—of belonging to a worthy group and of participating in decisions that affect the group's, and one's own, destiny.

National-level programs aimed at implementing the concept of a right to satisfaction of these universal needs have been adopted by over 120 countries, in most cases within the past four decades. In some of the countries, including the United States, the programs were preceded by many years of debate over the appropriateness of this presumed right and its actualization through provision of "safety-net" transfer payments or provision of services. Yet inequities in economic distribution far beyond anything that would be tolerated in any individual country exist between the rich and the poor internationally. Behind the rhetoric of the demands of the developing world for a new economic order is the proposition that *a concept of human welfare that has thus far been accepted and applied within a majority of individual nations should now be extended to the entire family of humankind.*

Despite inevitable opposition, ultimate acceptance of this proposition appears likely, in that it is an extension of an already accepted basic trend and that the various peoples of the world are increasingly aware of being one world, through communication and commerce (as well as shared fate of the planet).

Perhaps most central of all aspects of the development conundrum (which is intimately linked to the underemployment/unemployment dilemma) is that of meaning. Traditional society, whatever its drawbacks, had a place for everyone—a role to play, with its own inherent *meaning.* Modernization has involved the destruction of traditional meaning and the creation of marginal people—people who live at the margins of society and have no real place, whether unemployed, underemployed, or unemployable. It will not be allowed to continue to do so. The triumphs and horrors of anti-modernization movements in Iran and Cambodia are only early indicators of the irrational forces that will bring about change if more reasoned approaches do not.

To depict the problems of modernization is not to overlook the positive accomplishments of the same paradigm that contributes to the dilemmas. We are not simply indulging in a criticism of industrial society, rather, we are attempting to indicate one compelling reason that the future will inevitably differ from a continuation of past trends. It is of critical importance to understand what social forces propel us in a different direction—why a fundamental system change is unavoidable.

The development problem and the work problem are intimately related, and alike in one respect. They both arise out of the fundamental issue of modern society—namely, what is it all about? What is the meaning in the success of modernization? If the "learning society" is an answer for the technologically advanced countries, the "developing society" is an answer for the world: "developing society" in the sense of fostering the maximum possible development for each human individual.

Surely it is not too idealistic to imagine a future global commonwealth in which each of Earth's citizens has a reasonable chance to create through his or her own efforts a decent life for self and family; in which men and women live in harmony with the Earth and its creatures, cooperating to create and maintain a wholesome environment for all; in which there is an ecology of different cultures, the diversity of which is appreciated and supported; in which war and flagrant violation of human rights in the name of the state has no legitimacy anywhere, and there is universal support of the rule of law throughout the world; and in which throughout the entire human family there is a deep and shared sense of meaning in life itself.

If that goal is an inspiring definition of development, it will serve equally as a definition of true *security*.

FINDING GLOBAL SECURITY

In the foregoing, we have described the signs of shifting basic assumptions underlying American society in particular and Western-dominated society in general. This shift appears to be away from the M-1 assumptions, which for generations up to the 1950s at least had been steadily increasing in influence, and toward the M-3 assumptions. These M-3 assumptions have never had widespread popular approval in either Europe or America, although the undercurrent has always been present (from the Gnostics and mystery religions, to the Rosicrucians and Freemasons of later centuries, to the New England Transcendentalists of the mid-nineteenth century, and the still later Theosophy movement in England and America and the Anthroposophy movement on the Continent).

We have seen how the various interconnected dilemmas of modern society appear to be inherent in the basic paradigm of industrial society, and will become solvable only with a shift away from that paradigm to some as-yet-unspecified trans-industrial or postmodern paradigm. We have seen, also, how the M-3 assumptions are compatible with the diverse traditional societies around the globe. Thus one might hope that with a shift toward the M-3 metaphysic the scourge of war might be finally eliminated from the Earth. Let us explore that possibility in more detail.

Removing Legitimacy From War

In this nuclear age, virtually everyone is for peace. However, not all mean the same thing by the word. Some stress "peace with national security." Others insist that there must be "peace and social justice." Some praise the nuclear weapons for having "kept the peace for 50 years"; others find that being under perpetual threat of nuclear holocaust is a state that hardly qualifies as a definition of peace.

Whatever way the world eventually comes to handle the issue of peace, or more specifically, prevention of nuclear war, that task must be done *with 100 percent reliability*. Nothing less will do; the world cannot afford one nuclear war. It is sobering to realize that nowhere else in our experience is that kind of reliability demanded.

In considering this goal, it will be helpful to distinguish between two kinds of peace: (1) a long-term goal of "real peace," implying permanently low levels of conflict and prevailing attitudes of loving, caring, and peacefulness among persons and nations around the globe, and (2) a short-term goal of "practical peace," sufficient to remove the threat posed by presently available weapons of mass destruction and mass slaughter (nuclear, biological, chemical). The former goal is, in effect, a major step in social and psychological evolution. We have been urged toward it by spiritual leaders of East and West for thousands of years, but progress is slow. The latter goal we must achieve now.

By "practical peace" let us mean something even more specific. This goal would include, at a minimum, (a) delegitimation of both war and preparation for war as instruments of national policy; (b) outlawing of all weapons of mass slaughter; and (c) meaningful commitment by all the powerful nations to pool sovereignty to a sufficient extent to create and maintain an effective institution for peacekeeping and nonviolent conflict resolution.

The two goals, the long- and short-term, are of course intertwined. Progress toward one aids achievement of the other. Yet the differentiation is important in a practical sense. Some of the roots of conflict go very deep into the human psyche, and some of the perceived injustices involve long-standing characteristics of social and political institutions. Because the long-term goal involves extensive changes in powerful and deep-rooted social and politico-economic institutions, and major transformations in the lives of hundreds of millions of people, it is easy to be overwhelmed by the magnitude of the task. One may be so intimidated that one may overlook the achievability of the short-term goal, which could be realized within a reasonably short time, in a generation or less.

Although it has become fashionable in the United States to malign the United Nations, the Charter of this organization (1945) and the Universal Declaration of Human Rights (1948) must rank among the most noble political documents in history. They have been agreed to by nearly all of the nations and peoples of the Earth. They provide one—perhaps not the only—framework within which the goal of "practical peace" could be achieved, if we really wanted it. The plain fact is that the people and leaders of the most powerful nations have not manifested the will to delegitimate war. It is not a matter of lack of appropriate mechanisms, or of need for new technologies, but a moral choice.

We should not overlook the progressive delegitimizing of certain forms of war that has been quietly taking place. Until around 1914, *offensive* war was considered permissible and legitimate, at least under certain conditions. Some of the European nations rather frequently fought wars that were frankly offensive in purpose. By the end of World War II wars of aggression and territorial gain were generally considered to be not permissible, and since about mid-century most military engagements around the world have been justified on defensive grounds. (In 1947 the United States changed the name of its War Department to the "Department of Defense.") The "gunboat diplomacy" in which powerful, technically advanced nations intervened at will in weak Third World nations, although it may still go on to some extent, must be well disguised if it is to be considered legitimate even by the people of the nation committing the intervention.

Attitudes toward war have been changing rapidly as the fundamental nature of war changed. Since World War II, war is no longer a contest between trained armies; it is the desolation of civilian populations. In World War I approximately 15 percent of the casualties were civilian; in World War II, over 50 percent; in the Vietnam War, close to 90 percent; in the breakup of Yugoslavia, over 90 percent. One can only imagine what the figure would be for a nuclear war. Serving one's country in war, which as recently as World War I was regarded as "glorious" and "heroic," has so lost its glamour that the veterans of Vietnam complained about being treated like pariahs. It is difficult to be enthusiastic about being a participant in the mass slaughter of innocent victims.

We have before us the example of progressive withdrawal of legitimacy from various forms of slavery, oppression, torture, and murder (including attempted genocide) that were formerly condoned or even encouraged. Delegitimating war and preparation for war, seeking national and global security through other means, is the next logical step in the sequence.

Throughout history, the really fundamental changes in societies have come about not from dictates of governments and the results of battles but through vast numbers of people changing their minds— sometimes only a little bit. Some of these changes have amounted to profound transformations—for instance the transition from the Roman empire to medieval Europe, or from the Middle Ages to modern times. Others have been more specific, such as the constitution of democratic governments in England and America, or the termination of slavery as an accepted institution. In the latter cases, it is largely a matter of people recalling that no matter how powerful the economic or political or even military institution, it persists because it has legitimacy, and that legitimacy comes from the perceptions of people. People give legitimacy, and they can take it away. *A challenge to legitimacy is the most powerful force for change to be found in history.*

The nineteenth century Prussian strategist Karl von Clausewitz defined war as "an extension of state policy by other means." To move from this rational argument for war to a complete delegitimating of war would be one of the more profound shifts in the history of humankind. Yet like other major shifts in attitude throughout history (for example the end of feudalism, the delegitimating of political colonies), it can come about when the people of the world change their minds and demand it. The only kind of war that retains the cloak of legitimacy is that for which the preparation was in the name of "defense" and the initiation is non-deliberate. *That is precisely the kind of war that is most hazardous—the one that the world fearfully awaits.*

Beliefs And Perceptions In International Conflict

The main obstacle to the removal of legitimacy from all war is lack of belief in the feasibility of peace. We have alluded earlier to the extent to which our perceptions, motivations, values, and behaviors are shaped by partially unconscious beliefs such as "This is fundamentally a world of scarcity," or "People with other-colored skins are alien." Scientific research has been progressively disclosing the surprising extent to which this "inner map" of beliefs underlies perceptions, which in turn underlie conflict and the perceived impossibility of peace.

If it is these inner beliefs that are really at the core of intergroup conflicts, the nature of the task of achieving peace becomes more clear. It is not human nature that has to change—as has sometimes been claimed—but, rather, the unconscious "programming." (Observing this, some scientists have actually urged interventions such as implanted electrodes with reconditioning signals to bring about desired "peaceful" behavior. We restrict our discussion here to self-chosen reconditioning.)

We humans have a truly awesome ability to deceive ourselves. Once we have settled on one perception of "reality," all evidence to the contrary tends to become invisible; all hints that our picture might be wrong or even seriously incomplete are deftly (and unconsciously) warded off. This is true even if the perception doesn't serve our self-interest. For example, the paranoid sees the environment in a way that causes much self-anguish, and rational argument or even contradictory experience may fail to change that perception. It does not serve us well to perceive the world in such a way that there is no viable alternative to the impasse of weapons of mass destruction, yet that is the all too common perception. In fact it appears that *a vast number of persons would risk the destruction of civilization rather than risk fundamentally changing their perceptions of the world.*

Consider the implications if we were to be persuaded that *the fundamental causes of conflict on the planet are to be found mainly in the collective beliefs of the various societies—beliefs that are partly consciously held, but are in great measure unconscious.* We are used to seeking explanations of the state of global non-peace in national competitions, in the ambitions and frustrations of leaders in those countries, in the flaws of past treaties, in conflicts between religious and ideological factions. No doubt these explanations are partially accurate. But underlying them, as a more fundamental breeding ground of non-peace, are the largely collective beliefs that so subtly create barriers, separations, tensions, and collisions. These beliefs are difficult to even become aware of, and certainly to challenge, mainly because the people around us in our own society tend to share the same beliefs and tacitly to take them for granted.

Naturally enough we all have our own internal resistance to perceiving how the underlying paradigm of Western industrial society (both forms: capitalist and Marxian) leads inexorably to the kinds of problems and global dilemmas we now face. We have earlier described how we unwittingly "buy into" a belief system in which technical solutions are sought for problems that are basically sociopolitical in nature—including the futile attempt to buy "national security" through more powerful weapons. We are most reluctant to recognize how powerfully the world's belief systems, including our own, lock us into a death march toward the future.

Collectively held unconscious beliefs shape the world's institutions, and are at the root of institutionalized oppression and inequity. "Peace" will always be no more than a temporary truce if there exist widespread perceptions of basic injustice, needs unmet, and wrongs unrighted.

To the empowering principle that the people can withhold legitimacy, and thus change the world, we now add another: *By deliberately changing their internal images of reality, people can change the world.*

We have spoken earlier of the principle (so puzzling to the M-1 assumptions; so matter-of-fact to the M-3) that what we deeply believe and image to be true tends to become real. But what we deeply believe and image to be true can be changed through changing what we persistently affirm to ourselves. A large portion of the Earth's population is using this principle, unwittingly. In myriad ways we see people reaffirming fear, despair, the inevitability of nuclear holocaust, and their powerlessness to do anything about it. Think of the power this collective negative affirmation wields in bringing about the very thing we fear and wish to avoid. And think of the power it would have if the world were to deliberately affirm the feasibility of "practical peace" within a generation.

One's initial reaction to the idea of imagining a peaceful world is likely to be that it sounds like a simplistic version of "the power of positive thinking." It may seem difficult at first to convince oneself that by such an affirmation one is actually doing anything. True, it may be simplistic to believe that if we all just love one another and speak peace, peace will come into the world. It may be simplistic because powerful unconscious forces make our love ambivalent, and our peace tinged with hidden conflict.

Despite such justifiable caution, it remains the case that a collective belief in the achievability of global peace will contribute toward realizing that goal, just as the collective disbelief is now thwarting it. However, for affirmation to work well we need to be as specific as possible. The affirmation of sustainable peace will be most effective if it is not simply a general "pray for peace" outlook, but rather affirmation of a fairly specific plausible scenario based on an informed view of the factors and forces involved.

People sincerely busy with some sort of peace activity often fail to recognize the subtleties of the principles involved here. Holding a negative image—dwelling on and even trying to generate the fear that a nuclear exchange might come about, or holding anger toward our leaders who continue to escalate the numbers of missiles (while talking arms limitation)—contributes very directly to bringing about what is feared or hated. *Being against war is not at all the same thing as being for peace.* Holding a positive image, vividly imagining a state of peace to exist, contributes to that state's coming about in ways that may seem quite mysterious if we have too limited a belief about the capabilities of the human mind. Because of the interconnectedness of all minds, affirming a positive vision may be about the most sophisticated action any one of us can take.

POLITICS AND VALUES

We have implicitly raised the question of what business might be like if it were restructured on the base of an M-3 set of assumptions—and found, perhaps to our surprise, that it already shows signs of moving in that direction. We raised a similar question regarding development, and saw that although in the past development has been equated with modernization and has tended to overrun and drive out transcendental beliefs in traditional cultures, a small "alternative development" movement is seeking new patterns of development—at least some of which implicitly contain something like the M-3 assumptions. If we now look to political systems, we may notice that there is an element of M-3 hidden away in the orientations of the "Green" parties in various countries.

Green Politics A Portent?

Green politics in West Germany arose out of the feeling that the most fundamental and critical issues of the day were not addressed by the central positions of any of the existing parties. Among the broad spectrum of citizens who rallied during the mid-1970s to stop the spread of nuclear reactors, the pollution of rivers, and the death of the forests, there arose an understanding that we humans are part of nature, not above it; all our complex structure of governmental and economic institutions—indeed human life itself—ultimately depends on wise, respectful interaction with the life-support processes of the planet. As a growing group of people perceived the interconnections among principles of ecological wisdom, sustainable peace, an economy with a future, and a participatory democracy with power channeled directly from the grassroots level, they conceived of Green politics as the political expression of these concerns.

Green-related parties have played significant political roles in fifteen European countries and another half-dozen elsewhere. The Green parties are sometimes misidentified as being on the left. "Left" is usually associated with a tendency toward the welfare state, public ownership of critical industrial and service organizations, and strong emphases on egalitarian and human rights issues. Although Green politics is concerned with human rights and social responsibility, its primary focus is quite different from that of the classical Left. The Left tends to take for granted the goals of technological progress, economic growth, and material standard of living, assuming that increasing wealth will enable resources to be applied to problems of social justice and human rights. Green politics finds a fundamental flaw in this logic, and judges that more fundamental change will be required. As the Green parties tend to claim, "We are neither right nor left; we are in front."

The Green outlook includes emphasis on a holistic view, ecological awareness, ending the nuclear arms race, decentralization, human-scale technologies and enterprises, feminine perspective, trans-materialist beliefs, social responsibility, nonviolent change, and the empowerment of people. There is a keen sensitivity to the destructive aspects of patriarchal industrial society; specialization and bureaucratization; and masculine competitive, aggressive, exploitative values. What is sought is a balance of these values with a more holistic view, and with the feminine nurturing, cherishing, cooperative, conserving values. There is an emphasis on self-realization, transcendent meaning, and inner growth leading to wisdom and compassion. That there is a dimension of spirituality to Green politics seems unquestionable, yet there is a reluctance to identify the movement as such in so many words. The concept of "deep ecology" is one of the adopted ways of talking about spirituality in terms that are inoffensive to those who, for various reasons, eschew religious language. "Deep ecology" goes beyond the scientific framework to a subtle awareness of the oneness of all life, the interdependence of its manifold manifestations, and the irrepressibility of its tendencies toward evolution and transformation.

M-3 In The Founding Of The United States

For the most important example of a political system based on M-3 principles, however, we need to look back two centuries to the early shaping of the United States of America. Most Americans seem unaware that a particular embodiment of the "perennial wisdom" in the Freemasonry of the time was a key factor in the American democratic experiment. The philosophy that underlies Freemasonry has gone by many names since its progenitor appeared in the Egyptian mystery religions. It was a behind-the-scenes influence throughout the development of Western civilization, and in the latter half of the eighteenth century it played a leading role in the emergence of democratic philosophies of government.

Freemasonry as it existed at that time was both esoteric and political (in contrast to contemporary Masonic lodges, which are much more in the nature of social organizations). The essential premise of Freemasonry was that there are transcendental realms of reality in which we coexist, and of which we potentially can have conscious knowledge. While the patterns and forces of these realms are inaccessible to the physical senses, they are available for exploration through looking into the deep mind. They play important roles in shaping evolutionary and human events, and can be called upon for power and guidance.

The Freemasonry network of the eighteenth century transcended national boundaries; there were lodges in Great Britain, France, and Poland as well as America. Freemasonry was concerned with more than the development of individual awareness. Most particularly, its concern focused on the development of human knowledge and the arts, and on the reformation of governments toward a "philosophic commonwealth" and democratic forms.

The most obvious evidence of this influence in the shaping of the United States is in its Great Seal, adopted in essentially its present form in 1782. (Considerable opposition was expressed to the Presidential decision in 1935 to place on the new dollar bill this "dull emblem of a Masonic fraternity," as professor Charles Eliot Norton referred to the central symbol in the reverse side—the unfinished pyramid capped by the "All-seeing Eye.") If one imagines that the founders of this country were a motley citizenry of farmers, shopkeepers, and country gentlemen, the Great Seal symbols from the ancient traditions of Freemasonry seem a puzzling choice. But Benjamin Franklin and George Washington were both active and high-ranking Masons. Of the 56 signers of the Declaration of Independence, at least 50 were Masons; so were all but 5 of the 55 members of the Constitutional Convention. Many Freemasons from other countries supported the American Revolution, including Lafayette, Kosciusko, de Kalb, and Pulaski. Offshoots of the secret Masonic societies of Europe were transplanted to the New World at least 15 years before the Revolution, with the express purpose of initiating a democratic experiment that had not found fertile soil in Europe.

The Great Seal of the United States with its symbolic references to development of individual awareness, human knowledge, and the arts, and to the reformation of governments toward a "philosophic commonwealth."

The symbols of the Great Seal depict a vision that not only sustained and guided the new nation through most of its history, but also for a time provided inspiration to the poor and downtrodden around the world. Bearing in mind that it is the essence of a powerful symbol that it says many things to many levels of the mind (so that any "explanation" of its meaning is necessarily a dilution and distortion), let us examine the symbols of the Great Seal as they appear on the back of any dollar bill.

The most obviously Masonic symbol is the uncompleted pyramid capped by a radiant triangle enclosing the All-seeing Eye, which occupies the center of the reverse side of the seal. Whatever other meanings this ancient symbol may have had (such as significance attached to the numbers of levels and stones; or resemblance to the Great Pyramid of Gizeh, shrine tomb of Hermes who personifies Universal Wisdom), it clearly proclaims that the works of humans (either individual character or external works) are incomplete unless they incorporate divine insight. This symbol is meant to indicate that the nation will flourish only as its leaders are guided by supraconscious intuition.

The phrase *novus ordo seclorum* (from Virgil), meaning a new order of the ages is born, declares that this event is not just the formation of another nation but of a new spiritually based order for the world. The project is launched with confidence because *annuit cœptis*, "He [God] looks with favor upon our undertaking."

Dominating the obverse of the seal is the bird that is now an eagle, but in earlier versions was the Phoenix, the ancient symbol of human aspiration toward universal good, of being reborn through enlightenment and higher awareness. The olive branch and arrows in the bird's talons announce that the new order covets peace but intends to protect itself from those who would destroy it.

E pluribus unum, "unity from many," refers to the nation made up of states, and probably also to the higher unity. The star-studded glory over the bird's head traditionally symbolizes the cosmic vision.

The "great debunking" of religion by M-1 based science that took place over roughly a century extending into the 1960s took its toll as regards the values underlying the great American democratic experiment. By the 1970s, the prevailing mood was largely oblivious to the meaning of the symbols and cynicism with regard to the goals. The power of these symbols on the collective psyche is such, however, that if the American nation is to regain its earlier position of moral leadership in the world it will be through an effort focused around these symbols and meanings, and no other.

LEADING EDGE CHANGE: AN EXAMPLE

We remarked earlier that one might (somewhat paradoxically) anticipate that the world of business, which is so totally a product of the Western industrial paradigm, would at the same time be one of the first sectors to adapt to the new—first co-opting some of its slogans, lifestyles, and superficial values, but in the end being transformed by it. The early signs of this are already apparent in the organizational development and executive development fields. It will be fruitful to look at one example.

Larry Wilson is a several-times successful entrepreneur, earlier the founder of Wilson Learning Corporation, purveying courses in sales, administration, management, and leadership. Upon retiring from that corporation he founded the Pecos River Learning Center on a 2,000-acre ranch in northeastern New Mexico, which aimed at providing advanced training for tomorrow's top executives. Its clients tended to be the no-nonsense managements of large to very large corporations.

Larry had become convinced that a new day is dawning for business leadership. Most of those who passed through his workshops were, too. What they learned is of interest, not only because it points toward new characteristics of the business world, but because it summarizes the key insights of the leading edge of our culture.

The following four "learnings," said Wilson, are the key to successful leadership (and living) in the new era. It will be helpful to think of them as exemplifying the sort of understanding that makes obvious sense from the vantage point of the M-3 assumptions, and would have seemed dubious at best viewed through the M-1 lens.

Trust

Fear and inability to trust are two of the most important limiting factors for executives (and the rest of us). Fear of criticism, of ridicule, of failure keeps us from actualizing our potentialities—to a far greater extent than is immediately apparent. Because we can't trust, we try to do by ourselves what can't be done alone. The most important thing to learn about fear and trust is that both are *choices*—unconscious choices, but choices nonetheless. That is to say, we can choose to trust and not to fear.

One of the good ways to learn about fear and trust is experientially. For example, fear can be faced in attempting to scale a cliff or performing some feat in a high place (with a safety harness), so that one is faced with the necessity of dealing with the fear of (seemingly) risking one's life. Trust is learned in a group activity in which the goal can clearly not be reached without depending on one another. (In one such exercise, the team goes over an eighteen-foot wall without the use of any aiding implements. To do this they have to form a human pyramid to get the first person over—and eventually a human chain to hoist over the last person. The lesson of the necessity for trust and cooperation is learned at a deep experiential level.)

Another effective approach to fear and trust is through affirming something like the following: There is nothing in the universe to fear. I can trust. I can trust my own mind (although the teachings of my culture are that in the unconscious lurk evil and unsavory things, and one must not go exploring without the aid of a psychiatrist). I can trust others (although life seems to present much evidence to the contrary). I can trust the universe to provide for my needs. (We may recall the advice: "Do not be anxious. . . . Consider the lilies in the field, how they grow; they neither toil nor spin; yet . . . even Solomon in all his glory was not arrayed like one of these. . . . Therefore do not be anxious about tomorrow.")

To affirm "I have no fear," or "I trust," is in a sense to lie to myself—just as the athlete is lying to himself when he or she affirms "I am leaping gracefully over the bar set at 7 feet 10 inches," knowing full well that that level exceeds all previous achievement. But the point is that the affirmation amounts to programming oneself to do just that. Similarly, in the process of affirming absence of fear and total trust, one is programming the self to perceive the world as different—and to find it different in experience. (Recall in firewalking the temporary suspension of belief that "burning coals barbecue bare feet" results in immunity to harm.)

Purpose

The second learning is that each of us can discover, deep within ourselves, a sense of purpose—of having chosen to come here to do something. To align our lives with that purpose is the closest thing to a "secret of life" that can be given. To structure an organization around the goal of helping each individual find and act from that deep sense of purpose is to ensure a limitless source of motivation.

Yet we typically experience great resistance to that inner alignment. We do not have to seek very far for the reason. To have the goal of aligning one's desires with the deep inner purpose implies having *no other goals*. No other aims, ambitions, plans, hopes, ideals, desires, preferences, predilections, formulas of morality, reputation for virtue or consistency or good sense, rational analyses of preferred actions— nothing else. (We will recognize the familiar emphasis in the Eastern traditions on nonattachment, or in the Christian tradition on "losing all to find all.") The ego-mind balks, feeling its control threatened.

Again we can use the "reprogramming" power of affirmation and inner imagery. An affirmation such as "I have only the desire to know the deepest part of myself, and to follow that," vividly imagined to be true, and repeated many times daily over months, will produce changes that are startling.

Creating A Vision

The sense of purpose is not specific enough to form a basis for action; it is necessary to create a vision. We do this all the time, without thinking. Often as not the vision does not serve us well— such as the vision "I'm afraid I may fail," or "I am trying hard to achieve" (thus affirming that it is difficult).

Once the vision is created and there is commitment to it, the factors and forces to bring about its realization are already set in motion. "Coincidences," "lucky breaks," and "following hunches" are likely to play a part; actualization of the vision comes about in ways that feel mysteriously like something more than planned steps plus chance events. Exertion is unnecessary—exertion is the inner struggle between conditioning and the deep intuition.

The more vividly and persistently the vision is held, the stronger the tendency for it to actualize. If it is the collective vision of a group or an organization, that is even more powerful. Thus it follows that real leadership is helping the group to create a vision that is as nearly as possible in alignment with their individual sense of purpose, thus ensuring the motivation to achieve it without the need of external carrots or sticks. Effective management seeks to foster commitment to a shared vision of the future and to develop a high degree of alignment around that vision among members at all levels.

The same insight has application in the area of fundamental societal change. The key step in our bringing about change is eschewing the negative visions to which we have unwittingly been contributing, and choosing a vision that befits our inner purpose and that of those around us.

Acting With Feedback

The vision is the basis for action, and action is essential. But because none of us can discern clearly just what action will lead to achievement of the goal, whatever action we take is likely to be off target. The essence of the fourth learning is to consider *whatever* happens—success or failure, good luck or bad, opposition or unexpected help—as simply feedback, informing us on the application of the action.

Thus one is unattached to a specific outcome. It doesn't matter whether the action achieves the goal. It doesn't matter if the action generates opposition, or encounters obstacles, or seems to end in failure. It doesn't even matter if the goal turns out not to be what we really want. Only one thing is essential—the inner decision to follow the deep sense of purpose and to consider all else as feedback from a basically friendly universe.

As this way of life becomes a habit, we look back over our lives and discover much more of a pattern than we were able to discern at the time. Past decisions were somehow made in a way that contributes to our present competence and understanding, even though we were unaware of it at the time. Skills developed along the way, knowledge gained, will all be used in the tasks to which our inner leanings now direct us. Our external lives are much as they were before; enlightenment has not led to the necessity for putting on white robes, gathering followers, and building temples. Life is as it was before—but with a profound difference. It could be characterized as a deep, quiet knowing, and a deep joy. The joy is unaffected by adversity, or apparent failure, or opposition, or criticism—because, again, these are all accepted as feedback signals nudging us toward the path we most deeply desire for ourselves.

Because of the interconnectedness of all minds with the universal mind, we can be sure that the tasks to which we are directed will be most effective in solving the world's fundamental illness, of which hunger and poverty and plague and pestilence and war are all a part. We need not fear that in pursuing our own real self-interest we will fail to contribute maximally to the real self-interest of others.

CONCLUDING THOUGHTS

We have concluded with these four "learnings" because it would be difficult to improve on them as a concise summary of the way of life that comes from, or is implied by, betting one's life on an M-3 set of assumptions. Just random informal conversation is enough to demonstrate that the number of those who are so basing their lives is growing rapidly. The crisis in meaning and values that was so evident in the 1960s is quietly being resolved. What once seemed a conflict between science and religion is being healed by one simple observation: There is no conflict between the "perennial wisdom" of the world's spiritual traditions and a science based on M-3 assumptions. The number of scientists who are reconciling their science with the M-3 assumptions is small, but increasing. Leading-edge institutions such as some small entrepreneurial corporations are choosing corporate goals, following personnel practices, and encouraging leadership in accordance with the same assumptions. Those are the signs that suggest the global mind change is well underway.

It is difficult for any of us to fully comprehend what is undoubtedly true: *If* the basic assumptions underlying modern society are indeed shifting in the way we have suggested, it follows that *society will, only a few generations from now, be as different from modern industrial society as that is from the society of the Middle Ages.* Furthermore, it will be different in ways that we can only vaguely intuit, just as a Renaissance futurist would have had a hard time trying to describe modern society.

We do have an advantage over any other time in history. When other profound change took place, those living through it tended to be unaware of the historical significance, and were aware mostly of the transition pains and difficulties. We are fortunate enough not only to be able to watch major change take place within a single lifetime, but also to possess enough knowledge to have a good picture of what is going on. Our part in it can be exhilarating and fun. Given the choice, why not perceive it that way?

REFERENCES AND FURTHER READING

John Adams, ed., *Transforming Work;* Miles River Press, 1984.

Michael Baigent et al., *The Messianic Legacy;* Dell, 1989.

William Baldwin, *Spirit Releasement Therapy;* Human Potential Foundation Press, Falls Church, Virginia, 1993.

Henri Bergson, *Creative Evolution;* University Press of America, 1984.

Henri Bergson, *The Creative Mind;* The Philosophical Library, 1946.

Morris Berman, *The Reenchantment of the World;* Cornell University Press, 1981.

Thomas Berry, *The Dream of the Earth;* Sierra Club Books, 1988.

David Bohm, *Wholeness and the Implicate Order;* Routledge and Kegan Paul, 1980.

Elise Boulding, *Building a Global Civic Culture;* Syracuse University Press, 1990.

John Briggs and David Peat, *Looking Glass Universe: The Emerging Science of Wholeness;* Simon and Schuster, 1984.

Fritjof Capra, *The Turning Point: Science, Society, and the Rising Culture;* Bantam, 1984.

Bill Devall and George Sessions, *Deep Ecology: Living as if Nature Mattered;* Peregrine Smith, 1985.

Riane Eisler, *The Chalice and the Blade;* Viking, 1987.

Marilyn Ferguson, *The Aquarian Conspiracy: Personal and Social Transformation in the 1980s;* J. P. Tarcher, 1980.

Stephen Jay Gould, *Wonderful Life;* W. W. Norton, 1990.

Willis Harman and Howard Rheingold; *Higher Creativity: Liberating the Unconscious for Breakthrough Insights;* J. P. Tarcher, 1984.

Willis Harman and Jane Clark, eds., *New Metaphysical Foundations of Modern Science;* Institute of Noetic Sciences, 1994.

Willis Harman and Christian de Quincey, *The Scientific Exploration of Consciousness:*

Toward an Adequate Epistemology; Institute of Noetic Sciences report no. CP-6, 1994.

Hazel Henderson, *The Politics of the Solar Age;* Knowledge Systems, Inc., 1981.

Ernest Hilgard, *Divided Consciousness: Multiple Controls in Human Thought and Action;* John Wiley, 1977.

Morton Hunt, *The Universe Within;* Simon & Schuster, 1982.

Robert Hutchins, *The Learning Society;* Praeger, 1968.

Aldous Huxley, *The Perennial Philosophy;* Harper Brothers, 1945.

Brian Inglis, *Natural and Supernatural;* Prism Press, 1992.

William James, *The Varieties of Religious Experience;* Viking Penguin, 1982.

Raynor C. Johnson, *Nurslings of Immortality;* Harper and Brothers, 1957.

John Maynard Keynes, *Essays and Persuasions;* Cambridge University Press, 1978.

Charles Kiefer and Peter Senge, in *Transforming Work;* John D. Adams, ed.; Miles River Press, 1984.

Arthur Koestler, *Beyond Reductionism;* Beacon Press, 1971.

David Korten, *When Corporations Rule the World;* Berrett-Koehler, 1995.

Pat Kubis and Mark Macy, *Conversations Beyond the Light;* Griffin Publishing (Box 11036, Boulder CO 80301), 1995.

Thomas Kuhn, *The Structure of Scientific Revolutions;* 2nd edition; University of Chicago Press, 1970.

James E. Lovelock, *Gaia: A New Look at Life on Earth;* Oxford University Press, 1979.

James E. Lovelock, "Geophysiology: A New Look at Earth Science," *Bull. Amer. Meteorological Society;* vol. 67, no. 4, April 1986, pp. 392-397.

David Loye, *The Evolutionary Outrider: The Impact of the Human Agent on Evolution;* Praeger, 1998.

David Loye, *Darwin's Lost Theory;* forthcoming.

Winafred Lucas, *Regression Therapy: A Handbook for Professionals;* Deep Forest Press, 1993.

Abraham Maslow, *Toward a Psychology of Being;* 2nd edition; Van Nostrand Reinhold, 1968.

Robert Muller, *New Genesis: Shaping a Global Spirituality;* Doubleday, 1979.

Lewis Mumford, *The Transformations of Man;* Harper Brothers, 1956.

Frederic W. H. Myers, *Human Personality and Its Survival of Bodily Death* (abridged); Peregrin Books, 1992.

Jacob Needleman, *A Sense of the Cosmos;* E. P. Dutton, 1976.

Perry Pascarella, *The New Achievers;* Free Press, 1984.

F. David Peat, *Synchronicity: The Bridge Between Matter and Mind;* Bantam, 1987.

Kenneth Pelletier, *A New Age: Problems and Potentials;* Robert Briggs Associates, 1985.

Michael Polanyi, *Personal Knowledge;* University of Chicago Press, 1962.

Karl Popper, *Conjectures and Reflections: The Growth of Scientific Knowledge,* 2nd edition; Basic Books 1965.

Karl R. Popper and John C. Eccles, *The Self and Its Brain;* Springer International, 1981.

Frank Putnam, *Diagnosis and Treatment of Multiple Personality Disorder;* Guilford Press, 1989.

Milton Rokeach, *The Open and Closed Mind;* Basic Books, 1960.

Theodore Roszak, *Person-Planet: The Creative Disintegration of Industrial Society;* Anchor/Doubleday, 1978.

E. F. Schumacher, *Small is Beautiful: Economics as if People Mattered;* Abacus, 1974.

Rupert Sheldrake, *A New Science of Life;* Frederick Muller, 1981.

Henryk Skolimowski, *Participatory Mind;* Arkana (Penguin), 1994.

Pitirim Sorokin, *The Crisis of Our Age;* E. P. Dutton, 1941.

Roger Sperry, "Changing Priorities," *Annual Review of Neuroscience* (1981), vol. 4, pp. 1-15.

Roger Sperry, "Structure and Significance of the Consciousness Revolution," *Jour. Mind and Behavior;* Winter 1987, vol. 8, no. 1, pp. 37-66.

Ian Stevenson, *Children Who Remember Previous Lives;* University Press of Virginia, 1987.

Charles Tart, *Waking Up: Overcoming the Obstacles to Human Potential* (based on the principles of G. I. Gurdjieff); New Science Library/Shambhala, 1986.

Pierre Teihard de Chardin, *The Phenomenon of Man;* Harper Torchbooks, 1961.

Roger Terry, *Economic Insanity;* Berrett-Koehler, 1995.

Robert Theobald, *The Rapids of Change: Social Entrepreneurship in Turbulent Times;* Knowledge Systems, Inc., 1987.

Alvin Toffler, *The Third Wave;* William Morrow, 1980.

Arnold Toynbee, *A Study of History* (abridgement by D. C. Somervell); Oxford University Press, 1947.

United Nations, *Charter* (1945) and *Universal Declaration of Human Rights* (1948); Available from United Nations, New York.

Paul Wachtel, *The Poverty of Affluence;* New Society Publishers, 1989.

Renée Weber, *Dialogues with Scientists and Sages: The Search for Unity;* Routledge and Kegan Paul, 1986.

Ken Wilber, *Eye to Eye: The Quest for the New Paradigm;* Anchor/Doubleday, 1983.

Ken Wilber, "The Great Chain of Being," *Journal of Humanistic Psychology;* Vol. 33, no. 3; Summer 1993, pp. 52-65. (Also in Roger Walsh and Frances Vaughan, *Paths Beyond Ego: The Transpersonal Vision;* J. P. Tarcher, 1993.)

Ken Wilber, *Sex, Ecology, Spirituality: The Spirit of Evolution;* Shambhala, 1995.

INDEX

Abolitionist movement, 131
Aborigines, Australian, 135, 175
Adams, John, 195
Affirmation, 69–70, 73–74, 145, 192
Agriculture, organic, 134
Alice in Wonderland, 123
Altered states of consciousness, 96, 136
American Medical Association, 42
American Revolution, 188
Amerindian, *see Indian, American*
Amnesia under hypnosis, 60
Analgesia under hypnosis, 60–61
    and employment, 156–159, 176
    and metaphysics, 28–29
Animal magnetism, 60
Animism, 100
Annual Review of Neuroscience, 9
Anthroposophy, 179
Appropriate technology, 139-140, 171
Aquarian Conspiracy, The (Ferguson), 130, 195
Aristotle, 4, 102
    aspects of, 149–194
Astrology, 100
Astronomy, 106
Attention, 43–45, 95
Authority, external versus internal, 159
Autogenic training, 77
Automatic writing, 45, 72, 85-86
Autopoiesis, 92
Autosuggestion, 62
Babylonians, 106
Bacon, Sir Francis, 6, 104, 105, 109, 110
Baigent, Michael, 29, 195
Baldwin, William, 88, 195
    banking in, 171–174
Banking, 171–174
Basques, 135
Becker, Ernest, 27
Bedouin, 175
Behaviorism, 10, 93, 98, 110, 112
Belief systems, 12–18, 131–132
Belief, unconscious, 12–18, 78
Beliefs, collective, 182–185
Bell's theorem, 120–121
Benoit, Hubert, 33
Bergson, Henri, 28–29, 49, 195

Berman, Morris, 195
Berry, Thomas, 195
Beyond Human Personality (Cummins), 86–87
Beyond Reductionism (Koestler), 195
"Big Bang" theory of creation, 47, 160
Biofeedback, 17–18, 67, 78-79
Biological sciences, 92-101, 102
Black Elk, 142-143
Bohm, David, 121, 195
Bohr, Niels, 59, 120–121
Boulding, Elise, *xiv,* 195
Boyle, Robert, 29, 102
Brain studies, 8–9
Briggs, John, 195
Bruno, Giordano, 57, 103
Buddhism, 56, 63, 93, 96, 101
Building a Global Civic Culture (Boulding), *xiv,*
195
Business community
California Institute of Technology, 8
Capra, Fritjof, 130, 195
Causality
    central myth of, 160–161
Chalice and the Blade, The (Eisler), 138, 195
    challenges to, 150–194
    change in, 144–147, 189-200, 194
"Changing Priorities," *The Annual Review of Neuroscience* (1981) (Sperry), 8–9, 23, 196
Channeling, 51, 66
Chicanos, 135
Children Who Remember Previous Lives (Stevenson),
87, 196
China, 174
Choice, 80
Christianity, 6, 69, 74, 136
Civil rights movement, 131
Clairvoyance, 51, 60
Clark, Jane, 195
Community, 130, 134
Complementarity principle (Bohr), 59, 120–121
Congressional Institute for the Future, *xiv*
Connectedness, 159
Connection, necessary, 107
Consciousness as a causal reality, 8–12, 19–34,
88, 95, 113–115, 159, 160
Consciousness, 23, 30, 43–44, 72, 77–78, 112–

115, 141, 142-143
Consciousness, unembodied, 84–88
Constitutional Convention, US, 188
Contiguity, 107
Conversations Beyond the Light (Kubis and Macy), 87, 195
Copernican Revolution, 2–10, 11, 18, 33
Copernicus, Nicolaus, 2–5, 7, 11
Cosmologies, 111-112
Course in Miracles, A, 33
Creative Evolution (Bergson), 49, 195
Creative/intuitive mind, 69–70, 79–80
Creativity, 67–73, 79–80, 144–145
Crick, Sir Francis, 26
Crisis of Our Age, The (Sorokin), 128, 196
Croatians, 135
Cuckoo, European, 46
Cummins, Geraldine, 86
Daisyworld, 141-142
Darwin's Lost Theory (Loye), xv, 196
Darwin, Sir Charles, 47–48, 57, 99-100, 107
de Quincey, Christian, 112, 195
de Kalb, Baron Johann, 188
Death, existence after, 84–88
Debt, 171–174
Decentralization, 137, 139–140
Declaration of Independence, The, 188
Dee, John, 104
Deep ecology, 133–134, 186
Deep Ecology: Living As If Nature Mattered (Devall and Sessions), 195
Defense, US Department of, 180
Dematerialization, 51, *see also Paranormal phenomena*
Desargues, 104
Descartes, René, 21, 31, 102, 104, 105, 106, 107-108, 110
Devall, Bill, 195
Developing world, 153–156, 174–178
Dialogue on the Two Chief Systems of the World (Galileo), 4–5
Dialogues with Scientists and Sages: The Search for Unity (Weber), 196
Discourse on Method (Descartes), 106
Divided Consciousness: Multiple Controls in Human Thought and Action (Hilgard), 44, 195
downward and upward, 32, 97–98, 114, 115
"Dominator" model of society, 138
"Downward causation," 32, 97–98, 114, 116
Dr Jekyll and Mr Hyde, 63
Dream of the Earth, The (Berry), 195
Dreaming, 31, 34, 77
Dualism, 30, 31, 104–105

Eastern Europe, 132
Eccles, Sir John, 31, 44, 196
Eco-feminist movement, 131
Ecology of cultures, 139–140
Economic growth, 156–159, 165, 168–169
Economic Insanity (Terry), 196
Economics, 121–126, 151, 155–156, 161, 162–178
Efficient cause, 102, 106, 109
Egyptian mystery religions, 187
Eighteenth century, 21, 59, 107–108, 162–163
Einstein, Albert, 59
Einstein-Podolsky-Rosen paradox, 120
Eisler, Riane, 138, 195
Elliotson, John, 60
Embryology, 109
Emerson, Ralph Waldo, 77–78
Employment/underemployment/unemployment, 156–157, 166–169, 176, *see also Work*
Empowerment, sense of, 136–137
Enlightenment, 33–34
Environmental movement, 131, 133–134
Environmental sustainability, 150, 152–153
Epistemology, 29
Equity/inequity, 150, 153–156, 157–158
Esdaile, James, 60
Esoteric systems, 33, 50, 74–76, 179
Essays and Persuasions (Keynes), 162, 195
Ethics, 155–156
European Convention for the Protection of Human Rights and Fundamental Freedoms (1950), 154
Evolution, 45–49, 93, 100–102, 160
Evolutionary Outrider: The Impact of the Human Agent on Evolution (Loye), xv, 196
Exceptional capabilities, 49–53
Extrasensory perception (ESP), 50–51, 60–61, 78
Eye to Eye: The Quest for the New Paradigm (Wilber), 196
Eysenck, H. J., 37, 52
Fear of death, 84
Fear, 146, 190-191
Federal Reserve, 172
Feedback, 193–194
Ferguson, Marilyn, 130, 195
Fermat, 104
Fields, 46–47, 108
Fifteenth century, 21, 103
Final cause, 102–103, 106, 109
Firewalking, 16–17, 52, 67–68, 191
Food and Drug Administration, US, 42
Formal cause, 102, 109
Formative causation, 46

Fortune, 145
Fourteenth century, 21
Franklin, Benjamin, 29, 60, 188
Frauenberg, Cathedral of, 2
Free will, 43–45, 98
Freemasons, 29, 179, 187–189
French Academy, 57–58
Freud, Sigmund, 12, 57, 76, 80, 107
    fundamentalist, 99, 136
Gaia hypothesis, 93, 140-143
Gaia: A New Look at Life on Earth (Lovelock), 93, 195
Galileo, 3, 4–5, 57, 104, 105
"Geophysiology: A New Look at Earth Science," *Bull. Amer. Meteorological Society* (Lovelock), 195
Germany, West, 185–186
Gestalt, 10, 56
Giorgi, Francesco, 103
"Global casino," 173
Gnosis, 33, 79, 103
Gnostics, 179
Gould, Stephen Jay, 100, 195
Great Seal of the United States, 187–189
Great Society, 165
Greece and Greek culture, 3, 22, 106, 140, 143–144, 170
Green politics, 132, 185–186
Greenhouse effect, 142
Greens Party, *see Green politics*
Grimaldi, Francesco, 58
Gurney, Edmund, 86
Hallucination, 60
Harman, Willis W., *xiii–xv*, 112, 195
Harmonia mundi, De (Giorgi), 104
Harmony, 137–138
Harvard Business Review, 145
Harvey, Sir William, 57, 102–103
Hauntings, *see Paranormal phenomena*
Healing, 38–42, 67–68, 99
Healthcare, holistic, 93, 133, 134
Hebb, D. O., 61
Henderson, Hazel, *xiv-xvii*, 195
Hermes, 189
Hermetic tradition, 29
"Hidden observer," 45
Higher Creativity (Harman and Rheingold), 195
Hilgard, Ernest, 44–45, 195
    history and philosophy, 101–115, *see also Consciousness as a causal reality*
    history of work in, 162–165
Hobbes, Thomas, 107
Holarchy, 90-101
Holistic models, 90-92, 113–115

Holon, 90-91, 92-93
Hopi, 175
Hubbard, Alfred M., dedication
Hubris, *xv*
Human Personality and Its Survival of Bodily Death (Myers), 86, 196
Human rights, 154–155, 180
    human, 92-101
Hume, David, 106, 109
Hunt, Morton, 43
Hutchins, Robert, 143–144, 195
Huxley, Aldous, 75–76, 195
Hypersuggestibility and compliance, 60
Hypnosis, 15–16, 27, 77, 41, 44–45, 60–61, 69, 78, 100
Hypnosis, cultural, 17, 33, 78
Iberia, 104
Identity, 134–135
Imagery, inner, 62, 69–70, 73, 145, 192
Immune system, 38–42, 91, 94, 97
In Search of the Miraculous (Ouspensky), 33
    in science, 101–115
India, 17, 22, 154, 174
Indians, American, 135, 142–143, 175
Industrial-society paradigm, 122-130
Industry Week, 146
Information Society, 165, 166, 169
Inglis, Brian, 86, 195
"Inner self helper," 65
Inspiration, 66
Instinct, 45–49, 90, 97, 99, 100, 112
International Labour Organization, UN, 154, 176
Introduction to Metaphysics (Bergson), 28–29
Introspectionism, 10, 56
Intuition, 66–68, 70–73, 144–145, 159
Jaeger, Werner, 144
James, William, 74, 85, 113, 195
Johnson, Raynor C., 86, 195
Justice, 146, 149–152
Kalb, Baron Johann de, 188
Kant, Immanuel, 109
Kelvin, William, Lord, 59
Kepler, Johannes, 3–4
Keynes, John Maynard, 162, 164, 168, 195
Kiefer, Charles, 145, 195
Kierkegaard, Søren, 72
Koestler, Arthur, 90, 195
Kornhuber, H. H., 44
Korten, David, 130, 195
Kosciusko, Thaddeus, 188
Krebiozen, 41–42
Kubis, Pat, 87, 195

Kuhn, Thomas, 8, 195
Labor movement, 131
Lafayette, Marquis de, 188
Lamarck, Jean Baptiste Chevalier de, 48
Lavoisier, Antoine, 60, 57–58
Learning Society, The (Hutchins), 143–144, 195
Learning society, the, 143–144, 170–171
    learning, 143–144, 170–171
Legitimacy challenge, 132
Legitimacy of war, removal of, 179–182
Leibniz, 105
Leigh, 29
Levitation, *see Paranormal phenomena*
    life, 92-101, 102-103
Light, scientific study of, 58–59
Lodge, Sir Oliver, 85
Logical empiricism, 110–111
Looking Glass Universe: The Emerging Science of Wholeness (Briggs and Peat), 195
Lourdes (France) International Medical Commission, 99
Lovelock, James E., 93, 140–142, 195
Loye, David, *xv*, 196
Lucas, Winafred, 87, 195
Lull, Ramon, 103
Luther, Martin, 104
Macy, Mark, 87, 195
Malinowski, Bronislaw, 28
Management, 145–147
Marginalization, 150–151
Mark, Book of, 69
Marx, Karl, 164, 183
Mary, the Virgin, 57
Maslow, Abraham, 70, 139, 195
Masons, *see Freemasons*
Material cause, 102, 109
Materialization, 51, *see also Paranormal phenomena*
Maudsley Hospital, London, 52
Maxwell, James, 59
McDougall, William, 46–47, 48
Mead, Margaret, 157
Meaning, search for, 135–136
Medici court, 103
Medieval period, *see Middle Ages*
Meditation, 77, 75, 131, 136
Mediumship, 51, 66, 85–87
Mentalism, 32
Mersenne, 104
Metaphors, 113
Metaphysic M-1 (Materialistic Monism), 31, 32, 42, 43–45, 49–50, 128, 142, 189
Metaphysic M-2 (Dualism), 30, 31, 104–105

Metaphysic M-3 (Transcendental Monism), 30, 31, 32–35, 52–53, 136, 137, 138, 143, 147, 179, 185, 194
Metaphysical perspectives, 28–34
Metaphysics M-1, M-2, M-3, 28–35, 38, 42, 47, 52–53, 72–73, 137, 178–179, 184
Meteorites, 57–58
Middle Ages, 7, 20–21, 22, 57, 85, 181, 194
Mill, John Stuart, 107
Mind-body interaction in healing, 38–42
Mitchell, Edgar, *x*
Models, 113-114
Money, 171–174
Moray, Robert, 29
Morphogenesis, 99
Morphogenic fields, 46–47
Muller, Robert, 195
Multiple personality, 63–67, 96
Mumford, Lewis, 1, 7, 119, 129, 143, 196
Myers, F.W.H., 60, 85–86, 87, 196
Mystery religions, 179, 187
Myth, of modern society, 160–161
National Aeronautics and Space Administration, US, 141
Native American, *see Indian, American*
Natural and Supernatural (Inglis), 195
Nature philosophy, Renaissance, 103
Near-death experiences, 31, 65
Needham, Joseph, 27
Needleman, Jacob, 196
Nehru, Jawaharlal, 154
Nervous system, 38–41, 44
Neuropeptides, 40
New Achievers, The (Pascarella), 146, 196
New Age, A: Problems and Potentials (Pelletier), 196
New Genesis: Shaping a Global Spirituality (Muller), 195
New International Economic Order (NIEO), 154, 176–177
New Metaphysical Foundations of Modern Science (Harman and Clark), 195
New Science of Life, A (Sheldrake), 45–46, 196
Newton, Sir Isaac, 4, 29, 58, 105, 106, 107
Nineteenth century, 21, 60–61, 85, 107, 108, 163
Nobel Prize of 1981, 8
Nonattachment (Buddhism), 63, 96, 192
Norton, Charles Eliot, 187
Nuclear weapons, 122, 124, 126, 132, 136, 140, 158, 179–180, 182–183, 185
Nurslings of Immortality (Johnson), 86, 195
Objectivity in science, 56–63, 84, 92, 95–96, 105, 113, 159–160

Observers, 114
On the Revolutions of the Celestial Spheres (Copernicus), 4
Oneness, 78–79
"On the Need to Know and the Fear of Knowing" (Maslow), 70
Ontology, 29, 101-102, 103, 109, 115–116
Open and Closed Mind, The (Rokeach), 12, 196
Open inquiry, 113
Opium, effect of, 59–60
Organic agriculture, 134
    origins of, 124–130
Ouspensky, P. D., 33
Out-of-body experience, 65
Paideia, 143–144, 170
Panpsychism, 32
Paradigm change, 8–12, 121–137, 149–194
Paradigm shift, *see Paradigm change*
Paranormal phenomena, 11, 30, 37, 49–53, 60, 61, 84–88
Parapsychology, 107, *see also Paranormal phenomena*
Parsimony, principle of, 100-101
Participatory methodology, 114
Participatory Mind (Skolimowski), 114, 196
"Partnership" model of society, 138
Pascal, 104
Pascarella, Perry, 146, 196
Past lives therapies, 87-88, *see also Paranormal phenomena*
Pasteur, Louis, 57
Peace movement, 130, 131
Peace, 179–180, 182–185
Peat, F. David, 195, 196
Pecos River Learning Center, 190
Peirce, Charles Sanders, 110
Pelletier, Kenneth, 196
Perception, 78
Perennial Philosophy, The (Huxley), 75–76, 195
"Perennial wisdom," 31, 73–81, 115–116, 121, 187, 194
Person-Planet: The Creative Disintegration of Industrial Society (Roszak), 130, 196
Personal Knowledge (Polanyi), 196
Phenomenology, 10, 56, 113, 114
Phenomenon of Man, The (Teilhard de Chardin), 49, 196
Philosophy of science, 101–115
    philosophy of, 101–115
    physical, 92-101
Placebo effect, 41, 61
Plato, 108–109
Poland, 4, 187

Polanyi, Michael, 196
Politics of the Solar Age (Henderson), *xiv*
Pollution index, 157
Poltergeists, *see Paranormal phenomena*
Popper, Sir Karl, 44, 92, 109, 111, 196
Populist movement, 131
Positivism, 9–10, 30, 31, 38, 43, 84, 91, 110–111, 112, 125, 136, 159–160
Postmodern age, 32, 130, 144
Poverty of Affluence (Wachtel), 196
Precognition, 51, *see also Paranormal phenomena*
Primitive cultures, 17, 24, 30, 131, 137, 175
Principle of local causes, 120–121
Production-focused society, 158–159, 169
    proposed levels of, 92–101
    proposed, 112–115
Psychedelics, 131, 136
Psychic healing, 51, 60
Psychic research, *see Paranormal phenomena*
Psychic surgery, *see Paranormal phenomena*
Psychoanalysis, 85
Psychokinesis, 51, 62, *see also Paranormal phenomena*
Ptolemy, 2–3, 4, 16, 42
Pulaski, Count Casimir, 188
Purpose, 191–192
Qualitative methodology, 114
Quantum physics, 120–121
Quebecois, 135
Quine, W.V.O., 110
Radical empiricism, 113
Radical impersonalism, 105
Radicalization, 131
Rapids of Change, The (Theobald), 196
Reagan, Ronald, *xiv*
Reductionism, 9–10, 20, 38, 42, 88, 92, 94, 97, 105, 110, 112, 121, 125, 159–160
Reenchantment of the World, The (Berman), 195
Reformation, Protestant, 7, 22, 104
Regeneration, in healing, 42, 97
Regression Therapy: A Handbook for Professionals (Lucas), 87, 195
Reincarnation, 31, 87-88
Relationship, 134
Remote viewing, 17, 60
Renaissance nature philosophy, 103
Renaissance, 108, 194
Replicability in science, 56–63, 96
Resistance, 79
Retrocognition, 51, *see also Paranormal phenomena*
Reuchlin, Johannes, 103, 104
Revelation, 66

Rheingold, Howard, 195
Road to Immortality, The (Cummins), 86
Roentgen, Wilhem Conrad, 59
Rokeach, Milton, 12, 196
    role of, 151–152
Rolfs, Henry, dedication
Roman Empire, 7, 181
Rosicrucians, 29, 179
Roszak, Theodore, 130, 196
Royal Society, British, 29, 58–59
Rule of Law, 154–155
Russell, Bertrand, 26
Saint-Exupéry, Antoine de, 55, 77
Salk, Jonas, *xiv*
Sanai of Afghanistan, 33
Scholasticism, 5, 20, 57
Schumacher, E. F., 171, 175, 196
Science
Sciences
Scientific causality, philosophy of, 101-112
Scientific Exploration of Consciousness, The: Toward an Adequate Epistemology (Harman and de Quincey), 195
Scientific method, 89, 110
Scientific revolution, *xvii*, 5, 22, 85, 105–106
Scientific worldview, 159–161
Self and Its Brain, The (Eccles and Popper), 44, 196
Self-realization, 139
Semmelweis, Ignaz Philipp, 57
Senge, Peter, 145,195
Sense of the Cosmos, A (Needleman), 196
Seventeenth century, 8, 20–21, 31, 57, 59, 104, 105–107, 108–109
Sex, Ecology, Spirituality: The Spirit of Evolution (Wilber), 90, 196
Shamanism, 50, 76, 100
Sheldrake, Rupert, 45–47, 99, 196
Sherrington, Sir Charles, 25–26
Sidgwick, Henry, 86
Simplicius, 5
Sixteenth century, 104
Skinner, B. F., 26
Skolimowski, Henryk, 114, 196
Skutch, Judith (Whitson), dedication
Slavery, 181
Small is Beautiful: Economics As If People Mattered (Schumacher), 175, 196
Smith, Adam, 164
Social and Cultural Dynamics (Sorokin), 128
Social movements, 130–137, 139
Society
Society for Psychical Research, 83

Socrates, 66
Soft energy path, 134, 176
Solomon, 191
Sorcery, 50
Sorokin, Pitirim, 128, 196
South Africa, 133
Sperry, Roger, 8–9, 11, 19, 23, 32, 97, 196
Spirit attachment, 88
Spirit Releasement Therapy (Baldwin), 88, 195
    spiritual, 92-101
Spiritualism, 50
Stevenson, Ian, 87, 196
Stress disorders, 40–41
Stress, 11, 40–41, 91
Stress-response system, 38–39
"Structure and Significance of the Consciousness Revolution," *Journal of Mind and Behavior* (Sperry), 196
Structure of Scientific Revolutions, The (Kuhn), 8, 195
Study of History , A (Toynbee), 128–129, 196
Succession, 108
Supreme Court, US, 99
Survival after death, 84–88
Sustainability, 150, 152–153
Synchronicity: The Bridge Between Mind and Matter (Peat), 196
System of Logic, A (Mill), 108
Tart, Charles, 196
Technology assessment movement, 136
Teilhard de Chardin, Pierre, 49, 196
Teleology, 6, 94, 106
Telepathy, 51, 60, 78–79
Teleportation, 51
Temple, Paul N., dedication
Terry, Roger, 196
Theobald, Robert, 196
Theosophy, 179
Third Wave, The (Toffler), 129–130, 196
Third World groups, 135, 137
Thirteenth century, 21, 104
Thought photography, 51, *see also Paranormal phenomena*
Tibetan Buddhism, 56, 93, 101
Toffler, Alvin, 129–130, 196
Toward a Psychology of Being (Maslow), 70, 195
Toynbee, Arnold, 128–129, 196
Transcendentalists, 179
Transformations of Man, The (Mumford), 7, 129, 196
Transforming Work (Adams), 145, 195
Transpersonal psychology, 75, 90, 131, 159
Treatise of Human Nature (Hume), 106

Trobriand Islanders, 28
Trust, 190–191
Turning Point, The (Capra), 130, 195
Twelfth century, 21
Twentieth century, 18, 60, 85, 108–111, 120, 134–135, 161, 165
Unconscious belief, 12–18, 78–79
Unconscious knowing, 67–68
Unconscious mind, 87, 88, *see also Creative/intuitive mind*
Unembodied existence, 84–88
Unidentified Flying Objects (UFOs), 58
United Nations Charter, 180, 196
United Nations Conference on Climate Change, *xiv–xv*
United Nations, 154, 176, 180
United States
Unity of experience, 114–115
Universal Declaration of Human Rights, 154, 180
Universal Mind, 80, 193
Universe Within, The (Hunt), 43, 195
    unspoken assumptions of, 24–28
Upanishads, 65
"Upward causation," 32, 97–98, 114, 115
USSR Communist Party, 132
Varela, Francisco, 92
Varieties of Religious Experience, The (James), 74, 195
Vietnam War, 136, 181
Virgil, 149, 189
Virgin Mary, the, 57
Vision quests, 76
Vitalism, 99, 108, 117
Vivekananda, Swami, 34
Volition, 43–45, 95
Wachtel, Paul, 196
Waking Up: Overcoming the Obstacles to Human Potential (Tart), 196
War Department, US, *see Defense, US Department of*
War, 179–182
Washington, George, 188
Weber, Renée, 196
West Germany, *see Germany, West*
West, Philip, 41–42
When Corporations Rule the World (Korten), 130, 195
Whewell, 107
White House Conference on the Industrial World Ahead, *xiii–xiv*
Whitson, Judith Skutch, dedication
Wholeness and the Implicate Order (Bohm), 195

Wholeness, search for, 133–134
Wilber, Ken, 90, 115, 196
Wilson Learning Corporation, 190
Wilson, Larry, 190
Witchcraft, 60, 100
Women's movement, 130–131, 135, 139
Women, 130–132, 135, 137, 139
Wonderful Life (Gould), 100, 195
Wordsworth, William, 87
Work, 145, 156–159, 161–171, 177–178
World macroproblem, 119–147
Worldview challenge, 159–160
Wren, Christopher, 29
Writing, automatic, 45, 72, 85–86
Yoga, 17, 76, 131, 136
Yoga, tantric, 50
Young, Thomas, 58

WILLIS HARMAN (1918-1997)

Widely recognized as one of the practical visionaries of our time, Willis Harman was deeply committed to working with the global transformation that is evidently part of our immediate future. He exemplified the integration of spiritual and intellectual knowing that is at the heart of the work of the Institute of Noetic Sciences, where he was president until his death in 1997.

For 16 years, Harman was Senior Social Scientist at SRI International, a global-futurist think-tank in Menlo Park, California. He was emeritus professor of Engineering-Economic Systems at Stanford University, and a member of the Board of Regents of the University of California.

His books include *An Incomplete Guide to the Future, Changing Images of Man, Higher Creativity, Paths to Peace, New Metaphysical Foundations of Science,* and *Biology Revisioned,* as well as a number of monographs including "A Reexamination of the Metaphysical Foundations of Modern Science" and "The Scientific Exploration of Consciousness."

About The Institute Of Noetic Sciences

An Overview

The Institute of Noetic Sciences (IONS) is a research foundation, an educational institution and a membership organization. It was founded in 1973 and currently has approximately 50,000 members worldwide.

The word *noetic* is derived from the Greek word *nous*, for mind, intelligence or ways of knowing. The "noetic sciences" bring the full range of knowing to the interdisciplinary study of consciousness, the mind, and human potential. Research topics at the Institute range from mind-body health and healing, meditation, and exceptional human abilities, to emerging paradigms in science, business, and society. The Institute conducts its research by providing seed grants to leading-edge scientific and scholarly researchers, organizing lectures, and sponsoring conferences. New ideas are disseminated through publication of selected books, a review, research reports, and a monograph series commissioned from leading scientists, philosophers and scholars. The Institute also publishes a member magazine, and supports a variety of member research projects, networking opportunities, and local group activities.

The Central Role Of Research At The Institute

Research informs the Institute's work. The Institute's seed grants build and sustain fruitful relationships with key researchers and organizations doing work in the field of consciousness studies, resulting in a stimulating cross-fertilization of ideas. While maintaining scientific rigor and scholarly integrity, these working partnerships are enlivened by the creativity, vision, and hope that inevitably accompany the exploration of new ideas.

The Institute's research strategy supports ideas and individuals judged to be both at the forefront of the exploration of consciousness, and particularly significant to its understanding. This strategy incorporates the following elements:

- Identifying key ideas and researchers

- Providing modest seed grants to support their work

- Linking them to other researchers
- Supporting recognition and legitimacy by publishing their work and providing opportunities to speak
- Creating a forum for open exploration of innovative ideas
- Assisting in making key ideas accessible to an informed public.

Scope Of Research

The Institute has a threefold interest in the exploration of consciousness:

I. Emerging Worldviews: Many agree society is undergoing a profound transition. The Institute has been addressing this transformation for two and a half decades, and today it continues to occupy a central place in research efforts. Unlike many other institutions in our society, the Institute is addressing social change at the level of worldview, beliefs and values. It is inquiring into the process of transformation for the individual, for organizations, and for key sectors of society (business, medicine, and science). The Institute's work is based on a belief that this transformation is fundamentally about an emerging worldview in which science and spirit are understood as integrated aspects within a unified whole, leading to such emerging concepts as "sustainable development" and "deep ecology."

II. The Nature Of Consciousness: Work here focuses on detailed inquiries into ancient consciousness traditions, as well as recent Western scientific work arising from quantum physics, biology and the neurosciences. The Causality Project, a current major program, involves leading Western scientists in questioning the metaphysics of contemporary science based on challenges arising from within science itself. Research into consciousness over twenty-five years points out the inadequacies of our Western scientific paradigm and strongly confirms the need to identify a suitable answer to the question: How is knowledge validated in subjective areas? The Institute believes that the time is opportune to examine the fundamental assumptions on which Western science has been based for hundreds of years, and to forge an alternative set of assumptions— and a new epistemology which offers the tools currently lacking to strengthen inquiries into consciousness, mind, spirit and related areas.

III. Applied Research Areas: The third major focus is in selected applied research areas that are particularly relevant to emerging worldviews and an understanding of consciousness. Foremost among these has been work in health and healing. IONS has funded research in imagery, biofeedback, psychoneuroimmunology (the role of the mind, emotions, beliefs, and personality in physical health), the role of the spirit in health and healing, the importance of "connection" (family, community, and support groups). Documenting and attempting to understand spontaneous remissions has been an area of special focus. Altruism has been a research interest both because it appears to be a natural outcome of personal transformation and because research in healing suggests that altruism positively affects health. The role of consciousness in human performance has included the study of peak performance in athletics and the work place, remote viewing, psychokinesis, and channeling. The Institute also has maintained a long-standing research program into different states of consciousness, as exemplified by meditation and the exploration of other altered states. Redefining health and healing also involves reconceptualizing death; the role of spirit in our lives and the question of survival after death of the physical body are long-standing and current research interests.

The Role Of Research
In Membership At The Institute

Institute members are at the forefront of positive social change—committed to their own development and to societal transformation. In partnership with members, the Institute explores both the inner dimensions of human experience and the implications of consciousness research for personal and social change. We feel it is important to link what we do to the growing segment of contemporary society committed to exploring these ideas and integrating them into the social structures of our time. This grounding effect delivers an essential element of practicality to our work. As a consequence, the Institute's efforts are tied to fundamental changes as they emerge both in research and in members' lives.

Berrett-Koehler Publishers

BERRETT-KOEHLER is an independent publisher of books, periodicals, and other publications at the leading edge of new thinking and innovative practice on work, business, management, leadership, stewardship, career development, human resources, entrepreneurship, and global sustainability.

Since the company's founding in 1992, we have been committed to supporting the movement toward a more enlightened world of work by publishing books, periodicals, and other publications that help us to integrate our values with our work and work lives, and to create more humane and effective organizations.

We have chosen to focus on the areas of work, business, and organizations, because these are central elements in many people's lives today. Furthermore, the work world is going through tumultuous changes, from the decline of job security to the rise of new structures for organizing people and work. We believe that change is needed at all levels—individual, organizational, community, and global—and our publications address each of these levels.

We seek to create new lenses for understanding organizations, to legitimize topics that people care deeply about but that current business orthodoxy censors or considers secondary to bottom-line concerns, and to uncover new meaning, means, and ends for our work and work lives.

See next page for other books from Berrett-Koehler Publishers

Other leading-edge business books
from Berrett-Koehler Publishers

Building a Win-Win World

Life Beyond Global Economic Warfare

Hazel Henderson

WORLD-RENOWNED futurist Hazel Henderson extends her twenty-five years of work in economics to examine the havoc the current economic system is creating at the global level. She demonstrates how the global economy is unsustainable because of its negative effects on employees, families, communities, and the ecosystem, and shows that win-win strategies can become the norm at every level when people see the true current and future costs of short-sighted, narrow economic policies.

Hardcover, 320 pages, 6/96 • ISBN 1-881052-90-7 CIP
Item no. 52907-249 $29.95

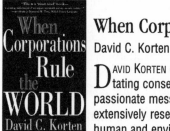

When Corporations Rule the World

David C. Korten

DAVID KORTEN offers an alarming exposé of the devastating consequences of economic globalization and a passionate message of hope in this well-reasoned, extensively researched analysis. He documents the human and environmental consequences of economic globalization, and explains why human survival depends on a community-based, people-centered alternative.

Paperback, 384 pages, 9/96 • ISBN 1-887208-01-1 CIP
Item no. 0801-249 $19.95

Hardcover, 09/95 • ISBN 1-887208-00-3 CIP • Item no. 08003-249 $29.95

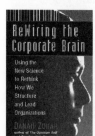

Rewiring the Corporate Brain

Using the New Science to Rethink
How We Structure and Lead Organizations

Danah Zohar

DRAWING ON a solid background in the contemporary sciences, Zohar shows how organizational structures mirror the organization of the human brain and how to utilize the capacity of the whole corporate brain. She presents a fundamentally new conceptual model for deep transformational change to the structure and leadership of organizations.

Hardcover, 250 pages, 11/97 • ISBN 1-57675-022-1 CIP
Item no. 50221-249 $27.95

Available at your favorite bookstore, or call (800) 929-2929

Put the leading-edge business practices you read about to use in your work and in your organization

D O YOU EVER WISH there was a forum in your organization for discussing the newest trends and ideas in the business world? Do you wish you could explore the leading-edge business practices you read about with others in your company? Do you wish you could set aside a few hours every month to connect with like-minded coworkers or to get to know others in your business community?

If you answered yes to any of these questions, then the answer is simple: Start a business book reading group in your organization or business community. For step-by-step advice on how to do just that, visit the Berrett-Koehler website at <www.bkpub.com> and click on "Business Literacy 2000." There you'll find specific guidelines to help in all aspects of creating a successful reading group—from locating interested participants to selecting books, and facilitating discussions.

The website is part of the Business Literacy 2000 program launched by the Consortium for Business Literacy—a group of 19 business book publishers whose primary goal has been to promote the formation of business reading groups within corporations and business communities.

Business Literacy 2000 is dedicated to providing you with tools to help you build a dialog with others in your company or business community, share ideas, build lasting relationships, and bring new ideas and knowledge to bear in your work and organizations. On our website, you'll find guidelines for starting and running a reading group, suggested readings, study guides, and activities to help ensure lively and useful discussions.

For more information on Business Literacy 2000, guidelines for starting a business book reading group, or copies of any of our study guides, please visit our website at: <www.bkpub.com>.

If you do not have Internet access, you may request information by contacting us at:

Berrett-Koehler Publishers
450 Sansome St., Suite 1200
San Francisco, CA 94111
Fax: (415) 362-2512
Email: bkpub@bkpub.com

Please be sure to include your name, address, phone number, email address, and the information you would like to receive.

IF YOU LIKE THE IDEAS in *Global Mind Change* and would like to explore them with others, please fill out the form below and mail, fax, or email the information to:

Berrett-Koehler Publishers
450 Sansome St., Suite 1200
San Francisco, CA 94111
Fax: (415) 362-2512
Email: bkpub@bkpub.com

Name _____

Title _____

Company _____

Address _____

_____

Telephone _____

Fax_ _____

Email _____

Where did you buy this book? _____

_____

Please be sure to include complete information.